Learning JavaScript

Other resources from O'Reilly

Learning JavaScript

Shelley Powers

O'REILLY®

Beijing · Cambridge · Farnham · Köln · Paris · Sebastopol · Taipei · Tokyo

Learning JavaScript
by Shelley Powers

Copyright © 2007 O'Reilly Media, Inc. All rights reserved.
Printed in the United States of America.

Published by O'Reilly Media, Inc., 1005 Gravenstein Highway North, Sebastopol, CA 95472.

O'Reilly books may be purchased for educational, business, or sales promotional use. Online editions
are also available for most titles (*safari.oreilly.com*). For more information, contact our
corporate/institutional sales department: (800) 998-9938 or *corporate@oreilly.com*.

Editor: Simon St.Laurent	**Indexer:** Johnna VanHoose Dinse
Production Editor: Rachel Monaghan	**Cover Designer:** Karen Montgomery
Copyeditor: Mary Anne Weeks Mayo	**Interior Designer:** David Futato
Proofreader: Rachel Monaghan	**Illustrators:** Robert Romano and Jessamyn Read

Printing History:

October 2006:   First Edition.

 This book uses RepKover™, a durable and flexible lay-flat binding.

ISBN-10: 0-596-52746-2
ISBN-13: 978-0-596-52746-4
[M]   [1/07]

Table of Contents

Preface . . . . **ix**

1. Introduction and First Looks **1**

Twisted History: Specs and Implementations   2

Cross-Browser Incompatibility and Other Common JavaScript Myths   4

What You Can Do with JavaScript   5

First Look at JavaScript: "Hello World!"   6

The JavaScript Sandbox   16

Accessibility and JavaScript Best Practices   17

2. JavaScript Data Types and Variables **25**

Identifying Variables   25

Scope   29

Simple Types   33

Constants: Named but Not Variables   42

Questions   43

3. Operators and Statements **44**

Format of a JavaScript Statement   44

Simple Statements   45

Conditional Statements and Program Flow   53

The Conditional Operators   59

The Logical Operators   64

Advanced Statements: The Loops   65

Questions   69

4. The JavaScript Objects **70**

The Object Constructor   70
The Number Object   71
The String Object   73
Regular Expressions and RegExp   78
Purposeful Objects: Date and Math   84
JavaScript Arrays   92
Associative Arrays: The Arrays That Aren't   96
Questions   97

5. Functions **98**

Defining a Function: Let Me Count the Ways   98
Callback Functions   105
Functions and Recursion   108
Nested Functions, Function Closure, and Memory Leaks   109
Function As Object   112
Questions   114

6. Catching Events **115**

The Event Handler at DOM Level 0   116
Questions   133

7. Forms and JiT Validation **134**

Accessing the Form   134
Attaching Events to Forms: Different Approaches   135
Selection   136
Radio Buttons and Checkboxes   140
Input Fields and JiT Regular Expressions   145
Questions   148

8. The Sandbox and Beyond: Cookies, Connectivity, and Piracy **149**

The Sandbox   150
All About Cookies   152
Alternative Storage Techniques   157
Cross-Site Scripting (XSS)   160
Questions   163

9. The Basic Browser Objects **164**

BOM at a Glance 164

The window Object 164

Frames and Location 174

history, screen, and navigator 179

The all Collection, Inner/Outer HTML and Text, and Old and New
Documents 188

Something Old, Something New 191

Questions 192

10. DOM: The Document Object Model **193**

A Tale of Two Interfaces 194

The DOM and Compliant Browsers 195

The DOM HTML API 196

Understanding the DOM: The Core API 202

The DOM Core Document Object 210

Element and Access in Context 213

Modifying the Tree 215

Questions 218

11. Creating Custom JavaScript Objects **219**

The JavaScript Object and Prototyping 220

Creating Your Own Custom JavaScript Objects 222

Object Detection, Encapsulation, and Cross-Browser Objects ... 226

Chaining Constructors and JS Inheritance 231

One-Off Objects 233

Advanced Error-Handling Techniques (try, throw, catch) 235

What's New in JavaScript 238

Questions 241

12. Building Dynamic Web Pages: Adding Style to Your Script ... **242**

DHTML: JavaScript, CSS, and DOM 243

Fonts and Text 248

Position and Movement 251

Size and Clipping 259

Display, Visibility, and Opacity 263

Questions 269

13. Moving Outside the Page with Ajax **270**

Ajax: It's Not Only Code   271

How Ajax Works   273

Hello Ajax World!   273

The Ajax Object: XMLHttpRequest and IE's ActiveX Objects   277

Working with XML—or Not   280

Google Maps   287

Questions   290

14. Good News: Juicy Libraries! Amazing Web Services! Fun APIs! **291**

Before Jumping In, A Word of Caution   291

Working with Prototype   292

Script.aculo.us: More Than the Sum of Its Periods   297

Sabre's Rico   301

Dojo   303

The Yahoo! UI   308

MochiKit   310

Questions   315

Appendix: Answers **317**

Index **329**

Preface

JavaScript was originally intended to be a scripting interface between a web page loaded in the browser client (Netscape Navigator at the time), and the application on the server. Since its introduction in 1995, JavaScript has become a key component of web development, and has found uses elsewhere as well.

This book covers the JavaScript language, from its most primitive data types that have been around since the beginnings of the language, to its most complex features, including those involved with Ajax and DHTML. By the end of the book, you will have the basics you need to work with even the most sophisticated libraries and web applications.

Audience

Readers of this book should be familiar with web page technology, including CSS and HTML/XHTML. You may well have seen some JavaScript in that work. Previous programming experience isn't required, though some sections may require extra review if you have no previous exposure to programming.

This book should help:

- Anyone who wants, or needs, to integrate JavaScript into his own personal web site or sites
- Anyone who uses a content-management tool, such as a weblogging tool, and wants to better understand the scripting components incorporated into her tool templates
- Web developers who seek to integrate JavaScript and some of the DHTML/Ajax features into their web sites
- Web service developers who want to develop for a new market of clients
- Teachers who use web technologies as either the focus or a component of their courses

- Web page designers who wish to better understand how their designs can be enlivened with interactive or animated effects
- Anyone interested in web technologies

Assumptions and Approach

As stated earlier, this book assumes you have experience with (X)HTML and CSS, as well as a general understanding of how web applications work. Programming experience isn't necessary, but the book covers all aspects of JavaScript, some of which are relatively sophisticated. Though the heavier pieces are few, you will need to understand JavaScript enough to work with the newer Ajax libraries.

The book is broken into four sections:

Chapters 1 through 3 provide an introduction to the structure of a JavaScript application, including the simple data types supported in the language, as well as the basic statements and control structures. These establish a baseline of understanding of the language for the sections that follow.

Chapters 4 through 8 introduce the main JavaScript objects, including the all-important function, script access for web-page forms, event handling, scripting security, and working with cookies. Combined, these topics comprise the core of JavaScript, and with these chapters, you can validate form elements, set and retrieve cookies, capture and provide functionality for events, and even create JavaScript libraries. The functionality covered in these chapters has been basic to JavaScript for 10 years, and will remain so for at least another 10.

Chapters 9 through 11 delve into the more sophisticated aspects of web-page development. These chapters cover the Browser Object Model and the newer Document Object Model, and show how you can create your own custom objects. Understanding these models is essential if you wish to create new windows, or individually access, modify, or even dynamically create any page element. In addition, with custom objects, you can then move beyond the capabilities that are prebuilt into either language or browser.

Chapters 12 through 14 get into the advanced uses of JavaScript, including DHTML, Ajax, and some of the many wonderful new libraries that support both.

Chapter 1, *Introduction and First Looks*
> Introduces JavaScript and provides a quick first look at a small web-page application. This chapter also covers some issues associated with the use of JavaScript, including the many tools that are available, as well as issues of security and accessibility.

Chapter 2, *JavaScript Data Types and Variables*
> Provides an overview of the basic data types in JavaScript, as well as an overview of language variables, identifiers, and the structure of a JavaScript statement.

Chapter 3, *Operators and Statements*
> Covers the basic statements of JavaScript, including assignment, conditional, and control statements, as well as the operators necessary for all three.

Chapter 4, *The JavaScript Objects*
> Introduces the first of the built-in JavaScript objects, including Number, String, Boolean, Date, and Math. The chapter also introduces the RegExp object, which provides the facilities to do regular-expression pattern matching. Regular expressions are essential when checking form fields.

Chapter 5, *Functions*
> Focuses on one other JavaScript built-in object, the function. The function is key to creating custom objects, as well as packaging blocks of JavaScript into pieces that can be used, again and again, in many different JavaScript applications. This JavaScript function is relatively simple, but certain aspects can be complex. These include recursion and closure, both of which are introduced in this chapter and detailed in Chapter 11.

Chapter 6, *Catching Events*
> Focuses on event handling, including both the original form of event handling (which is still commonly used in many applications), as well as the newer DOM-based event handling.

Chapter 7, *Forms and JiT Validation*
> Introduces using JavaScript with forms and form fields, including how to access each field type—such as text input fields and drop-down lists—and validate the data once retrieved. Form validation before the form is submitted to the web server helps prevent an unnecessary round trip to the server, and thus saves both time and resource use.

Chapter 8, *The Sandbox and Beyond: Cookies, Connectivity, and Piracy*
> Covers script-based cookies, which store small pieces of data on the client's machine. With cookies, you can store usernames, passwords, and other information so that users don't have to keep reentering data. In addition, since discussion of cookies inevitably leads to discussions of security, the section also covers some security issues associated with JavaScript.

Chapter 9, *The Basic Browser Objects*
> Begins to look at object models accessible from JavaScript, starting with the Browser Object Model—a hierarchy of objects including the window, document, forms, history, location, and so on. Through the BOM, JavaScript can open windows; access page elements such as forms, links, and images; and even do some basic dynamic effects.

Chapter 10, *DOM: The Document Object Model*
> Focuses on the Document Object Model, a straightforward, but not trivial, object model that provides access to all document elements and attributes. You'll see documents that are based in XML (such as XHTML) as well as HTML. Though

the model is comprehensive and its coverage is fairly straightforward, there could be some challenging moments in the chapter for new programmers.

Chapter 11, *Creating Custom JavaScript Objects*
Demonstrates how to create custom objects in JavaScript and covers the entire prototype structure that enables such structures in the language. Some programming language concepts are discussed, such as inheritance and encapsulation, but you don't need experience with these concepts.

Chapter 12, *Building Dynamic Web Pages: Adding Style to Your Script*
Provides a general introduction to some of the more commonly used Dynamic HTML effects, including drag and drop, collapsing and expand page sections, visibility, and movement. Some understanding of CSS is required.

Chapter 13, *Moving Outside the Page with Ajax*
Introduces Ajax, which, despite all the excitement it has generated, is actually not a complicated use of JavaScript. In addition to covering the components of Ajax, the chapter also provides one example of an application that has promoted Ajax probably more than any other: Google Maps.

Chapter 14, *Good News: Juicy Libraries! Amazing Web Services! Fun APIs!*
Covers some of the more popular libraries you can download and use for free. This includes Prototype, Sabre's Rico, Dojo, MochiKit, Yahoo! UI, and script. aculo.us. Between these libraries and the book, you'll have all you need to create incredible, and useful, web applications.

Conventions Used in This Book

The following typographical conventions are used in this book:

Italic
Indicates new terms, URLs, email addresses, filenames, and file extensions.

`Constant width`
Indicates computer code in a broad sense, including commands, arrays, elements, statements, options, switches, variables, attributes, keys, functions, types, classes, namespaces, methods, modules, properties, parameters, values, objects, events, event handlers, XML tags, HTML tags, macros, the contents of files, and the output from commands.

`Constant width bold`
Shows commands or other text that should be typed literally by the user.

`Constant width italic`
Shows text that should be replaced with user-supplied values or by values determined by context.

This icon signifies a tip, suggestion, or general note.

 This icon indicates a warning or caution.

Web sites and pages are mentioned in this book to help you locate online information that might be useful. Normally both the address (URL) and the name (title, heading) of a page are mentioned. Some addresses are relatively complicated, but you can probably locate the pages easier using your favorite search engine to find a page by its name, typically by writing it inside quotation marks. This may also help if the page cannot be found by its address; it may have moved elsewhere, so the name may still work.

Using Code Examples

This book is here to help you get your job done. In general, you may use the code in this book in your programs and documentation. You do not need to contact us for permission unless you're reproducing a significant portion of the code. For example, writing a program that uses several chunks of code from this book does not require permission. Selling or distributing a CD-ROM of examples from O'Reilly books does require permission. Answering a question by citing this book and quoting example code does not require permission. Incorporating a significant amount of example code from this book into your product's documentation does require permission.

We appreciate, but do not require, attribution. An attribution usually includes the title, author, publisher, and ISBN. For example: "*Learning JavaScript* by Shelley Powers. Copyright 2007 O'Reilly Media, Inc., 978-0-596-52746-4."

If you feel your use of code examples falls outside fair use or the permission given above, feel free to contact us at *permissions@oreilly.com*.

How to Contact Us

Please address comments and questions concerning this book to the publisher:

O'Reilly Media, Inc.
1005 Gravenstein Highway North
Sebastopol, CA 95472
800-998-9938 (in the United States or Canada)
707-829-0515 (international or local)
707-829-0104 (fax)

We have a web page for this book that lists errata, examples, and any additional information. You can access this page at:

> *http://www.oreilly.com/catalog/learningjvscpt*

You can also visit the author's web site for the book at:

> *http://learningjavascript.info*

To comment or ask technical questions about this book, send email to:

> *bookquestions@oreilly.com*

For more information about our books, conferences, Resource Centers, and the O'Reilly Network, see our web site at:

> *http://www.oreilly.com*

Safari® Enabled

 When you see a Safari® Enabled icon on the cover of your favorite technology book, that means the book is available online through the O'Reilly Network Safari Bookshelf.

Safari offers a solution that's better than e-books. It's a virtual library that lets you easily search thousands of top tech books, cut and paste code samples, download chapters, and find quick answers when you need the most accurate, current information. Try it for free at *http://safari.oreilly.com*.

Acknowledgments

With some books, you have a terrific team behind you, and this book is one of those. I want to thank my editor, Simon St.Laurent, for his patience, enthusiasm, and guidance as the book metamorphosed during the writing process. In addition, I want to thank the tech and content reviewers, Steven Champeon, Roy Owens, and Alan Herrell for their excellent suggestions, as well as help in finding the gotchas and rough spots.

I also want to acknowledge Rachel Monaghan, production editor for this book; Mary Anne Weeks Mayo, copyeditor; Johnna VanHoose Dinse, indexer; and Marlowe Shaeffer, production manager.

Finally, I want to send thanks to those who I have met online, in the tech community and out. You were in mind as I wrote the book. In a way, you can say this book was written for you—you know who you are.

CHAPTER 1

Introduction and First Looks

JavaScript is one of the most widely used programming languages; it is also one of the most misunderstood. Its growth has exploded in the last few years, and most web sites use it in some form. Its component-based capabilities simplify the creation of increasingly complicated libraries—most providing effects in web pages that previously required the installation of an external application. It can also be tightly integrated with server-side applications that are created with a variety of languages and interface with any number of databases. Yet for all of this, JavaScript is often considered lightweight and unsophisticated—not like a "real" programming language.

In some ways, JavaScript is too easy to use. To its detractors, it lacks discipline; its object-oriented capabilities aren't really OO; it exists within a simplified environment with only a subset of functionality; it isn't secure; it's loosely typed; it doesn't compile into bytes or bits. I remember reading in a JavaScript introduction years ago that you shouldn't let the name fool you: JavaScript has little to do with Java. After all, Java is *hard* to learn.

So what's the reality? Is JavaScript a fun little scripting language—lightweight, helpful, but not to be taken seriously? Or is it a powerful programming language you can trust with some of your site's most important functionality? The reality of JavaScript, and hence the confusion, is that it's two languages in one.

The first is a friendly, easy-to-use scripting language built into web browsers and other applications, offering functions such as form validation and cool stuff like drop-down menus, color fades during data updates, and in-place page edits. Because it's implemented within a specific environment—usually a web browser of some form—and within a protected environment, JavaScript doesn't need to have functionality to manage files, memory, or many of the other programming language basic components, making it leaner and simpler. You can begin programming in JS with little or no background, training, or even prior programming experience.

The second language, however, is a mature, full-featured, carefully constrained, object-based language, which *does* require more in-depth understanding. Used correctly, it can help web applications scale (increase their number of users) with little or no change to the application on the server. It can simplify web-site development and add a level of sophistication, making a good site appear even better to its visitors.

Used incorrectly, JavaScript can also open security holes to your site, especially when used in combination with other functionality, such as a web service or database form. It can also make a page unusable, unreadable, and less accessible.

In *Learning JavaScript*, I'm going to introduce you to both languages just described: the fun scripting language, as well as the powerful object-oriented programming language. More importantly, I'm going to show you how to use JavaScript correctly.

Twisted History: Specs and Implementations

Learning a programming language doesn't require learning its history—unless you're a language like JavaScript, whose history is reflected in web pages today.

JavaScript originated with Netscape, back when it was first developing its LiveConnect server-side development. The company wanted a scripting language that could interface with the server-side components and created one called "LiveScript." Later, after an initial partnership with Sun, owner of the Java programming language, the Netscape engineers renamed LiveScript to JavaScript, even though there was and is no connection between either programming language. Well-known JavaScript guru Steven Champeon wrote:

> Rewind to early 1995. Netscape had just hired Brendan Eich away from MicroUnity Systems Engineering, to take charge of the design and implementation of a new language. Tasked with making Navigator's newly added Java support more accessible to non-Java programmers, Eich eventually decided that a loosely typed scripting language suited the environment and audience, namely the few thousand web designers and developers who needed to be able to tie into page elements (such as forms, or frames, or images) without a bytecode compiler or knowledge of object-oriented software design.
>
> The language he created was christened "LiveScript," to reflect its dynamic nature, but was quickly (before the end of the Navigator 2.0 beta cycle) renamed JavaScript, a mistake driven by marketing that would plague web designers for years to come, as they confused the two incessantly on mailing lists and on Usenet. Netscape and Sun jointly announced the new language on December 4, 1995, calling it a "complement" to both HTML and Java.
>
> (From "JavaScript: How Did We Get Here?" O'Reilly Network, April 2001.)

Not to be out-engineered, Microsoft countered Netscape's effort with the release of Internet Explorer and its own scripting language—VBScript—derived from the company's popular Visual Basic. Later, it also released its own version of a JavaScript-like language: JScript.

The competition between browsers and languages impacted the early adoption of Java-Script within many companies, especially as the difficult challenge of maintaining cross-browser compatible pages increased—not to mention confusion about the name.

In an effort to cut through the compatibility issues, Netscape submitted the Java-Script specification to the European Computer Manufacturer's Association (ECMA) International in 1996, to reissue it as a standardized work. Engineers from Sun, Microsoft, Netscape, and other companies holding a stake in the language were invited to participate, and the result was the release of the first ECMAScript specification—ECMA-262—in June 1997. Since that time, most companies that support a version of JavaScript (or JScript or ECMAScript) have agreed to, at a minimum, support ECMA-262.

 You can download a PDF of ECMA-262 at *http://www.ecma-international.org/publications/standards/Ecma-262.htm*. It's not exciting reading, but it does make a good companion reference.

The second version of ECMA-262 was strictly a maintenance release. The third, and current, version was released in December 1999.

However, this wouldn't be JavaScript if the confusion ended with the passing of ECMA-262. Scattered about the Web is discussion of a new version of ECMAScript, designated ECMA-357. However, this isn't a new edition or version of ECMAScript; it's an extension known as E4X. The purpose of the extension is to add native XML capability to ECMA-262. ECMA-357 was published in 2004, and at this time, Java-Script 1.6 has partially implemented E4X.

What's important to remember from all of this is that many of these older versions of scripting langauges are still in use, even today. It's not uncommon to find old JScript or the earliest versions of JavaScript. To clarify all the versions of scripting languages and how they relate to one another, Table 1-1 provides an approximate correspondence between JavaScript, JScript, and ECMAScript version, and what version of each is supported by today's most popular web browsers.

Table 1-1. Script support in browsers

Browser	Script support	Documentation URL
Internet Explorer 6.x	ECMA-262 (v3) /JScript 5.6	*http://msdn.microsoft.com/library/default.asp?url=/library/en-us/script56/html/1e9b3876-3d38-4fd8-8596-1bbfe2330aa9.asp*
Internet Explorer 7.x (Windows XP)	ECMA-262 (v3) /JScript 5.6	*http://msdn.microsoft.com/ie/*
Opera 8 and 8.5	ECMA-262 (v3) /JavaScript 1.5	*http://www.opera.com/docs/specs/js/ecma/*

Table 1-1. Script support in browsers (continued)

Browser	Script support	Documentation URL
Firefox 1.5	ECMA-262 (v3) with partial support for ECMA-357 (E4X) /JavaScript 1.6	JavaScript 1.5 core reference: *http://developer.mozilla.org/en/docs/Core_JavaScript_1.5_Reference/*
		JavaScript 1.6 core reference: *http://developer.mozilla.org/en/docs/New_in_JavaScript_1.6*
Safari 2.x on Tiger	ECMA-262 (v3)	*http://developer.apple.com/documentation/AppleApplications/Conceptual/SafariJSProgTopics/index.html*
Camino 1.0	ECMA-262 (v3) /JavaScript 1.5	*http://www.caminobrowser.org/*
Netscape 8.1	ECMA-262 (v3) /JavaScript 1.5	*http://browser.netscape.com/ns8/*
Various wireless device browsers	Varies	Site that contains reference to several emulators and testing tools: *http://www.wirelessdevnet.com/channels/printlinks.phtml?category=4*

When you're visiting web pages and curious as to how they implement a specific feature, you can usually tell what version of JavaScript they're using by how they declare the script block. In addition, there are pieces of these old languages that still influence the more modern versions of JS. We'll look more closely at the script block later in this chapter, and at the influences of older browsers throughout the book, but it's important to be aware that old versions of JavaScript and its variations still impact today's applications.

 Throughout the book, I use both JavaScript and JS interchangeably. In addition, unless otherwise noted, examples in this book are based on EMCA-262 and JavaScript 1.5/1.6.

Cross-Browser Incompatibility and Other Common JavaScript Myths

The JavaScript language runs in multiple environments and on many platforms. It can be used to develop web pages (and other applications) that work in operating systems such as Mac OS X, Windows, and Linux. It doesn't require any special download or installation, because JavaScript is built into whatever browser you decide to use.

Most browsers implement a common subset of the language, making most code quite compatible across browsers. This can lead to confusion: if the language implementation is similar, where do the issues of cross-browser incompatibilities arise?

Most cross-browser incompatibilities are based on differences in the underlying Document Object Model (DOM) exposed by the browser, rather than on the language itself. For instance, a JavaScript language object would be Date or String; it will remain a Date or a String whether implemented in Safari or Navigator. An instance of an object from the DOM would be the document object, which represents that portion of the browser that holds the web page. How these DOM objects are exposed and manipulated within the browser's respective implementation of JavaScript (or ECMAScript) is what leads to cross-browser incompatibility.

Another area of confusion has to do with what in the web page is managed by JavaScript and what is managed through the use of Cascading Style Sheets (CSS). The most that JavaScript can do with an element in a page is create it, remove it, or alter its attributes. Among such attributes are those defined through the CSS style attribute.

CSS defines the look and even some of the behavior of elements within the web page. It can hide or show elements, change color or font, move, resize, or clip, and so on. How each browser implements CSS can vary, and this can also lead to some issues of cross-browser incompatibility. All JavaScript does, though, is alter an element's CSS style attributes.

 ECMAScript compliance asserts that all built-in JavaScript objects be the same, but some small variations can exist between browsers. However, for the most part, cross-browser problems in the past have been based on DOM or CSS differences.

What You Can Do with JavaScript

JavaScript achieved early widespread use for simple tasks: validating form contents, or setting and retrieving *cookies* (small bits of information that persist even when the browser is closed). In the late 1990s, with the introduction of Dynamic HTML (DHTML), JavaScript was also used to provide a more dynamic user experience through drop-down menus and the like.

JavaScript's popularity has grown—exploded, really—most recently because it is a key component in Ajax (Asynchronous JavaScript and XML), which promises to restructure the way web applications interact with users. Over time, many cross-platform problems have been resolved, and the language has become more sophisticated—so much so that JavaScript is no longer just a scripting language; it's a full-featured programming language.

So what can you do with JavaScript? Well, for starters:

Validate form fields
  Validate form input before submitting the contents to the server. This saves time and server resources, and provides immediate feedback.

Set and retrieve web cookies
  Persist information such as usernames, account numbers, or preferences in a controlled, safe environment—saving users time the next time they access a site.

Dynamically alter the appearance of a page element
Provide feedback by highlighting incorrect form entries; increase the size of a section's font based on the reader's request.

Hide and show elements
Based on personal preference or user actions, show or hide page content, such as form elements, expanding writing, and changing the displayed size of an image.

Move elements about the page
Create a drop-down menu, or provide an animated cursor to accent page elements.

Capture user events and adjust the page accordingly
Based on keyboard or mouse actions, make a section of the page editable.

Scroll content
For larger images or content areas, provide a way to grab the element with a mouse or keyboard, and scroll it right or left, up or down.

Interface with a server-side application without leaving the page
This is the basis of Ajax and is used to populate selection lists, update data, and refresh a display—all without having to reload the page. This helps eliminate round trips to the server, which can be costly in both time and resources.

What can you do? Perhaps the better question is what *can't* you do.

First Look at JavaScript: "Hello World!"

One reason JavaScript is so popular is that it's relatively easy to add JavaScript to a web page. All you need to do, at a minimum, is include HTML script tags in the page, provide the JavaScript language for the type attribute, and add whatever Java-Script you want:

```
<script type="text/javascript">
...some JavaScript
</script>
```

Traditionally, script tags are added to the head element in the document (delimited by opening and closing head tags), but they can also be included in the body element—or even in both sections.

Example 1-1 shows a complete, valid web page, including a JavaScript block that uses the built-in alert function to open a message box containing the "Hello, World!" text.

Example 1-1. JavaScript block in the document head

```
<!DOCTYPE html PUBLIC "-//W3C//DTD XHTML 1.0 Transitional//EN"
"http://www.w3.org/TR/xhtml1/DTD/xhtml1-transitional.dtd">
<html>
<head>
<title>Example 1-1</title>
```

Example 1-1. JavaScript block in the document head (continued)

```
<meta http-equiv="Content-Type" content="text/html; charset=utf-8" />

<script type="text/javascript">
   var dt = Date( );

   // say hello to the world
   var msg = 'Hello, World! Today is ' + dt;
   alert(msg);
</script>
</head>
<body onload="hello( );">
</body>
</html>
```

Copying this into a file and opening the file in any web browser should result in a box popping up as soon as the page as loaded. If it doesn't, chances are that JavaScript is disabled in the browser, or, something very rare these days, JavaScript isn't supported.

Though the example is simple, it does expose the basic components of most JavaScript applications in use today. It deserves a closer look.

 The examples in this book were all designed to validate as XHTML, which means that they include DOCTYPE, document title, and content type. You can discard these when recreating the examples. However, a better approach might be to create a skeleton web page including the DOCTYPE, title, content type, head, and body, and then copy it for most of the examples.

The script Tag

JavaScript, unlike some other languages, is almost always embedded within the context of another language, such as HTML and XHTML (both of which are actual languages, though the moving parts may not be as obvious). By this I mean that there are restrictions in how the script is added to the page. You can't just plop JS into the page wherever and however you want.

 Even when used in other, non-Web, contexts, JavaScript is frequently part of a document or template.

In Example 1-1, the (X)HTML script element tag encloses the JavaScript. This lets the browser know that when it encounters this tag, it shouldn't process the tag's contents as HTML or XHTML. At this point, control over the contents is turned over to another built-in browser agent, the scripting engine.

Not all script embedded in web pages is JavaScript, and the tag contains an attribute defining the type of script. In the example, this is given as a text/javascript. Other allowable values for the type attribute are:

- text/ecmascript
- text/jscript
- text/vbscript
- text/vbs

The first is an alternative for JavaScript, the next a variation of JavaScript implemented by Microsoft in Internet Explorer, and the next two are for VBScript.

All these type values describe the MIME type of the content. *MIME*, or Multipurpose Internet Mail Extension, is a way to identify how the content is encoded (i.e., text), and what specific format it is (javascript). The concept arose with email, but spread to other Internet uses, such as designating the type of script in a script block.

By providing a MIME type, those browsers capable of processing the type do so, while other browsers skip over the section. This ensures that the script is accessed only by applications that can process it.

Earlier versions of the script tag took a language attribute, and this was used to designate the version of the language, as well as the type: javascript as compared to javascript 1.2. However, the use of language was deprecated in HTML 4.01, though it still shows in many JavaScript examples. And therein lies one of the earliest cross-browser techniques.

Years ago, when working with cross-browser compatibility issues, it wasn't uncommon to create a specific script for each browser in a separate section or file and then use the language attribute to ensure only a compatible browser could access the code. Looking through some of my old DHTML examples (circa 1997), I found the following:

```
<script src="ns4_obj.js" language="javascript1.2">
</script>

<script src="ie4_obj.js" language="jscript">
</script>
```

The philosophy of this approach was that only a browser capable of processing JavaScript 1.2 would pick up the one block (Netscape Navigator 4.x, primarily, at that time) and only a browser capable of processing JScript would pick up that file (Internet Explorer 4). Kludgey? Sure, but it also worked through the early years of trying to deal with frequently broken cross-browser DHTML.

Eventually, though, the preference shifted to an approach called *object detection*—a move only encouraged when the language attribute was deprecated. We'll look at object detection more closely in the later chapters, particularly those associated with Ajax. For now, object detection involves testing to see if a particular object or property of an object exists, and if so, one batch of JavaScript is processed; otherwise, a different batch is run.

Returning to the script tag, other valid attributes for this tag are src, defer, and charset. The charset attribute defines the character encoding used with the script. Unless you need a different character encoding than what's defined for the document, this usually isn't set.

One attribute that can be quite useful is defer. If you set defer to a value of "defer," it indicates to the browser that the script is not going to generate any document content, and the browser can continue processing the rest of the page's content, returning to the script when the page has been processed and displayed:

```
<script type="text/javascript" defer="defer">
...no content being generated
</script>
```

Using this can help speed up page loading when you have a larger JavaScript block or include a larger JS library. The last attribute, src, has to do with loading such libraries, and we'll explore it next.

JavaScript Code Location

In Example 1-1, the JavaScript block is embedded in the head element of the web page. The script can also be included in the body, as a modification of the application demonstrates in Example 1-2.

Example 1-2. Embedding JavaScript into the document body

```
<!DOCTYPE html PUBLIC "-//W3C//DTD XHTML 1.0
Transitional//EN" "http://www.w3.org/TR/xhtml1/DTD/xhtml1-transitional.dtd">
<html>
<head>
<title>JavaScript Code Block Example</title>
<meta http-equiv="Content-Type" content="text/html; charset=utf-8" />
</head>
<body>
<script type="text/javascript">
//<![CDATA[

var dt = Date();
var msg ='<h3>Hello, World! Today is ' + dt + '</h3>';
document..writeln(msg);

//]]>
</script>
</body>
</html>
```

Note in this example, rather than the alert function, the DOM document object is used to write directly to the page.

There are differing viewpoints on when JS should be included in the head and when in the body, but the following rules apply:

1. Place the JavaScript in the body when the JavaScript dynamically creates web page content as the page is being loaded.

2. JavaScript defined in functions and used for page events should be placed in the head tag, as this is loaded before the body.

A good rule of thumb with script placement is to embed the script in the body only when the script creates web page contents as it's loaded; otherwise, put it in the head element. This way, the page won't be cluttered with script, and the script can always be found in one location on each page.

Inserting JavaScript into the body can be avoided altogether by using the DOM to generate new content and attach it to page elements. I'll be introducing this approach later in the book.

Hiding the Script

In Example 1-2, the script block was included within a XHTML CDATA section. A CDATA section holds text that the XHTML processor doesn't interpret.

The reason for the CDATA section is that XHTML processors interpret markup such as the header (H3) opening and closing tags, even when they're contained within JavaScript strings. Though the page may display correctly, if you try to validate it without the CDATA, you will get validation errors.

JavaScript that is imported into the page using the SRC attribute is assumed to be compatible with XHTML and doesn't require the CDATA section. Inline or embedded JS, though, should be delimited with CDATA, particularly if it's included within the BODY element.

For most browsers, you'll also need to hide the CDATA section opening and closing tags with JavaScript comments (//), or you'll get a JavaScript error.

JavaScript Best Practice: The use of both the CDATA section and the JavaScript comments is important enough that these form the first of many JavaScript Best Practices that will be covered in this book.

When using an XHTML DOCTYPE, enclose inline or embedded Java-Script blocks in CDATA sections, which are then commented out using JavaScript comments. And always assume your web pages are XHTML, so always use CDATA.

Of course, the best way to keep your web pages uncluttered is to remove the Java-Script from the page entirely, through the use of JavaScript files. Many of this book's examples are embedded into the page primarily to make them easier to create.

However, the Mozilla Foundation recommends that all inline or embedded Java-Script be removed from a page and placed in separate JS files. Doing this prevents problems with validation and incorrect interpretation of text, regardless of whether the page is processed as HTML or XHTML.

 JavaScript Best Practice: Place all blocks of JavaScript code within external JavaScript files.

JavaScript Files

As JavaScript became more object-oriented and complex, developers began to create reusable JS objects that could be incorporated into many applications created by different developers. The only efficient way to reuse these objects was to create them in separate files and provide a link to each file in the web page.

JavaScript files are beneficial for reasons other than facilitating reuse. For example, rather than repeat the same code over many pages and have to update it in many places when it changes, the code is created in a file, and any modifications are then made to only one place. Nowadays, all but the most simple JavaScript is created in separate script files. Whatever overhead is incurred by using multiple files is more than offset by the benefits.

To include a JavaScript library or script file in your web page, use this syntax:

```
<script type="text/javascript" src="somejavascript.js"></script>
```

The `script` element contains no content, but the closing tag is still required.

Script files are loaded into the page by the browser in the order in which they occur in the page and are processed in order unless `defer` is used. A script file should be treated as if the code is actually included in the page; the behavior is no different between script files and embedded JavaScript blocks.

The entire second half of the book covers creating and using custom libraries, but Chapter 11 covers many of the basics.

Comments

A line that begins with the double-slash (//) is a JavaScript comment, usually an explanation of the surrounding code. Comments in JavaScript are an extremely useful way of quickly noting what a block of code is doing, and whatever dependencies it has. It makes the code more readable and more maintainable.

There are two different types of comments you can use in your own applications. The first, using the double-slash, just comments out a specific line:

```
// This line is commented out in the code
```

The second makes use of opening and closing JavaScript comment delimiters, (/*) and (*/), to mark a block of comments that can extend one or more lines:

```
/* This is a multiline comment
that extends through three lines.
Multiline comments are particularly useful commenting on a function */
```

Single-line comments are relatively safe to use, but multiline comments can generate problems if the beginning or ending bracket characters are accidentally deleted.

Typically, single-line comments are used before a block of JS performing a specific process or creating a specific object; multiline comment blocks are used in the beginning of a JavaScript file.

 JavaScript Best Practice: Begin every JavaScript block, function, or object definition with at least one line of comments. In addition, provide a more detailed comment block at the beginning of all JavaScript library files; include information about author, date, and dependencies, as well as a detailed purpose of the script.

Browser Objects

Examples 1-1 and 1-2, small as they were, used a powerful set of global, built-in browser objects to communicate with the user.

The first example used the alert function to create a small pop-up window (usually called a *dialog* window) with the provided message. Though not specifically included in the text, the alert dialog is a function of the window object—the top-most object in the Browser Object Model (BOM). The BOM is a basic set of objects implemented in most modern browsers.

The second example also used an object from the BOM—the document object—to write the message out to the page. The document, window, and all BOM objects are covered in Chapter 9.

 The BOM is a variation of the DOM mentioned earlier, and it is sometimes referred to as *DOM Version 0.*

JavaScript Built-in Objects

Examples 1-1 and 1-2 also use two other built-in objects, though only one is used explicitly. The explicit object is date; it accesses today's date. The second, implicit, object is string, which is the type of object that's returned when the date function is called. In fact, the following are all comparable implementations of the same code:

```
var dt = String(Date());
var dt = Date().toString();
```

The JavaScript built-in objects string and date are covered in more detail in Chapter 4.

JavaScript User-Defined Functions

The global function and built-in object are used within the context of a user-defined function (UDF) in Example 1-1. The typical syntax for creating a UDF is:

```
function functionname(params) {
   ...
}
```

The keyword function is followed by the function name and parentheses containing zero or more parameters (function arguments), followed by the function code contained within curly brackets. The function may or may not return a value. A user-defined function encapsulates a block of JavaScript for later or repeated processing.

Functions are technically another kind of a built-in JavaScript object. They look like statements, and you don't need to worry much about the distinction until you're building lots of them. However, they are objects, and they are complex enough and important enough to have their own chapter, Chapter 5.

Event Handlers

In the opening body tag of Example 1-1, an attribute named onload is assigned the hello function. The onload attribute is what's known as an *event handler*. This event handler, and others, are part of the underlying DOM that each browser provides. They can attach a function to an event so that when the event occurs, some code is processed.

There are several events that can be captured in various types of elements, each of which can then be assigned code to be implemented when the event occurs.

Adding an event handler directly to the element tag is one way to attach an event handler. A second technique occurs directly within JavaScript using a syntax such as the following:

```
<script type="text/javascript">
document.onload=hello( );

function hello( ) {
   var dt = Date( );
   var msg = 'Hello, World! Today is ' + dt;
   alert(msg);
}
</script>
```

Using this approach, you don't have to add event handlers as attributes into tags, but instead can add them into the JS itself. We'll get into more details on event handlers in Chapter 6. Though not demonstrated, events are frequently used in conjunction with HTML forms to validate the form data before submittal. Forms are covered in Chapter 7.

Mozilla has provided a good documentation set covering the Gecko engine (the underlying engine that implements JavaScript within browsers such as Camino and Firefox). The URL for the event handlers is *http://www.mozilla.org/docs/dom/domref/dom_event_ref.html*.

The var Keyword and Scope

We've looked at the built-in objects and functions, the user-defined function, and event handlers. Now it's time to take a brief look at the individual lines of JavaScript code.

Examples 1-1 and 1-2 use the var keyword to declare the variables dt and msg. By using var with variables, each is then defined within a local scope, which means they're only accessible within the function in which they're defined. If I didn't use var, the variables would have global scope, which means the variable would then be accessible by all JavaScript anywhere in the web page (or within any external JS libraries included in the page).

Setting the scope of a variable is important if you have both global and local variables with the same name. Example 1-1 doesn't have global variables of any name, but it's important to develop good JavaScript coding practices from the beginning. One such practice is to explicitly define the variable's scope.

Here are the rules regarding scope:

- If a variable is declared with the var keyword in a function, its use is local to that function.
- If a variable is declared without the var keyword in a function, and a global variable of the same name exists, it's assumed to be that global variable.
- If a variable is declared locally with a var keyword but not initialized (i.e., assigned a value), it is accessible but not defined.
- If a variable is declared locally without the var keyword, or explicitly declared globally, but not initialized, it is accessible globally but not defined.

By using var within a function, you can prevent problems when using global and local variables of the same name. This is especially critical when using external JavaScript libraries. (See Chapter 2 for more details on JS variables and simple data types.)

The Property Operator

There are several operators in JavaScript: those for arithmetic (+,–), those for conditional expressions (<, >), and others detailed more fully later in the book. Example 1-2 introduces your first operator: the dot (.), which is also known as the property operator.

In the following line from Example 1-2, the `property` operator accesses a specific property of the document object:

```
document.writeln(msg);
```

Data elements, event handlers, and object methods are all considered properties of objects within JavaScript, and all are accessed via the `property` operator.

Statements

The examples demonstrated a basic type of JavaScript statement: the assignment. There are several different types of JS statements that assign values, print out messages, look through data until a condition is met, and so on. The last component of our quick first look at JavaScript is the concept of a JS statement, including its terminator: the semicolon (;).

The statement lines in Example 1-1 end with a semicolon. This isn't an absolute requirement in JavaScript unless you want to type many statements on the same line. If you do, you'll have to insert a semicolon to separate the individual statements.

When typing a complete statement on one line without a semicolon, a line break terminates the statement. However, just as with the use of `var`, it's a good practice that helps avoid some kinds of mistakes. I use the semicolon for all of my JS development.

The use of the semicolon, other operators, and statements are covered in Chapter 3.

What You Didn't See

Ten years ago when most browsers were in their first or second version, JavaScript support was sketchy, with each browser implementing a different version. When browsers, such as the text-based Lynx, encountered the `script` tag, they usually just printed the output to the page.

To prevent this, the script contents were enclosed in HTML comments: <!-- and -->. When HTML comments were used, non-JS enabled browsers ignored the commented-out script, but newer browsers knew to execute the script.

It was a kludge, but it was a very widespread kludge. Most web pages with JavaScript nowadays feature the added HTML comments because the script is copied more often than not. Unfortunately, today, some new browsers may process XHTML as strictly XML, which means the commented code is discarded. In these situations, the JavaScript is ignored. As a consequence, HTML comments have fallen out of favor and aren't used in any examples in this book.

 JavaScript Best Practice: Do not use HTML commenting to "hide" JavaScript. Browsers that don't understand JS are long gone, and their use conflicts with pages created as XHTML.

The JavaScript Sandbox

When JavaScript was first released, there was understandable concern about opening a web page that would execute a bit of code directly in your machine. What if the JavaScript included something harmful, such as code to delete all Word documents or worse, copy them for the script originator?

To prevent such occurrences and to reassure browser users, JavaScript was built to operate in a *sandbox*: a protected environment in which the script can't access the resources of the browser's computer.

In addition, browsers implement security conditions above and beyond those established as a minimum for the JavaScript language. These are defined in a browser-specific *security policy*, which determines what the script can and cannot do. One such security policy dictates that a script may not communicate with pages other than those from the same domain where the script originated. Most browsers provide the means to customize this policy even further, making the environment in which the script operates more, or less, restrictive.

Unfortunately, even with the JavaScript sandbox and browser security policies, JavaScript has had a rough time, and hackers have discovered and exploited several JavaScript errors—some browser-dependent, some not. One of the more serious is known as cross-site scripting (XSS). This is actually a class of security breaks (some coming through JavaScript, others through holes in the browsers, and still others through the server) that can lead to cookie theft and exposure of client or site data and a host of other serious problems.

We'll look at this later in much more detail, as well as how to prevent XSS, along with other security problems and preventions, and that infamous little goodie, the cookie, in Chapter 8.

 The CERT site is the most authoritative on security issues, and the page discussing XSS can be found at *http://www.cert.org/advisories/ CA-2000-02.html*. The CGISecurity.com site has an in-depth FAQ on XSS and can be found at *http://www.cgisecurity.com/articles/xss-faq. shtml*.

It's important to be aware that JavaScript can be vulnerable, even with the best of intentions on the part of browser vendors. However, this shouldn't dissuade you from using JavaScript; most problems can be prevented by understanding their nature and following steps recommended by security experts.

Accessibility and JavaScript Best Practices

In an ideal world, everyone who visits your web site would use the same type of operating system and browser, and have JavaScript enabled. Your site would never be accessed via mobile phone or other odd-sized device; blind people wouldn't need screen readers, and the paralyzed wouldn't need voice-enabled navigation.

This isn't an ideal world, but too many JS developers code as if it is. We get so caught up in the wonders of what we can create that we forget that not everyone can share them.

There are many best practices associated with JavaScript, but if there's one to take away from this book, it's the following: whatever JavaScript functionality you create, it must not come between your site and your site's visitors.

What do I mean by "come between your site and your site's visitors"? Avoid using JavaScript in such a way that those who cannot, or will not, enable JavaScript are prevented from accessing essential site resources using a nonscript-enabled browser. If you create a drop-down menu using JS, you also need to provide navigation for people not using a JS-enabled device. If your visitors are blind, JS must not interfere with audio browsers; if your visitors use a cellphone with a black and white screen, or they are color blind, your page shouldn't depend on color to provide feedback.

Many developers don't follow these practices because they assume the practices require extra work, and for the most part, they do. However, the work doesn't have to be a burden—not when the results can increase the accessibility of your site. In addition, many companies now require that their web sites meet a certain level of accessibility. It's better to get into the habit of creating accessible pages in the beginning than to try to fix the pages, or your habits, later.

Accessibility Guidelines

The WebAIM site (*http://www.webaim.org*) has a wonderful tutorial on creating accessible JavaScript (available at *http://www.webaim.org/techniques/javascript/*). It covers the ways you shouldn't use JavaScript, such as using JS for menus and other navigation. However, the site also provides ways you can use JS to make a site more accessible.

One suggestion is to base feedback on events that can be triggered whether or not you use a mouse. For instance, rather than capture mouse click, capture events that are triggered if you use a keyboard or a mouse, such as onfocus and onblur. If you have a drop-down menu, add a link to a separate page, and then provide a static menu on the second page.

After reviewing the tutorial at WebAIM, you might want to spend some time at the W3C's Web Accessibility Initiative (at *http://www.w3.org/WAI/*). From there you can also access the U.S. Government's Section 508 web site, which discusses what is known as "508 compliance." Sites that comply with Section 508 are accessible regardless of physical constraints. At the web site, you can access various tools that evaluate your site for accessibility, such as Cynthia Says (at *http://www.cynthiasays. com/*); convert your nonaccessible Word or Adobe PDF documents into HTML, such as the Illinois Accessible Web Publishing Wizard (at *http://cita.rehab.uiuc.edu/ software/office/*); and help you develop accessible content from the beginning, such as the Web Accessibility Toolbar (at *http://cita.rehab.uiuc.edu/software/office/*).

Whether your site is located within the United States or not, you want it to be accessible; therefore a visit to Section 508 is useful regardless of your locale.

Of course, not all accessibility issues are related to those browsers in which JavaScript is limited or disabled by default, such as with screen readers. Many people don't trust JavaScript, or don't care for it and choose to disable it. For both groups of people—those who prefer not to use JavaScript, and those who have no choice—it's important to provide alternatives when no script is present. One alternative is noscript.

noscript

Some browsers or other applications are not equipped to process JavaScript, or are limited in their interpretation. If the JavaScript is not essential to navigation or interaction, and the browser ignores the script, no harm. However, if the JavaScript is essential to access the site's resources and you don't provide alternatives, you're basically telling these folks to go away.

Years ago when JavaScript was fairly new, one popular approach was to provide a plain or text-only page accessible through a link, usually placed at the top of the page. However, the amount of work to maintain the two sites could be prohibitive, not to mention the constant worry about keeping the sites synchronized.

A better technique is to provide static alternatives to the dynamic, script-generated content. When you use JavaScript to create a drop-down menu, also provide a standard hierarchical linked menu; when you use script to expose form elements for editing based on user interaction, provide the more traditional links to a second page to do the same.

The tag that enables all of this is noscript. Wherever you need static content, add a noscript element with the content contained within the opening and closing tags. Then, if a browser or other application can't process the script (because JavaScript is not enabled for some reason), the noscript content is processed; otherwise, it's ignored.

Example 1-3 shows our original example with the addition of noscript. Accessing the page with a JavaScript-enabled browser should display it with the link labeled "First Example." If, however, you disable JavaScript in your browser's preferences, the page should display with the link labeled "Original Example."

Example 1-3. The use of noscript for non-JavaScript-enabled browsers

```
<!DOCTYPE html PUBLIC "-//W3C//DTD XHTML 1.0 Transitional//EN"
"http://www.w3.org/TR/xhtml1/DTD/xhtml1-transitional.dtd">
<html>
<head>
<title>Example 1-3</title>
<meta http-equiv="Content-Type" content="text/html; charset=utf-8" />
</head>
<body>
<script type="text/javascript">
var dt = Date();
var msg ='<a href="js1.htm">First Example</a>';
document.writeln(msg);
</script>
<noscript>
<a href="js1.htm">Original Example</a>
</noscript>
</body>
</html>
```

The example is just a simplified use of noscript; you'll see more sophisticated uses later in the book.

As useful as noscript is, in a more complicated page, it can become tedious working with embedded noscript elements scattered about. The next section introduces an alternative approach.

 A second instance in which noscript content is processed is when a browser or other application has scripting enabled but can't work with the MIME type of the scripting block. This is also a time when the script can't be executed, and the noscript content should be processed. However, many popular browsers such as Firefox and Safari don't process the noscript content in these circumstances. This is an error, and one you should be aware of if you depend on noscript.

An Alternative to noscript

The more you add to a web page, the harder it becomes to maintain. If you use Java-Script to provide a great deal of functionality and then use noscript to provide alternatives, your pages could get large and complicated.

Another approach, one I recommend when you're hiding and showing web content based on user interaction, is to design the page with static elements, and then use script to either hide these elements and provide the alternative dynamic content, or actually leave the static elements in and then provide the dynamic as an additional option.

The popular photo site Flickr (*http://flickr.com*) uses this technique. If you access an individual photo page as the photo owner, whether or not you have JavaScript enabled, you'll see a link to click to edit the photo title, tags, and description. When you have JavaScript enabled, clicking on the title or the description area opens up a space to edit both; clicking a separate "Add a tag" link opens a space for adding a new tag, as shown in Figure 1-1.

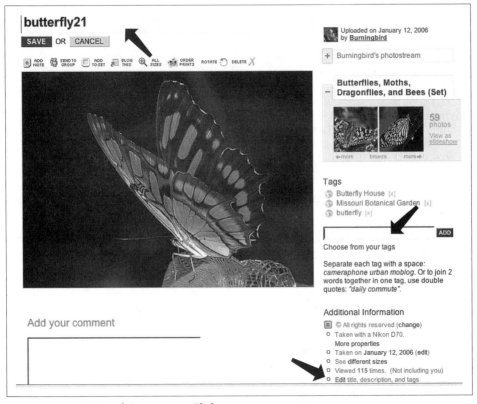

Figure 1-1. DHTML and Ajax in use at Flickr

When JavaScript is disabled, clicking on the title and description doesn't cause any change in the page, and the link to add the tags doesn't show. Because the CSS attribute display isn't dependent on JavaScript, the items are hidden regardless of whether or not script is enabled.

When script is enabled, by associating event handlers with page elements such as the title and description, you can use JavaScript to display the previously hidden objects when the web-page reader clicks the items.

Where I disagree with Flickr is in its message to users to the effect that *if only* they had a JavaScript-enabled browser, they could see such-and-such functionality, as shown in Figure 1-2. The issue is that some people may not be able to use Java-Script. Those that can but choose to disable JavaScript usually do so for a good reason, one that they're not likely to change because of one web site—no matter how much they like that site. Adding an "if only" message to a page is similar to the old "You need to use Internet Explorer to view these pages" that became very popular at the end of the 1990s. It was a bad idea then to tell web-page readers what they should and should not use; it's a bad idea now.

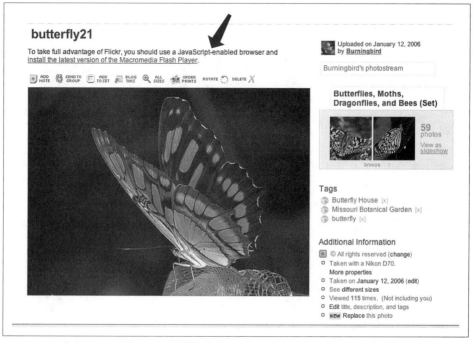

Figure 1-2. Flickr page with JavaScript disabled, and the "if only" message

You might as well put up a "Wow, you're really an annoyance" sign because that's basically what you're saying.

Using Your Browser and Other Developer Tools

When JavaScript was first implemented, acceptance was slow because there were no script debuggers or development tools for the language. Now, though, most browsers have built-in JavaScript consoles or other tools to simplify the JavaScript development and debugging process.

Firefox has a JavaScript console listing errors and warnings, accessible by clicking a symbol (either a stop sign for an error, a warning triangle, or a conversation bubble with a small *i*) in the toolbar or by clicking JavaScript Console in the Tools menu. This console provides debugging information for the JavaScript for each page, and persists this information until you specifically clear the Console contents, as shown in Figure 1-3.

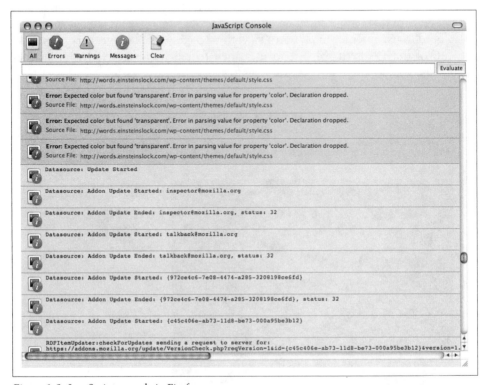

Figure 1-3. JavaScript console in Firefox

Firefox also provides what it calls the DOM Inspector. These very helpful utilities allow you to inspect the DOM objects within the page, including the following very useful information (the computed style is shown in Figure 1-4):

DOM Node
Node name, type, class, namespace URI, and value

Box Model
Position, x and y values

Computed style
The default styles for the object

XBL Binding

The Extensible Binding Language (not covered in this book)

CSS Style Rules

The CSS style rules that apply by default for an element and are given in the stylesheet

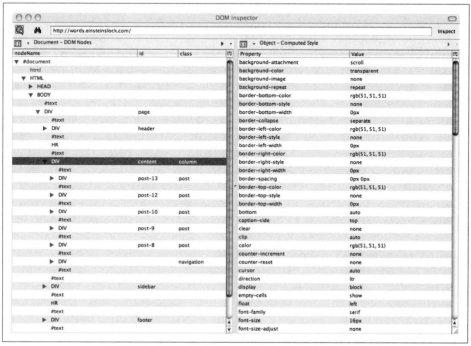

Figure 1-4. Computed style as shown in Firefox DOM Inspector

The JavaScript object, shown in Figure 1-5, is of particular importance because it provides a listing of events, properties, attributes, and functions accessible on the object from JavaScript.

In addition, there are any number of tools now—standalone or embedded—that can work with JavaScript. Rather than attempt to touch on a selection in one chapter, I include sidebars in several chapters that provide a brief overview of handy gadgets, libraries, and tools.

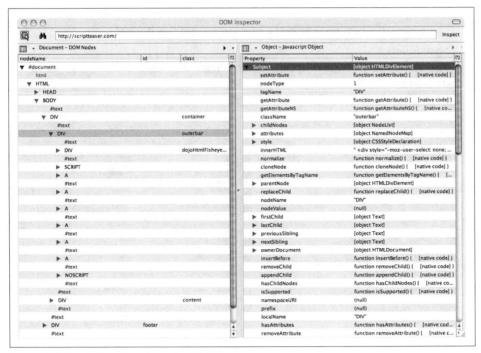

Figure 1-5. JavaScript object from the DOM Inspector

CHAPTER 2

JavaScript Data Types and Variables

The best part of JavaScript is that it's forgiving, especially in regards to data typing. If you start out with a string and then want to use it as a number, that's perfectly fine with the language. (Well, as long as the string actually contains a number and not something like an email address.) If you later want to treat it as a string again, that's fine, too.

One could also say that the forgiving nature of JavaScript is one of the worst aspects of the language. If you try to add two numbers together, but the JavaScript engine interprets the variable holding one of them as a string data type, you end up with an odd string, rather than the sum you were expecting.

Context is everything when it comes to JavaScript data typing, and also when it comes to working with the most basic of JavaScript elements: the variable.

This chapter covers the the three basic JavaScript data types: `string`, `boolean`, and `number`. Along the way, we'll explore escape sequences in strings and take a brief look at Unicode. The chapter also delves into the topic of variables, including variable scope and what makes valid and meaningful variable identifiers. We'll also look at the influences on identifiers that originate from the newest generation of JavaScript applications based on Ajax.

Identifying Variables

JavaScript variables have an identifier, scope, and a specific data type. Because the language is loosely typed, the rest, as they say, is subject to change without notice.

Variables in JavaScript are much like those in any other language; they're used to hold values in such a way that the value can be explicitly accessed in different places in the code. Each has an identifier unique to the scope of use (more on this later), consisting of any combination of letters, digits, underscores, and dollar signs. There is no required format for an identifier, other than that it must begin with a character, dollar sign, or underscore:

```
_variableidentifier
variableIdentifier
$variable_identifier
var-ident
```

Starting with JavaScript 1.5, you can also use Unicode letters (such as ü) and digits, as well as escape sequences (such as \u0009) in variable identifiers. The following are also valid variable identifiers for JS:

```
_&#252;valid
T\u0009
```

JavaScript is case-sensitive, treating upper- and lowercase characters as different characters. The following two variable identifiers are seen as separate variables in JS:

```
strngVariable
strngvariable
```

In addition, a variable identifier can't be a JavaScript keyword, a list of which is illustrated in Table 2-1. Other keywords will be added over time, as new versions of Java-Script (well, technically ECMAScript) are released.

Table 2-1. JavaScript keywords

break	else	new	var
case	finally	return	void
catch	for	switch	while
continue	function	this	with
default	if	throw	
delete	in	try	
do	instanceof	typeof	

Due to proposed extensions to the ECMA 262 specification, the words in Table 2-2 are also considered reserved.

Table 2-2. ECMA 262 specification reserved words

abstract	enum	int	short
boolean	export	interface	static
byte	extends	long	super
char	final	native	synchronized
class	float	package	throws
const	goto	private	transient
debugger	implements	protected	volatile
double	import	public	public

In addition to the ECMAScript reserved words, there are JavaScript-specific words implemented in most browsers that are considered reserved by implementation. Many are based in the Browser Object Model—objects such as document and window. Though not a definitive list, Table 2-3 includes the more common words.

Table 2-3. Typical reserved words in browsers

alert	eval	location	open
array	focus	math	outerHeight
blur	function	name	parent
boolean	history	navigator	parseFloat
date	image	number	regExp
document	isNaN	object	status
escape	length	onLoad	string

Naming Guidelines

Any name can be used for variables and functions within code, but there are several naming practices—many inherited from Java and other programming languages—that can make the code easier to follow and maintain.

First, use meaningful words rather than something that's thrown together quickly:

```
var interestRate = .75;
```

versus:

```
var iRt = .75;
```

You can also provide a data type clue as part of the name, using something such as the following:

```
var strName = "Shelley";
```

This type of naming convention is known as the *Hungarian notation* and is especially popular in Windows development. As such, you'll most likely see it used within the older JScript applications created for Internet Explorer but less often in more modern JS development.

Use a plural for collections of items:

```
var customerNames = new Array();
```

Typically, objects are capitalized:

```
var firstName = String("Shelley");
```

Functions and variables start with lowercase letters:

```
Function validateName(firstName,lastName) ...
```

Many times, variables and functions have one or more words concatenated into a unique identifier, following a format popularized in other languages, and frequently referred to as *CamelCase*:

```
validateName
firstName
```

This approach makes the variable much more readable, though dashes or underscores between the variable "words" work as well:

```
validate-name
first_name
```

The newer JavaScript libraries invariably use CamelCase.

 The term CamelCase is based on the popularity of mixed upper- and lowercase letters in Perl, and of the camel featured on the cover of the bestselling book, *Programming Perl,* by Larry Wall et al. (O'Reilly). Wikipedia has a fascinating and dynamic article on this and other naming notations at *http://en.wikipedia.org/wiki/CamelCase.* Another variation, somewhat tongue-in-cheek and also covered at Wikipedia, is StudlyCaps, at *http://en.wikipedia.org/wiki/Studlycaps.*

Though you can use the $, number, or underscore to begin a variable, your best bet is to start with a letter. Unnecessary use of unexpected characters in variable names can make the code harder to read and follow, especially for newer JavaScript developers.

However, if you've looked at some of the newer JavaScript libraries and examples, you might notice several new conventions for naming variables. The Prototype JavaScript library is a strong influence in this regard—so much so that I think of the rise of new naming conventions as the "Prototype effect."

The Prototype Effect and the Newer Naming Conventions

Many new or relatively newer naming conventions introduced into JavaScript are based less on making the language more readable and more on making JavaScript look and act like other programming languages, such as Java, Python, or Ruby.

As an example, JavaScript has several object-oriented-like capabilities, including the ability to create private members for an object. These are properties/methods that are accessible only within another function of the object, not directly by applications using the objects.

There is nothing inherent in JavaScript that marks an object as being private, as opposed to public. However, an increasing number of JavaScript developers are following both Java and Python naming conventions and are using the underscore (_) to mark a variable as private:

```
var _break    = new Object();
var _continue = new Object();
```

The Prototype library also introduced the use of the $ to designate *shortcut methods*—ways to access references to objects without having to write out the specifics:

```
$();
$A();
```

Class objects start with an uppercase character, functions and variables start with lowercase, and all use CamelCase, discussed earlier. Abbreviations are reformatted into this notation (i.e., `XmlName`, as compared to `XMLName`), and the only exceptions are *constants* (variables treated as unchanging static values), which are typically written out all uppercase: MONTH as compared to month or Month.

In names for functions, a verb should be used; nouns are used for variables:

```
var currentMonth;
function returnCurrentMonth...
```

If included in an isolated block of JavaScript meant for distribution (typically referred to as a JavaScript library or package), identifiers for functions and global variables should have a package reference to prevent *name collision* (conflict between names):

```
dojo_someValue;
otherlibrary_someValue;
```

Iterator variables (used in for loops and other looping mechanisms) should be simple, and consist of *i*, *j*, *k*, and so on, down the alphabet (a holdover from long, long ago when programming languages such as FORTRAN required that all integers begin with the letters *i*, *j*, etc.).

There are other conventions established with the newer JavaScript development, most of which are detailed quite nicely in a document put out by the Dojo organization, *JavaScript Programming Conventions* (available at *http://dojotoolkit.org/js_style_guide.html* at the time of this writing).

I agree with, and adhere to, many of the conventions covered in this section and the last. The one convention I do take exception to is the use of the dollar sign in the Prototype library. It adds an unnecessary element of obfuscation to the language that makes it difficult for newer developers to understand what's going on.

Regardless of personal preferences, there is nothing mandatory or magical about the naming conventions I've outlined, other than the few requirements enforced by the JavaScript engine. They are a convenience.

 We'll cover the Prototype library in detail in Chapter 14, but for now, when you see these naming conventions used in sample code at sites as you start to explore, you'll know that I haven't left great chunks of JavaScript functionality out of the book.

Scope

The next critical characteristic of a variable is its *scope*: whether it's local to a specific function or global to the entire JavaScript application. A variable with *local* scope is one that's defined, initialized, and used within a function; when the function terminates, the variable ceases to exist. A *global* variable, on the other hand, can be accessed anywhere within any JavaScript contained within a web page—whether the JS is embedded directly in the page or imported through a JavaScript library.

In Chapter 1, I mentioned that there is no special syntax necessary to specifically define a variable. A variable can be both created and instantiated in the same line of code, and it need not look any different from a typical assignment statement:

```
num_value = 3.5;
```

This is a better approach:

```
var num_value = 3.5;
```

The difference between the two is the use of the var keyword.

Though not required, explicitly defining a variable using the var keyword is strongly recommended; doing so with local variables helps prevent collision between local and global variables of the same name. If a variable is explicitly defined in a function, its scope is restricted to the function, and any reference to that variable within the function is understood by both developer and JavaScript engine to be that local variable. With the growing popularity of larger, more complex JS libraries, using var prevents the unexpected side effects created by using what you think is a local variable, only to find out it's global in scope.

To illustrate this type of side effect and the importance of explicitly declaring variables, Example 2-1 demonstrates a web page with separate blocks of JavaScript, each accessing the same variable, message. The page includes two external JavaScript files, both of which also set the same variable: one, globally, outside the function that uses it; the other, locally, within the function. None of the examples use the var keyword to expressly define the variable.

Example 2-1. The dangers of global variables and not declaring local variables explicitly

```
<!DOCTYPE html PUBLIC "-//W3C//DTD XHTML 1.0 Transitional//EN"
"http://www.w3.org/TR/xhtml1/DTD/xhtml1-transitional.dtd">
<html>
<head>
<title>Scope</title>
<meta http-equiv="Content-Type" content="text/html; charset=utf-8" />
<script type="text/javascript" src="global.js" >
</script>
<script type="text/javascript" src="global2.js">
</script>
<script type="text/javascript">

message = "I'm in the page";

function testScope() {
  message += " called in testScope()";
  alert(message);
}
```

Example 2-1. The dangers of global variables and not declaring local variables explicitly (continued)

```
</script>
</head>
<body onload="testScope();global2Print();globalPrint()">
<script type="text/javascript">

message += " embedded in page";
document.writeln(message);
</script>
</body>
</html>
```

When the page initially loads, the JS in the head element is processed first, and the message variable is set to a string with the words, I'm in the page. The variable is then output to a dialog window from a function, testScope, which is called when the page finishes loading. Before printing the message, though, the function also concatenates (adds to the end) the string, called in testScope() to the original text. Later in the web page, another block of JavaScript also accesses message and concatenates its own text to the message string: embedded in page. The modified string is then printed out to the web page.

The page also imports two JavaScript external files. The first, *global.js*, concatenates its own string, globally in globalPrint, to the message. The source file also has a function, globalPrint, which opens a dialog and publishes the message:

```
message += " globally in globalPrint";

function globalPrint() {
  alert(message);
}
```

The last component of this application, the JavaScript source file *global2.js*, has a function, global2Print, and also modifies message, this time by adding "also accessed in global2Print":

```
function global2Print() {
message += " also accessed in global2Print";
alert(message);
}
```

When the web page is first opened, message is initially set in the first script block, and then modified and printed out in the second script block as the page loads. The message at this point is:

```
I'm in the page embedded in the page
```

Nothing too surprising here. Via the onload event in the body tag, testScope is called as soon as the page is loaded. This function modifies the message string, and pops up a window with:

```
I'm in the page embedded in the page called in testScope()
```

Clicking the OK button closes the window, and the next function listed in `onload` is called: `global2Print` in *global2.js*. This function adds "Hi, you were here", resulting in a dialog with the following:

```
I'm in a page embedded in page called in testScope( ) also accessed in global2Print
```

The message is getting long and has been modified in multiple JS blocks across two files, but it's not finished yet. The last function called from the `onload` event is `globalPrint` in *global.js*. The JavaScript in this file modifies the string message, and `globalPrint` outputs it via an alert. The resulting text is:

```
I'm in a page embedded in a page called in testScope( ) also accessed in global2Print
```

Now, this is when what's happening with `message` may begin to get confusing. As you can see, the message didn't change between calling the function in *global2.js* and calling the function in *global.js*, but JavaScript in both files modified the string.

The discrepancy in the result is that *global2.js* modified the string directly within the function before printing, treating it as a local variable, while *global.js* modified it outside the function, treating it as if it were global. When the JavaScript source file is loaded, the JavaScript is processed as the page is loaded, and the message set globally is lost as soon as the JavaScript in the head element of the web page body is processed. This script block treats `message` as a local variable and sets, rather than modifies, the `message` variable's contents—overwriting the value set in the global variable of the same name.

After a few more directs and redirects, and mixing global and local access of a variable with nothing to differentiate the two, you'll be surprised at the result at some point no matter how carefully you follow the variable. Guaranteed.

 Though not demonstrated, a variable declared within a code block (delimited with curly braces) has scope beyond the block. It's accessible by the code for the entire function, or a script if the block is not within a function. JavaScript 1.7 adds block-level scoping, but this language version is not universally implemented in browsers at this time.

What's the moral of all of this, then? Well, there are two, really.

The first is to be especially careful when using global variables. Some would say that with JavaScript's ability to create objects and attach properties, as well as pass values as function parameters, you shouldn't use global variables. However, global variables can be very handy: they can keep running counts or hold timers, or any value necessary to more than one function.

Still, if you use large JavaScript libraries, no matter how careful you are, a global variable of the same name as the one you're using in your library can happen. When it does, you're going to get unexpected side effects.

An additional reason to avoid global variables is that they add to the overall memory burden of a JS application. Memory management for JavaScript is managed for us, but we can help the process. Unlike local variables, which are freed when the function ends, global variables hang around until the web page, and JS application, are no longer loaded in the browser.

If using extreme caution with global variables is one of the morals learned in this section, what's the second? It's this: always explicitly define a local variable using the var keyword. If you don't, it's treated as a global variable—pure and simple.

JavaScript Best Practice: Use the var keyword to define any variable regardless of scope: global or local. As the old saying goes, begin as you mean to continue. This is particularly true when you are learning JavaScript.

Widgets for JavaScript

After a long hard day of working with variable scope, I like to spend a little time playing around with what I call "geegaws"—fun utilities, toys, what have you, that can be installed quickly and are intuitively simple and easy to use.

I have both a Mac and a Windows notebook computer, and I like both, though I prefer my Mac. One of the items I especially like about my Mac is the number of widgets I can install into my Dashboard—the widget space that can overlay your contents. It's a wonderful spot for geegaws, including JavaScript geegaws.

Among the geegaws I have currently installed on my Mac are: HTML Test 2, which can be used to test JavaScript; ExecScript 2.0, which can run JS typed into a window; Regex, the regular expression survival kit; and Rob Rohan, a JavaScript shell.

Most JavaScript widgets can be found in the Developer category of the widget download site: *http://www.apple.com/downloads/dashboard/developer/*. Each is installable with just one click of a button, with a minimum of footprint (resource use).

Simple Types

JavaScript is a trim language, with just enough functionality to do the job—no more, no less. However, as I've said before, it is a confusing language in some respects.

For instance, there are just three simple data types: string, numeric, and boolean. Each is specifically differentiated by the literal it contains: string, numeric, and boolean. However, there are also built-in objects known as number, string, and boolean. These would seem to be the same thing, but aren't: the first three are classifications of primitive values, while the latter three are complex constructions with a type of their own: object.

Rather than mix type and object, in the next three sections, we'll look at each of the simple data types, how they're created, and how values of one type can be converted to others. In Chapter 4, we'll look at these and other built-in JS objects, and the methods and properties accessible with each.

The String Data Type

A string variable was demonstrated in Example 2-1. Since JavaScript is a loosely typed language, there isn't anything to differentiate it from a variable that's a number or a boolean, other than the literal value assigned it when it's initialized and the context of the use.

A string literal is a sequence of characters delimited by single or double quotes:

```
"This is a string"
'But this is also a string'
```

There is no rule as to which type of quote you use, except that the ending quote character must be the same as the beginning one. Any variation of characters can be included in the string:

```
"This is 1 string."
"This is--another string."
```

Not all characters are treated equally within a string in JavaScript. A string can also contain an *escape sequence*, such as \n for end-of-line terminator.

An escape sequence is a set of characters in which certain characters are encoded in order to include them within the string. The following snippet of code assigns a string literal containing a line-terminator escape sequence to a variable. When the string is used in a dialog window, the escape sequence, \n, is interpreted literally, and a new line is published:

```
var string_value = "This is the first line\nThis is the second line";
```

This results in:

```
This is the first line
This is the second line
```

The two different types of quotes, single and double, can be used interchangeably if you need to include a quote within the quoted string:

```
var string_value = "This is a 'string' with a quote.";
```

or:

```
var string_value = 'This is a "string" with a quote.';
```

You can also use the backslash to denote that the quote in the string is meant to be taken as a literal character, not an end-of-string terminator:

```
var string_value = "This is a \"string\" with a quote."
```

To include a backslash in the string, use two backslashes in a row:

```
var string_value = "This is a \\string\\ with a backslash."
```

The result of this line of code is a string with two backslashes, one on either side of the word string.

There is also a JavaScript function, escape, that encodes an entire string, converting ASCII to URL Encoding (ISO Latin-1 [ISO 8859-1]), which can be used in HTML processing. This is particularly important if you're processing data for web applications. Example 2-2 demonstrates how escape works with a couple of different strings.

Example 2-2. Using the escape function to escape strings

```
<!DOCTYPE html PUBLIC "-//W3C//DTD XHTML 1.0 Transitional//EN"
"http://www.w3.org/TR/xhtml1/DTD/xhtml1-transitional.dtd">
<html>
<head>
<title>Convert Object to String</title>
<meta http-equiv="Content-Type" content="text/html; charset=utf-8" />
</head>
<body>
<script type="text/javascript">
//<![CDATA[

var sOne = escape("http://oreilly.com");
document.writeln("<p>" + sOne + "</p>");

var sTwo = escape("http://burningbird.net/index.php?pagename=$1&page=$2");
document.writeln("<p>" + sTwo + "</p>");

//]]>
</script>
</body>
</html>
```

The result of the program is the following two escaped strings:

```
http%3A//oreilly.com

http%3A//burningbird%2Cnet/index.php%3Fpagename%3D%241%26page%3D%242
```

Characters that are escaped are spaces, colons, slashes, and other characters meaningful in an HTML context. To return the string to the original, use the unescape function on the modified string.

Though handy enough, the problem with escape is that it doesn't work with non-ASCII characters. There are, however, two functions—encodeURI and decodeURI—that provide encoding beyond just the ASCII character set. The encoding that's followed is shown in Table 2-4, replicated from the Mozilla Core JavaScript 1.5 Reference.

Table 2-4. Characters subject to URI encoding

Type	Includes
Reserved characters	; , / ? : @ & = + $
Unescaped characters	Alphabetic, decimal digits, - _ . ! ~ *' ( )
Score	#

If the body of the JavaScript block in Example 2-1 is replaced with the following:

```
var sURL = "http://oreilly.com/this_is_a_value&some-value='some value'";
sURL = encodeURI(sURL);
document.writeln("<p>" + sURL + "</p>");
```

Here's the resulting string printed to the page:

```
http://oreilly.com/this_is_a_value&some-value='some%20value'
```

The function decodeURI can then be used to retrieve the original, nonescaped string.

There are two other functions for URI encoding—encodeURIComponent and decodeURIComponent—that are used in Ajax operations because they also encode &, +, and =, but we'll look at those in Chapter 13.

You can also include Unicode characters in a string by preceding the four-digit hexa-decimal value of the character with \u. For instance, the following outputs the Chinese (simplified) ideogram for "love":

```
document.writeln("\u7231");
```

What displays is somewhat browser-dependent; however, most of the more commonly used browsers now have adequate Unicode support.

Learn more about Unicode and access relevant charts at *http://www.unicode.org/*.

The empty string is a special case; it's commonly used to initialize a string variable when it's defined. Following are examples of empty strings:

```
var string_value = '';
var string_value = "";
```

Which quote character you use makes no difference to the JavaScript engine. What's more important is to use one or the other consistently.

These are all demonstrations of how to explicitly create a string variable, and variations of string literals that incorporate special characters. The values within a specific variable can also be converted from other data types, depending on the context.

If a numeric or Boolean variable is passed to a function that expects a string, the value is implicitly converted to a string first, before the value is processed:

```
var num_value = 35.00;
alert(num_value);
```

In addition, when variables are added, depending on the context, nonstring values are also converted to strings. You've seen this in action when nonstring values are added (concatenated) to a string to be published in a dialog window:

```
var num_value = 35.00;
var string_value = "This is a number:" + num_value;
```

You can also explicitly convert a variable to a string using string (toString in ECMAScript). If the value being converted is a boolean, the resulting string is a text representation of the Boolean value: "true" for true; "false" for false. For numbers, the string is, again, a string representation of the number, such as "-123.06" for −123.06, depending on the number of digits and the precision (placement of the decimal point). A value of NaN (Not a Number, discussed later) returns "NaN".

Table 2-5 shows the results of using String on different data types.

Table 2-5. toString conversion table

Input	Result
Undefined	"undefined"
Null	"null"
Boolean	If true, then "true"; if false, then "false"
Number	See chapter text
String	No conversion
Object	A string representation of the default representation of the object

The last item in Table 2-5 discusses how a string conversion works with an object. Within the ECMAScript specification, the conversion routines first call the toPrimitive function, before the type conversion. The toPrimitive function calls the DefaultValue object method, if any, and returns the result. For instance, using toString on the String object itself returns a value of the following in some browsers:

```
[object Window]
```

This can be useful if you wish to drill into the value held in a variable for debugging purposes.

The Boolean Data Type

The boolean data type has two values: true and false. They are not surrounded by quotes; in other words, "false" is not the same as false.

The function Boolean (ToBoolean in ECMAScript) can convert another value to boolean true or false, according to Table 2-6.

Table 2-6. ToBoolean conversion table

Input	Result
Undefined	false
Null	false
Boolean	Value of value
Number	Value of false if number is 0 or NaN; otherwise, true
String	Value of false if string is empty; otherwise, true
Object	true

The Number Data Type

Numbers in JavaScript are floating-point numbers, but they may or may not have a fractional component. If they don't have a decimal point or fractional component, they're treated as integers—base-10 whole numbers in a range of -2^{53} to 2^{53}. Following are valid integers:

```
-1000
0
2534
```

The floating-point representation has a decimal, with a decimal component to the right. It could also be represented as an exponent, using either a superscript or exponential notation. All of the following are valid floating-point numbers:

```
0.3555
144.006
-2.3
44²
19.5e-2 (which is equivalent to 19.5-2)
```

Though larger numbers are supported, some functions can work only with numbers in a range of $-2e31$ to $2e31$ ($-2,147,483,648$ to $2,147,483,648$); as such, you should limit your number use to this range.

There are two special numbers: positive and negative infinity. In JavaScript, they are represented by Infinity and -Infinity. A positive infinity is returned whenever a math overflow occurs in a JS application.

In addition to base-10 representation, octal and hexadecimal notation can be used, though octal is newer and may be confused for hexadecimal with older browsers. A hexadecimal number begins with a zero, followed by an x:

```
-0xCCFF
```

Octal values begin with zeros, and there is no leading x:

```
0526
```

You can convert strings or booleans to numbers; two functions, parseInt and parseFloat, manage the conversion depending on the type of number you want returned.

The parseInt function returns the integer portion of a number in a string, whether the string is formatted as an integer or floating point. The parseFloat function returns the floating-point value until a nonnumeric character is reached. In Example 2-3, three strings containing numeric values are passed to either parseInt or parseFloat, and the values are written to the page.

Example 2-3. Converting strings to numbers using different global functions

```
<!DOCTYPE html PUBLIC "-//W3C//DTD XHTML 1.0 Transitional//EN" "http://www.w3.org/TR/
xhtml1/DTD/xhtml1-transitional.dtd">
<html>
<head>
<title>Convert String to Number</title>
<meta http-equiv="Content-Type" content="text/html; charset=utf-8" />
</head>
<body>
<p>
<script type="text/javascript">
//<![CDATA[

var sNum = "1.23e-2";
document.writeln(parseFloat(sNum));

var fValue = parseFloat("1.45inch");
document.writeln("<p>" + fValue + "</p>");

var iValue = parseInt("33.00");
document.writeln("<p>" + iValue + "</p>");

//]]>
</script>
</p>
</body>
</html>
```

Using Firefox as a browser, the values printed out are:

```
0.0123
1.45
33
```

Notice with the first value, the number is printed out in decimal notation rather than the exponential notation of the original string value. Also note that parseInt truncates the fractional component of the number.

The parseInt function can convert an octal or hexadecimal number back to base-10 representation. There is a second parameter to the function, base, which is 10 or base 10, by default. If any other base is specified, in a range from 2 to 36, the string is interpreted accordingly. If you replace the document output JavaScript in Example 2-3 with the following:

```
var iValue = parseInt("0266",8);
document.writeln("<p>" + iValue + "</p>");

var iValue = parseInt("0x5F",16);
document.writeln("<p>" + iValue + "</p>");
```

These octal and hexidecimal values are printed out to the page:

```
182
```

```
95
```

In addition to `parseInt` and `parseFloat`, the `Number` function also converts numbers. The type returned after conversion is dependent on the representation: floating-point strings return floating-point numbers; integer strings, integers. Conversion to numbers from each type is shown in Table 2-7.

Table 2-7. Conversion from other data types to numbers

Input	Result
Undefined	NaN
Null	0
Boolean	If `true`, the result is 1; otherwise 0
Number	Straight value
String	See chapter text
Object	Numeric representation of the default representation of the object

In addition to converting strings to numbers, you can also test the value of a variable to see if it's infinity through the `IsFinite` function. If the value is infinity or NaN, the function returns `false`; otherwise, it returns `true`.

There are other functions that work on numbers, but they're associated with the Number object, discussed in Chapter 4. For now, we'll continue to look at the primitive types with two special JavaScript types: null and undefined.

Null and Undefined

The division between literals, simple data types, and objects is blurred in JavaScript, nowhere more so then when looking at two that represent nonexistence or incomplete existence: null and undefined.

A *null* variable is one that has been defined, but hasn't been assigned a value. The following is an example of a null variable:

```
alert(sValue); // results in JavaScript error because sValue is not declared first
```

In this example, the variable sValue has not not been declared either through the use of the var keyword or by being passed as a parameter to a function. If the variable has been declared but not initialized, it is considered undefined.

```
var sValue;
alert(sValue); // no error, and a window with the word 'undefined' is opened
```

A variable is not null and not undefined when it is both declared and given an initial value:

```
var sValue = "";
```

When using several JS libraries and fairly complex code, it's not unusual for a variable to not get set, and trying to use it in an expression can have adverse effects— usually a JavaScript error. One approach to test variables if you're unsure of their state is to use the variable in a conditional test, such as the following:

```
if (sValue) ... // if not null and initialized, expression is true; otherwise false
```

We'll look at conditional statements in the next chapter, but the expression consisting of just the variable sValue evaluates to true if sValue has been declared and initialized; otherwise, the result of the expression is false:

```
if (sValue) // not true, as variable has not been declared, and is therefore null
```

```
var sValue;
if (sValue) // variable is not null, but it's still not true, as variable has not
been defined (initialized with a value)
```

```
var sValue = 1;
if (sValue) // true now, as variable has been set, which automatically declares it
```

Using the null keyword, you can specifically test to see whether a value is null:

```
if (sValue == null)
```

In JavaScript, a variable is undefined, even if declared, until it is initialized. It differs from null in that using a null value as a parameter to a function results in an error, while using an undefined variable usually does not:

```
alert(sValue); // JS error results, "Error: sValue is not defined"
var sValue; // no JS error and the window reads, "undefined" which is the value of
the object
```

A variable can be undeclared but initialized, in which case it is not null and not undefined. However, in this instance, it's considered a global variable, and as discussed earlier, not specifically declaring variables with var causes problems more often than not.

Though not related to existence, there is a third unique value related to the type of a variable: NaN, or Not A Number. If a string or Boolean variable cannot be coerced into a number, it's considered NaN and treated accordingly:

```
var nValue = 1.0;
if (nValue == 'one' ) // false, the second operand is NaN
```

You can specifically test whether a variable is NaN with the isNaN function:

```
if (isNaN(sValue)) // if string cannot be implicitly converted into number, return
true
```

By its very nature, a null value is NaN, so it is undefined.

 Author and respected technologist Simon Willison gave an excellent talk at O'Reilly's 2006 ETech conference titled, "A (Re)-Introduction to JavaScript." You can view his slides at his web site, *http://simon. incutio.com/slides/2006/etech/javascript/js-tutorial.001.html*. The whole presentation is a very worthwhile read, but my favorite is the following line:

> *0, "", NaN, null, and undefined are falsy. Everything else is truthy.*

In other words, zero, null, NaN, and the empty string are inherently false; everything else is inherently true.

For the most part, JavaScript developers create code in such a way that we know a variable is going to be defined ahead of time and/or given a value. In most instances, we don't explicitly test to see whether a variable is set, and if so, whether it's assigned a value.

However, when using large and complex JS libraries, and applications that can incorporate web service responses, it becomes increasingly important to test variables that originate and/or are set outside of our control—not to mention to be aware of how null and undefined variables behave when accessed in the application.

Constants: Named but Not Variables

There are times when you'll want to define a value once, and then have it treated as a read-only value from that time forward. The keyword const is used to create a JavaScript const:

```
const CURRENT_MONTH = 3.5;
```

The constant can be of any value, and since it can't be assigned or reassigned a value at a later time, it's initialized to its constant value when defined.

Just as with variables, a JavaScript constant has global and local scope. I use constants at a global level, primarily because they contain a value I want to be accessible (and unchanged) by a JavaScript block.

Questions

1. Of the following identifiers, which are valid, which are not, and why?

   ```
   $someVariable
   _someVariable
   1Variable
   some_variable
   som&#232;variable
   function
   .someVariable
   some*variable
   ```

2. Convert the following identifiers using the conventions outlined in the first section of the chapter:

   ```
   var some_month;
   function theMonth // function to return current month
   current-month // a constant
   var summer_month; // an array of summer months
   MyLibrary-afunction // a function from a JavaScript package
   ```

3. Is the following string literal valid? If not, how would you fix it?

   ```
   var someString = 'Who once said, "Only two things are infinite, the universe and
   human stupidity, and I'm not sure about the former."'
   ```

4. Given a number, 432.54, what JavaScript returns the integer component of the number, and then finds the hexidecimal and octal conversion?

5. You create a JavaScript function in a library that can be used by other applications. A parameter, someMonth, is passed to the function. How would you determine whether it's null or undefined?

Answers are provided in the appendix.

CHAPTER 3

Operators and Statements

The examples in the book so far have performed mostly simple tasks: a variable has been defined and its value set; a value is printed out in the page or in an alert window; a variable is modified through addition or multiplication or some other means. These all use JavaScript statements and operators.

There are a number of different types of statements in JavaScript: assignment, function call, conditional, and loops. Each is fairly intuitive, simple to use, and quick to learn. A snap, really. As with with most programming languages, in JavaScript the statements are easy to learn; the tricky part is lining them up, one after the other, so they do something useful.

This chapter takes a closer look at statements and operators, what they share, and how they differ.

Format of a JavaScript Statement

JavaScript statements terminate with a semicolon, though not all statements need the terminator expressly given. If the JavaScript engine determines that a statement is complete (whatever that is for each type of statement), and the line ends with a new line character, the semicolon can be omitted:

```
var bValue = true
var sValue = "this is also true"
```

If multiple statements are on the same line, though, the semicolon must be used to terminate each:

```
var bValue = true; var sValue = "this is also true"
```

However, not explicitly terminating each JavaScript statement is a bad habit to get into, and one that can result in unexpected consequences. As such, the use of the semicolon to terminate JavaScript statements is a JavaScript best practice.

JavaScript Best Practice: Explicitly terminate JavaScript statements with the semicolon, whether or not it's required.

The use of whitespace in JS has little impact on the code. For instance, the following two lines of code are interpreted exactly the same:

```
var firstName = 'Shelley'    ;
var firstName = 'Shelley';
```

Other than to delimit words within quotes or to terminate statements, extra whitespace—such as tabs, spaces, and new lines—is disregarded. In the following code, the variable assignment completes successfully, even though there is a line terminator separating the statement:

```
var firstName
= 'Shelley';
alert(firstName);
```

The engine didn't interpret the end-of-line character as a statement terminator in this instance because it evaluated the code and determined that it was incomplete. The JavaScript engine continues to process what it finds until either the semicolon is reached or until a statement is completed. In the case of the assignment statement, this state is reached when the right-side expression of the statement is provided.

Deciding whether to interpret an end-of-line terminator as a statement terminator is all a part of JavaScript's forgiving nature: JavaScript works on the side of successfully processing the code and does whatever is needed to facilitate this. Well, unless doing so introduces confusion. In the following code:

```
var firstName =
var lastName = 'Powers';
```

The JavaScript engine returns an error because the second line doesn't evaluate to a correct right-side assignment.

Returning to the discussion of whitespace, indentation is used throughout the book to make the examples more readable, but there's no programmatic reason to indent a line with a tab or spaces. The same holds true for whitespace surrounding operators such as assignment (=) or one of the math operators (such as +). Whitespace isn't necessary. Whitespace and comments, as well as meaningful identifiers, are there to make the code easier to maintain.

Simple Statements

Some JavaScript statements extend beyond a line, such as those for loops, which have a beginning and end. Others, though, stand all on their own: one statement, one line. Among these simple statements are those for assignment.

JavaScript "Compression"

The reasons to add whitespace make sense: readability, separation of key language elements, line termination, and so on. But what about removing such space?

JavaScript compressors take all noncode-specific whitespace out of a JavaScript application. The concept behind such tools is the more whitespace you put into JavaScript, the slower the download and the more client resources you consume. There are tools and sites that provide compressed JS, such as Packer, at *http://dean.edwards.name/packer/* (shown in Figure 3-1) and a host of others listed at Web Tools by Radok, at *http://www.radok.com/javascript-compression.html*.

Are these necessary? With small scripts, no, of course not. For larger JavaScript files? Hard to say: even the most complex JS library isn't more than a few hundred lines. Usually, I should add, because some of the newer Ajax libraries can be quite large.

Still, web pages today have 200K photos embedded in them and links to resource material served from half a dozen sites. Does the size of a JS library have as much of an impact as it once did? Again, it depends on the page, and what you know of your client's expectations and environments.

There are reasons not to use compression. If an error is introduced into the code, the compression makes it difficult to debug. The code is also unreadable, which inhibits sharing, a hallmark of the scripting community.

Of course, sometimes you want to limit sharing. The very nature of compression—obfuscation—may be one reason to use compressors. As Figure 3-1 demonstrates, Packer doesn't just compress the code, it also obfuscates it, making it difficult (if not impossible) to copy. There are several encryption and obfuscation tools that can make JS completely unreadable, though most (unlike Packer) are commercial products.

The Assignment Statement

The most common statement is the assignment statement. It's an expression consisting of a variable on the left side, an assignment operator (=), and whatever is being assigned on the right.

The expression on the right can be a literal value:

```
nValue = 35.00;
```

Or, a combination of variables and literals combined with any number of operators:

```
nValue = nValue + 35.00;
```

And it can be a function call:

```
nValue = someFunction( );
```

More than one assignment can be included on a line. For instance, the following assigns the value of an empty string to multiple variables, on one line:

```
var firstName = lastName = middleName = "";
```

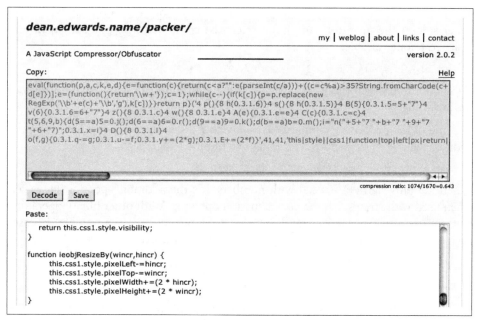

Figure 3-1. Packer, a JavaScript compression service

Following the assignment statement, the second most common type of statement is the arithmetic expression that involves the arithmetic operators, discussed next.

Arithmetic Statements

In the last section, the second example was a demonstration of a binary arithmetic expression: two operands are separated by an arithmetic operator, leading to a new result. When paired with an assignment, the result is then assigned to the variable on the left:

```
nValue = vValue + 35.00;
```

More complex examples can use any number of arithmetic operators, with any combination of literal values and variables:

```
nValue = nValue + 30.00 / 2 - nValue2 * 3;
```

The operators used in the expression come from this set of binary operators:

+   For addition

-   For subtraction

*   For multiplication

/   For division

%   To return the remainder after division

These are considered binary operators because they require two operands, one on either side of the operator. Any number can be combined into one statement and assigned to one variable:

```
var bigCalc = varA * 6.0 + 3.45 - varB / .05;
```

This code shows the binary operators working with numbers. How about if the values are strings?

In some of the previous examples, I *concatenated* (joined) strings together using the addition sign (+), just as if I were adding two numbers together:

```
var newString = "This is an old " + oldString;
```

When the plus sign (+) is used with numbers, it's the addition operator. However, when used with strings, it's the concatenation operator. With other binary operators, you can use a string as an operand, but the string has to contain a number. In cases such as this, the value is converted to a number before the expression is evaluated:

```
var newValue = 3.5 * 2.0; // result is 7
var newValue = 3.5 * "2.0"; // result is still 7
var newValue = "3.5" * "2.0"; // still 7
```

On the other hand (and it's important to be aware of the distinction), if you add a number literal or variable and a string, the number is the value that's converted from number to string.

In the following example, you might expect to get a value of 5.5 but instead get a new string, "3.52.0":

```
var newValue = 3.5 + "2.0"; // result is a string, "3.52.0"
```

This one can trip you up quite frequently. Be very, very careful when mixing types with implicit conversion; a simple accident in any of the values could lead to surprising results. When you think the data type of one variable is treated as a string by the JavaScript engine, a better approach is to use parseInt, parseFloat, or Number to explicitly convert the value:

```
var aVar = parseFloat(bVar) + 2.0;
```

The Unary Operators

In addition to the binary arithmetical operators just covered, there are also three unary operators. These differ from the earlier batch in that they apply to only one operand:

++ Increments a value

-- Decrements a value

- Represents a negative value

Here's an example of a unary operator:

```
someValue = 34;
var iValue = -someValue;
```

```
iValue++;
document.writeln(iValue);
```

In the second line, the number is converted to a negative value through the use of the negative unary operator. The value is incremented by one using ++, which is a shorthand version of:

```
iValue=iValue + 1;
```

The end result is –33.

The increment and decrement operators have another interesting aspect to them. In an expression, if the operator is listed first, the value is adjusted before the result is assigned. However, if the operator is listed after the variable, the initial value in the variable is assigned, and the value is adjusted:

```
var iValue = 3.0;
var iValue2 = ++iValue; //iValue2 is set to 4.0, iValue has a value now of 4.0
var iValue3 = iValue++; //iValue3 is set to 4.0; iValue now has a value of 5.0
var iValue4 = iValue;   //both iValue4 and iValue have a value of 5.0
```

Precedence of Operators

There is a level of precedence to operators in JavaScript. In statements, expressions are evaluated left to right when all operators have the same precedence. If more than one type operator with more than one precedence is used in a statement, the rule is that the operator with higher precedence is evaluated first, then the rest of the expression is evaluated left to right.

Let's consider the following code:

```
newValue = nValue + 30.00 /  2 - nValue2 * 3;
```

If the value of nValue is 3 and the value of nValue2 is 6, the result is 0.

In detail, the division of 30.00 by 2 is evaluated first because it has higher precedence than the addition, resulting in a value of 15. The multiplication operator has the same precedence as that of division, but it occurs after the division. Because expressions are evaluated left to right when precedence is the same, the division is done first, then the multiplication. In the latter, the value in variable nValue2 is multiplied by 3, resulting in a value of 18. From that point on, the expression consists solely of addition and subtraction (equal precedence), and is evaluated left to right as:

```
newValue = nValue + 15 - 18;
```

The assignment operator has the lowest precedence, and once the arithmetic expression is evaluated completely, the result is assigned to newValue.

To control the impact of precedence, use parentheses around expressions you want evaluated first. Returning to the example, the use of parentheses can lead to widely different results:

```
newValue = ((nValue + 30.00) / (2 - nValue2)) * 3;
```

Now, addition and subtraction are evaluated first, before division and multiplication. The result of this expression is −24.75.

You all knew this from your basic math classes. However, it doesn't hurt to get a little reaffirmation: although it's in JavaScript, the rules are the same.

 Note that in JavaScript, unlike in other languages, the division results in a floating-point result, not a truncated whole number. The following results in a value of 1.5 rather than a rounded value of 1:

```
iValue = 3 / 2;
```

In the examples so far, we're typed out the full expression when using binary operators. There is a shortcut method to these expressions, which we'll look at next.

Handy Shortcut: Assignment with Operation

Assignment and an arithmetic operation can be combined into one simple statement if the same variable appears on both sides of the operator, such as in the following:

```
nValue = nValue + 30;
```

The simplified statement is:

```
nValue += 3.0;
```

All of the binary arithmetic operators can be used in this type of shorthand technique, known as an *assignment with operation*:

```
nValue %= 3;
nValue -= 3;
nValue *= 4;
nvalue += 5;
```

This type of operation can also be used in combination with the four bitwise operators.

Bitwise Operators

 This section covers JavaScript bitwise operators, and assumes you have some experience with Boolean algebra. It's not a functionality that's used extensively in JavaScript and can be safely skipped during this first introduction to the language. If you're not familiar with Boolean algebra and want to continue with this section, there is excellent Boolean algebra reference, put together by the BBC (British Broadcasting Corporation), at *http://www.bbc.co.uk/dna/h2g2/A412642*.

Bitwise operators treat the operands as 32-bit values made up of a sequence of zeros and ones. The operators then perform, literally, a bitwise manipulation of the result; the type of manipulation depends on the type of operator:

& Bitwise AND operation, in which the resulting bit is 1 if, and only if, both values are 1.

| Bitwise OR operation on bits, in which the result is 1 only if one of the operand bits is 1.

^ Bitwise XOR operation on bits, in which the the combination of the two operand bits equals 1 if, and only if, both values are different. If the value of both is 1 or 0, the result is 0; otherwise, the result is 1.

~ Bitwise NOT operation on a bit, which returns the inverted value (complement) of the bit (i.e., 1 results in 0; 0 results in 1).

It might seem as if the bitwise operators don't have much use in JavaScript, except that they're a handy way of creating binary flags within a program. Binary flags are similar to variables except that they use much less memory (by a factor of 32). The Mozilla Core JavaScript 1.5 reference provides an example that uses binary flags: *http://developer. mozilla.org/en/docs/Core_JavaScript_1.5_Reference:Operators:Bitwise_Operators*. In the example, four flags are represented by the following variable:

```
var flags = 0x5;
```

This is equivalent to the binary value of 0101 (disregarding leading zeros):

```
flag A: false
flag B: true
flag C: false
flag D: true
```

Each bitmask flag is then represented as:

```
var flag_A = 0x1;
var flag_B = 0x2;
var flag_C = 0x3;
var flag_D = 0x4;
```

To test if flag_C is set in our flags variable, use the bitwise AND operator:

```
if (flags & flag_C) {
    do stuff
}
```

In Example 3-1, a binary flag and bitmasks are used to emulate the result of an imaginary form submission. In the example, we'll assume five fields are submitted, but only three have values: fields A, C, and E. If both A and C are filled in, a message to this effect is output in a dialog window.

Example 3-1. Use of binary flags and bitmask to create memory-friendly flags

```
<!DOCTYPE html PUBLIC "-//W3C//DTD XHTML 1.0 Transitional//EN"
 "http://www.w3.org/TR/xhtml1/DTD/xhtml1-transitional.dtd">
<html>
<head>
<title>Using Binary Flags</title>
<meta http-equiv="Content-Type" content="text/html; charset=utf-8" />
```

Example 3-1. Use of binary flags and bitmask to create memory-friendly flags (continued)

```
<script type="text/javascript">
//<![CDATA[

var FIELD_A = 0x1; // 00001
var FIELD_B = 0x2; // 00010
var FIELD_C = 0x4; // 00100
var FIELD_D = 0x8; // 01000
var FIELD_E = 0x10; // 10000

// assume fields A, C, and E are filled in
var fieldsSet = FIELD_A | FIELD_C | FIELD_E; // 00001 | 00100 | 10000 => 10101

if ((fieldsSet & FIELD_A) && (fieldsSet & FIELD_C)) {
   alert("Fields A and C are set");
}

//]]>
</script>
</head>
</body>
<p>Imagine a form with five fields and a button here...</p>
</html>
```

This is a way of conserving space in your application, as you can work with binary values within the space required for Boolean variables. However, this does compromise the code's readability.

 Another operator, the logical AND (designated by &&) is also introduced in Example 3-1. This is covered in detail later in the section "The Logical Operators."

There is more in the Mozilla reference regarding the use of bitwise operators as a test of input; it's an interesting technique and an affirmation that though memory management is handled behind the scenes with JavaScript, there are tricks and techniques you can use to get an edge when you need one.

 There are three other bitwise operators: shift left (<<), shift right with sign (>>), and shift right with zero fill (>>>). These move the bits of the operand to the right or left by the number of places designated by the second operand (a value between 0 and 31):

```
newValue = oldValue >>> 3;
```

This last example also introduces the concept of a different type of statement and set of operators: conditional statements, and relational and equality operators. We'll look at both in the next few sections.

Conditional Statements and Program Flow

Normally in JavaScript, the program flow is linear: each statement is processed in turn, one right after another. It takes deliberate action to change this. You can put the code in a function that is only called based on some action or event, or you can perform some form of conditional test and run a block of code only if the test evaluates to true.

One of the more common approaches to changing the program flow in JavaScript is through a conditional statement. As seen in the last few sections, the typical conditional statement has the following format:

```
if (value) {
statements processed
}
```

The term *conditional* comes from the fact that a condition has to be met before the block associated with the statement is processed. The example equates to: if some value (whether a result of an expression, a variable, or or a literal) evaluates to true, then do the following code; otherwise, jump to the end of the block, and continue processing at the very next line.

The use of the `if` keyword signals the beginning of the conditional test, and the parenthetical expression encapsulates the test. In the following code, the binary flag is tested against two bitmasks to see if either is matched. If so, and only then, the code contained in curly braces following the conditional expression is processed:

```
if ((fieldsSet & FIELD_A) && (fieldsSet & FIELD_C)) {
    alert("Fields A and C are set");
}
```

The use of curly braces isn't necessary in this example because only one line of JavaScript is processed if the condition evaluates to true. If more than one JS statement needs to be processed, all the code must be contained within curly braces. These are commonly referred to as *JavaScript blocks* or *blocks of code*, and the curly braces let the script engine know that all of the JavaScript contained in the block is processed if the condition evaluates to true.

Since it's not unheard of that additional code is added at a later time, it's good practice to use curly braces around a statement processed through some flow-of-control event (such as a conditional statement).

 JavaScript Best Practice: Use curly braces ({,}) around control blocks—statement(s) processed as a result of some flow-of-control action, such as a conditional statement.

To make the JavaScript more readable, it's also considered good form to indent the code that's contained within the curly braces. If the contained code has another conditional statement, the statements associated with it are indented the same amount, but from the original position and so on. Example 3-2 demonstrates three nested conditional statements—each with a block of code, each of which is indented. Change the variable's initial value to test the different conditional expressions.

Example 3-2. Three nested conditional statements, indented for easier reading

```
<!DOCTYPE html PUBLIC "-//W3C//DTD XHTML 1.0 Transitional//EN"
"http://www.w3.org/TR/xhtml1/DTD/xhtml1-transitional.dtd">
<html>
<head>
<title>Nested Indented Conditional statements</title>
<meta http-equiv="Content-Type" content="text/html; charset=utf-8" />
<script type="text/javascript">
//<![CDATA[

var prefChoice = 1;
var stateChoice = 'OR';
var genderChoice = 'F';

if (prefChoice == 1) {
   alert("You've picked option 1. Here is what will happen...");

   if (stateChoice == 'OR') {
      alert ("You've picked 1 and you're from Oregon.");

      if (genderChoice == 'M') {
         alert("You've picked 1 and you're from Oregon and you're a man.");

      } // innermost block

   } // middle block

} // outerblock


//]]>
</script>
</head>
<body>
<p>Imagine a form with five fields and a button here...</p>
</body>
</html>
```

Typically, code is indented three spaces with each block, and curly braces are lined up with the conditional statement. There's no fast rule on this; it doesn't impact the validity of the code.

In addition, the closing curly brace on each block is annotated with a comment. If the code is fairly long, complex, and full of nested blocks, such as those in Example 3-2, using comments to document the ending curly brace makes the code easier to read and maintain.

JavaScript Best Practice: In longer or more complex blocks of script, comment the ending brace to make it easier to identify exactly which block is being closed.

if...else

In many instances, a conditional test is performed, a block of one or more statements is processed, and the flow of the program continues at the end. However, not all logic can be expressed with just one test. Even within a spoken language, such as English, we have the concept of *if...then...else* to accommodate listing of various options:

> *If the sun is out, we'll go to the park; otherwise, we'll go to the movies.*

In JavaScript, the use of the keyword else performs the same functionality: it provides for processing an alternative set of statements if the condition being tested evaluates to false:

```
if (expression) {
    ...
} else {
    ...
}
```

In the following code snippet, if the value in stateCode is "MA" for Massachusetts, the tax value is set to 3.5; otherwise, the tax is set to 4.5:

```
if (stateCode == "MA") {
    taxPercentage = 3.5;
} else {
    taxPercentage = 4.5;
}
```

Either the state code is "MA" or it's not; the tax percentage is set regardless.

However, not all conditions are either/or. In some instances, there might be more than one possible conditional outcome of interest, and you'll need to capture a sequence of tests: if then...else if then...else if then... and so on. This is managed in JavaScript through the addition of a conditional expression immediately following the else clause:

```
if (conditional expression) {
    block of code
} else if (other conditional expression) {
    block of code
}
```

These can be chained, one after the other, until all conditions have been tested.

In Example 3-3, the variable holding the state code is set in the code (purely for testing purposes—normally you don't know what the variable is). The three state codes are tested, and a different tax percentage is assigned if any of the three matches.

Example 3-3. Testing a value with multiple conditional statements

```
<!DOCTYPE html PUBLIC "-//W3C//DTD XHTML 1.0 Transitional//EN"
"http://www.w3.org/TR/xhtml1/DTD/xhtml1-transitional.dtd">
<html>
<head>
<title>if...then...else...if</title>
<meta http-equiv="Content-Type" content="text/html; charset=utf-8" />
<script type="text/javascript">
//<![CDATA[

var stateCode = 'MO';

if (stateCode == 'OR') {
   taxPercentage = 3.5;
} else if (stateCode == 'CA') {
   taxPercentage = 5.0;
} else if (stateCode == 'MO') {
   taxPercentage = 1.0;
} else {
   taxPercentage = 2.0;
}

alert(taxPercentage);

//]]>
</script>

</head>
<body>
<p>Imagine a form with options to pick state code</p>
</body>
</html>
```

The program evaluates each expression in turn until it finds an expression that evaluates to true. At that point, the contained statements are processed, and the program continues on the first line after the complete conditional statement. If none of the expressions evaluates to true, the block of code following the else without a condition is processed, and the tax percentage is set accordingly.

You can continue adding additional else if statements testing the same variable, but after a time, the format is clumsy, hard to read, and inefficient. A better approach is to use the switch statement.

The switch Conditional Statement

The JavaScript switch statement is used when there are several possible outcomes resulting from a conditional expression. The JavaScript engine processes the expression and based on the result, one or more alternative options are processed:

```
switch (expression) {
    case firstlabel:
        statements;
        [break;]
    case secondlabel:
        statements;
        [break;]
    ...
    case lastlabel:
        statements;
        [break;]
    default:
        statements;
```

From the top, an expression that returns a value is given in the switch statement. case statements are then evaluated, in sequence from top to bottom, to see if any match. If a matching case is found, the statements contained within the particular case statement code block are processed. At this point, the program flow either continues processing each case statement, or the control of the program can be transferred to the first line following the end of the switch statement using the optional break.

If none of the cases match, the JavaScript engine looks for an optional default statement; if one is found, its code block is processed, and the program continues with the first line following the switch.

In the case where the same set of statements is processed for two or more case labels, the labels can be listed, with just the statements underneath:

```
case labelone:
case labeltwo:
case labelthree:
    statements;
    break;
```

With this technique, the statements are processed if any one of the three labels—labelone, labeltwo, or labelthree—are matched.

The switch statement is best explained with a demonstration. In Example 3-4, our state code is tested and if the value is OR, MA, or WI, the tax percentage is set to 3.5, and the state percentage to 0.5; if the code tested is MO, the tax percentage is set to 1.0, and the state percentage to 1.5; if the code tests out to CA, NY, and VT, the percentage is set to 4.5, and the state percentage to 2.6; if the code tests out to TX, the percentage is set to 3.0, with the state percentage left at 0.0; otherwise, the tax percentage is set to 2.0, with state set to 2.3.

Example 3-4. Using a switch statement to test expression against multiple values

```
<!DOCTYPE html PUBLIC "-//W3C//DTD XHTML 1.0 Transitional//EN"
"http://www.w3.org/TR/xhtml1/DTD/xhtml1-transitional.dtd">
<html>
<head>
```

```
<title>switch statement</title>
<meta http-equiv="Content-Type" content="text/html; charset=utf-8" />
<script type="text/javascript">
//<![CDATA[

var stateCode = 'NY';
var statePercentage = 0.0;
var taxPercentage = 0.0;

switch (stateCode) {
    case 'OR','MA','WI' :
      statePercentage = 0.5;
      taxPercentage = 3.5;
      break;
    case 'MO' :
      taxPercentage = 1.0;
      statePercentage = 1.5;
      break;
    case 'CA' :
    case 'NY' :
    case 'VT' :
      statePercentage = 2.6;
      taxPercentage = 4.5;
      break;
    case 'TX' :
      taxPercentage = 3.0;
      break;
    default :
      taxPercentage = 2.0;
      statePercentage = 2.3;
}

alert("tax is " + taxPercentage + " and state is " + statePercentage);

//]]>
</script>
</head>
<body>
<p>Imagine a form with options to pick state code</p>
</body>
</html>
```

From the top, the expression given in the `switch` statement is just the state code variable, `stateCode`. It can be any expression using any of the relational and logical operators (discussed in the next section). The case statements are then evaluated for a match. In the first, if the state code is OR, MA, or WI, the tax percentages are set to the same values. In this instance, the case values associated with the block are separated from the others by commas, which means any one of the three can match.

If the state code is TX or MO, the individual case blocks processed, but if the state code is CA, NY, or VT, the statements in the block associated with the last case, VT, are the ones processed. The other two state code cases have no statements of their own; neither do they have a break statement. This means, then, that if the state code is one of these, the program continues processing statements until the end of the switch statement, or until a break is reached. This is another approach that attaches the same statement block to more than one case value. It's identical in behavior to listing out the options, separated by a comma.

Finally if none of the cases match, the default is processed, and the program continues on the first statement after the switch.

Notice in the example that the only use of curly braces is around the switch control block itself. That's because with switch, program flow is controlled with the break statement, not curly braces. However, indentation still applies, thought it's not uncommon for the processed statements to be placed on the same line as the case condition:

```
case 'OR' : taxPercentage = 3.5; statePercentage = 2.0; break;
```

Most of the expressions being tested in the conditional control statements have been fairly simple equality tests. More complex conditional expressions, and even multiple expressions, can be used with conditional operators, discussed next.

The Conditional Operators

The conditional operators are a way of testing for specific conditions: equality, identity, relational, and logical. Though the processes may differ, and they range from simple to complex, the result of using such operators is one of two values: true or false.

The Equality and the Identity (String Equality) Operators

One of the most common operators used in a conditional expression is the equality operator, ==. It is used when a variable is compared with another variable or literal value, and based on the result, an action or set of actions is triggered:

```
// at some point  in application, assign 3 to variable nValue
var nValue = 3;
...
if (nValue == 3) ...
```

In this example, if the variable nValue is equal to 3, what follows (represented by the ellipses in the text) is processed. Otherwise, the flow of the program skips over the code block and goes to the first statement following.

Be careful not to leave off the second equals sign (=). If you do, the expression becomes one of assignment, not conditional testing. The variable nValue is assigned the value of 3. Since the assignment was successful, it returns true. It always returns true. A JavaScript error doesn't occur, and as such, it may be hard to spot this error in debugging.

As with the addition operator, the equality operator converts the variable's data type to facilitate the evaluation of the expression. If one value is numeric and the other is string, comparing both is successful if the value is "typographically" the same:

```
var nValue = 3.0;
var sValue = "3.0";
If (nValue == sValue) ...
```

This can lead to some interesting and unexpected side effects. In particular, the equality operator is implicitly used in the switch statement, which means that both of the following cases are applicable if the switch expression evaluates to "3.0":

```
case 3.0: ...
case "3.0": ...
```

Starting with JavaScript 1.3, a new operator—the identity, or strict equality operator—was added specifically to test on both value and type. Unlike standard equality, the strict equality operator won't return success unless both operands are the same *and* have the same data type:

```
if (nValue === sValue) ...
```

In addition to testing for both equality and identity, you can also test for not equals and strict not equals. The not equals operator is !=:

```
if (sName != "Smith") ...
```

The strict not equals operator is !==:

```
if (sName !== "Smith")...s
```

Here is where the difference between the two operators is most apparent. In Example 3-5, a numeric value is tested against a string with equality and strict equality, and a string value is tested against a numeric with not equals and strict not equals.

Example 3-5. Testing for precision between equals and strict equals

```
<!DOCTYPE html PUBLIC "-//W3C//DTD XHTML 1.0 Transitional//EN"
"http://www.w3.org/TR/xhtml1/DTD/xhtml1-transitional.dtd">
<html>
<head>
<title>Identity and Equality</title>
<meta http-equiv="Content-Type" content="text/html; charset=utf-8" />
<script type="text/javascript">
//<![CDATA[

var sValue = "3.0";
var nValue = 3.0;

if (nValue == "3.0") alert("According to equality, value is 3.0");

if (nValue === "3.0") alert("According to identity, value is 3.0");

if (sValue != 3.0) alert ("According to equality, value is not 3.0");

if (sValue !== 3.0) alert ("According to identity, value is not 3.0");
```

Example 3-5. Testing for precision between equals and strict equals (continued)

```
//]]>
</script>
</head>
<body>
<p>Some page content</p>
</body>
</html>
```

In the first case, the numeric 3.0 is tested against the string-based "3.0" with the equality operator. The result is true, and the dialog window opens. However, this comparison fails with strict equality, and the second dialog window is not opened.

In the third case, the string 3.0 is tested against the numeric 3.0. The not equals test fails, because to this operator, both values are the same. However, with the strict not equals operator, this comparison does evaluate to true, and the alert window opens.

 Example 3-5 also introduces a shortcut method of processing one statement associated with a conditional statement. In this case, curly braces aren't necessary because the association is quite readable, and there is only one statement being processed.

As you can see in Example 3-5, the strict equality operator is much more precise. If this is so, you might wonder why it's not more widely used.

The equality operator and its converse, not equals, have been around since the beginning of JavaScript and are supported by all JS engines. The strict equals/identity operator and its converse were added late in the game, with JavaScript 1.2. In addition, with the first release of the ECMA 262 specification, the strict equals operator was dropped, and only added back in with ECMA 262, Version 3.0. As such, support for strict equals isn't guaranteed in all browsers and by all JS engines.

Unless you can control which browser accesses your script, you need to assume that the identity or strict equals operator isn't supported. In a few years, as some of the older browsers finally die out, the strict equals operator will, most likely, become more widely used.

Testing for equality is helpful, but sometimes you need to test a range of values, not just for a specific value. Enter greater than and less than.

Other Relational Operators

A *relational operator* is one in which one operand is compared to another and depending on the result, one or more lines of code are processed. The equality and strict equality operators are relational operators, except sometimes we want relational operators to also match when a value is either greater than or less than another—not just equals.

The greater than operator (>) returns true if the right operand is of less value than the operand on the left. The greater than or equals operator (>=) returns true if the right operand is of less *or* equal value to the operand on the left:

```
var nValue = 1.0;
if (nValue > 3.0)  // false
...
if (nValue >= 1.0) // true
...
if (nValue >= 0.5) // true
...
```

The less than operator (<) returns true if the right operand is of greater value than the operand on the left. The less than or equals operator (<=) returns true if the right operand is greater than *or* equal to the value of the operand on the left, as demonstrated in the following test variations:

```
var nValue = 1.0

if (nValue < 3.0) // true
...
if (nValue <= 1.0) // true
...
if (nValue <= 0.5) // false
...
```

Like equality, type conversion occurs implicitly between numeric and string values with the less than/greater than operators. So the following evaluates to true:

```
sValue = "1.0";
if (sValue >= 2.0) // true
```

String conversion only occurs when the format is right. For instance, JavaScript does not convert "one" to "1" or "1.0" when doing implicit conversion.

Testing to see if a value is greater than or less than another is useful, but so is testing to see if a variable or expression result is within a range of values. In Example 3-6, a variable is tested to see if it falls within a given range, 0 to 100 inclusive, which means that the value could also be 0 or 100. It's also tested in the range between 0 and 100, excluding the values of 0 and 100. Final tests check whether the value is over 100, or less than zero (0). An appropriate message is displayed based on the result.

Example 3-6. Testing within a range of numbers

```
<!DOCTYPE html PUBLIC "-//W3C//DTD XHTML 1.0 Transitional//EN"
"http://www.w3.org/TR/xhtml1/DTD/xhtml1-transitional.dtd">
<html>
<head>
<title>Testing value in range</title>
<meta http-equiv="Content-Type" content="text/html; charset=utf-8" />
<script type="text/javascript">
//<![CDATA[
```

Example 3-6. Testing within a range of numbers (continued)

```
var nValue = 0;

if (nValue >= 0 && nValue <= 100) {
  alert("value between 0 and 100, inclusive");
} else if (nValue > 0 && nValue < 100) {
  alert("value between 0 and 100 exclusive");
} else if (nValue > 100) {
  alert ("value over 100");
} else if (nValue < 0) {
  alert ("value is negative");
}

//]]>
</script>
</head>
<body>
<p>Some page content</p>
</body>
</html>
```

The first two comparisons rely on additional operators to establish the range: the logical operators. One such, &&, was introduced in the bitwise operator section. We'll look at these in more detail later, but first, let's check out JavaScript's one and only ternary operator.

The One and Only JavaScript Ternary Operator

The operators we've looked at in this chapter have been unary (one operand), or binary (two operands). There is one ternary operator in JavaScript, the conditional operator, which works with three operands. Following is an example of its use:

```
var nValue = 1.0;
var sResult = (nValue > 0.5) ? "value over 0.5" : "value not over 0.5";
```

In this example, sResult is set to "value over 0.5" because the condition evaluates to true, resulting in the second operand being returned. Here's the format of the conditional operator:

```
condition ? value if true; value if false;
```

The conditional operator becomes, in effect, a shortcut method for the fairly common, "if (expression), do this; otherwise, do that," such as in the following code:

```
var stateCode = 'OR';
var taxPercentage = 0.0;
if (stateCode == 'OR') {
  taxPercentage = 3.5;
} else {
  taxPercentage = 4.5;
}
```

Converting for use in a conditional operator, the code becomes:

```
var taxPercentage = (stateCode == 'OR') ? 3.5 : 4.5;
```

It's both a handy shortcut, as well as a readable one, so its use is fairly common. There's more on this operator later in the book when it's used to resolve browser differences.

The Logical Operators

Most of the examples so far in the book show a conditional expression that consists usually of one operator and two operands, such as the following:

```
if (sValue == 'test')
```

However, many times a conditional expression is dependent on several different conditions being met, each represented by an expression and combined through the use of one of JavaScript's logical operators.

There are three logical operators—two binary and one unary. The first is the logical AND, represented by two ampersand characters, &&. When used in a conditional statement, the AND operator requires that expressions on both sides of the operator evaluate to true for the entire expression to evaluate to true:

```
var nValue = 10;
if ((nValue > 10) && (nValue <=100)) // true if nValue is greater than 10 and nValue
is less than or equal to 100
```

The result of using this expression joined by the AND operator is false because the variable, nValue, is equal to 10, which means the first expression is false. If the first expression evaluates to false, the JavaScript engine won't process the second expression because the entire statement is going to fail regardless.

The second operator is the logical OR operator, represented by two vertical lines, ||. When used in a conditional statement, the OR operator requires one or the other of its expressions on either side to be true in order for the entire expression to evaluate to true:

```
var nValue = 10;
if ((nValue > 10) || (nValue <= 100)) // true if nValue is either greater than 10 or
less than or equal to 100
```

The result of this code is that the conditional statement is true because the variable is less than 100. Both sides of the logical OR operator must be evaluated because the operator requires only a true expression on one side to return true.

The final logical operator is the logical NOT. This operator returns the logical negation of the expression. If the expression is true, it returns false; if false, it returns true:

```
var nValue = 10;
if (!(nValue > 10)) // returns true if nValue if less than or equal to 10; otherwise
it returns false
```

With both logical operators, the JavaScript engine does what is known as a short-circuit evaluation of the expression first. If the logical operator is AND (&&), and the first expression evaluates to false, the second isn't evaluated because the entire expression must evaluate to false.

If using the logical OR operator, if the first expression evaluates to true, the second is not evaluated. An OR operator evaluates to true when one of its operands is true.

By understanding how short-circuit evaluation works, you can use first expressions that are less CPU- or other resource-intensive, thereby adding a little efficiency to your application.

JavaScript Best Practice: Take advantage of short-circuit evaluation by placing the key expression or the less resource-intensive expression first when using logical AND/OR operators.

Also note that though the examples in this section use parentheses around the expressions, the use of parentheses isn't required; the relational operators have a higher precedence than do the logical operators and therefore are evaluated first. In Example 3-6, I didn't use the parentheses with the AND operator.

However, I've found they can make the entire expression more readable, as well as being a good visual double-check on it.

JavaScript Best Practice: Surround the expressions on either side of the logical operator (&& or ||) with parentheses.

Advanced Statements: The Loops

Before finishing up the remaining two built-in JavaScript objects, we'll take some time to look at the advanced JS statements: the loops. The looping statements are ones that have a conditional test, just like the conditional if...else... statements covered earlier. However, when the expression evaluates to true, the processor returns to the same condition again at the end of each loop.

The while Loop

The simplest JavaScript loop tests a condition at the start of each loop and continues if the expression evaluates to true. Something in the JavaScript contained in the loop changes at some point, forcing the expression to evaluate to false and the loop to terminate. The keyword while is used to designate this type of loop.

In Example 3-7, one of the test expression variables is incremented with each loop until its value exceeds 10. At that point, the loop terminates.

Example 3-7. Testing a value in a condition in a while loop

```
<!DOCTYPE html PUBLIC "-//W3C//DTD XHTML 1.0 Transitional//EN"
"http://www.w3.org/TR/xhtml1/DTD/xhtml1-transitional.dtd">
<html>
<head>
<title>While Loop</title>
<meta http-equiv="Content-Type" content="text/html; charset=utf-8" />
</head>
<body>
<script type="text/javascript">
//<![CDATA[

var iValue = 0;
while (iValue < 10) {
    iValue++;
    document.writeln("iValue is " + iValue + "<br />");
}

//]]>
</script>
</body>
</html>
```

Normally, you do more with a while loop than just increment a value, which you'll see in more detail throughout the rest of the book.

The do...while Loop

In the previous section, the while loop showed how a conditional expression is tested before the loop is executed. If the condition fails immediately, the contained code is never processed. There are times, though, when you might want the code to be processed at least once, regardless of the condition and its success or failure. Enter the do...while loop.

Unlike the while loop, the do...while loop doesn't evaluate the conditional expression until after the end of the code block. As such, the block is always processed at least once. The loop in Example 3-7 can be modified as follows if the code in the contained block is to be processed at least once:

```
do {
    iValue++;
    document.writeln("iValue is " + iValue + "<br />");
} while (iValue < 10)
```

With both the while loop and the do...while loop, the conditional operation determines whether the loop is processed. Any condition can work—including complicated ones, such as the following:

```
while (iValue < 10 && iValue >= 3) ...
```

There is another loop—the for loop—where you set the number of times the loop contents are processed.

The for Loops

Rather than use a condition, use a for loop to traverse the code contained within a loop a set number of times. There are two different types of for loops, though not all are implemented in all browsers.

The most common for loop, and one implemented in all browsers, has three stages: a variable is set to a starting value; it is updated with each loop; and when the value satisfies a specific condition, the loop is finished:

```
For (initial value; condition; update) {
...
}
```

The following code traverses a loop 10 times, printing out "hello" each time:

```
for (var i = 0; i < 10; i++) {
    document.writeln("hello<br />");
}
```

A variable, i, is set to zero. With each iteration of the loop, the value is tested to see if the condition is met (value still under 10); if not, the loop code block is processed, and the conditional variable is incremented. The condition can be set by a user variable or by traversing the elements of an array. (Arrays are explored in Chapter 4.)

The second version of the for loop is a for...in loop, which accesses each element of the array as a separate item. The syntax for this handy statement is:

```
for (variable in object) {
...
}
```

Before demonstrating the for...in loop, I want to digress for a moment and talk about objects as associative arrays. We'll get into arrays in Chapter 5 and objects starting in Chapter 9, but the for...in is especially useful for a construct known as an *associative array*.

An associative array is a hash, where each element can be accessed by a *key value*—a string associated with the value. Objects, such as the document object in JavaScript, are instances of associative arrays. The document object used in previous examples has one item, the writeln function, which is one member of its array of properties. There are actually many such document object properties. Rather than access these by some numeric index, as with most arrays, you use the property name.

Returning to the for...in loop, this control statement can be used to not only traverse an object's properties, but also each property's value. In Example 3-8, this approach is used to print out not only the properties of the object, but their value—using eval to evaluate the string as if it were a direct statement. The JavaScript for...in statement is used with the window object to find out what properties are available. Many of these will seem very unfamiliar because they're part of DOM Level 2, covered in Chapter 11.

Example 3-8. Using for...in to expose an object's properties

```
<!DOCTYPE html PUBLIC "-//W3C//DTD XHTML 1.0 Transitional//EN"
"http://www.w3.org/TR/xhtml1/DTD/xhtml1-transitional.dtd">
<html>
<head>
<title>Expose the Objects</title>
<meta http-equiv="Content-Type" content="text/html; charset=utf-8" />
</head>
<body>
<h1>Expose Me</h1>
<p>Going undercover to expose the document object's dirty little secrets..</p>

<script type="text/javascript">
//<![CDATA[

for (docprop in document) {
   document.writeln(docprop + "=");
   eval ("document.writeln(document.." + docprop + ")");
   document.writeln("<br />");
}

//]]>
</script>
</body>
</html>
```

Try this out with various browsers and various objects, and you'll get some interesting results. Though the object implementation is very similar across browsers, it isn't identical. Modifying the code to use different objects (JavaScript, Browser Object or Document Object models), you might also find, as I did, a bug—in this case, a bug in Firefox: an unhandled exception based on a nonimplemented property, domConfig.

 A third for loop is foreach, implemented in JavaScript 1.6 in Gecko-based browsers. This loop makes use of a callback function in the first parameter, and an object to act as primary reference within that callback function. Since foreach is not standard across browsers, and makes use of functionality we haven't discussed yet, I won't cover it other than to point you to the Mozilla organization documentation on the statement, *http://developer.mozilla.org/en/docs/Core_JavaScript_1.5_ Reference:Objects:Array:forEach.*

The use of in also works with conditional tests. For instance, to check whether a key (property) exists in an associative array (object), you can use:

```
if ("URL" in document) {
   alert(document.URL);
}
```

This syntax is not used frequently, and we'll get more into associative arrays in the next chapter and later in the book. However, if you see code of this nature in the future, you'll recognize it for what it is.

Now that we have much of the functionality of JavaScript behind us, it's time to take a closer look at the built-in JavaScript objects, covered in Chapter 4.

Questions

1. In the following, add parentheses to the expression so that it evaluates to 8:

   ```
   var valA = 37;
   var valB = 3;
   var valC = 18;
   var resultOfComp = valA - valB % 3 / 2 * 4 + valC - 3;
   ```

2. Using a switch statement, test an expression for a value of one, two, or three, and set a variable to OK if the expression is one or two; OK2 if the expression is three; and NONE if it doesn't match any.

3. You have three variables, varOne, varTwo, and varThree. How would you test all three such that a block of code is processed only if varOne is 33, varTwo is less than or equal to 100, but varThree is greater than 0?

4. Execute a loop and print out every number between 10 and 20.

5. Now do the same counting backward.

Answers are provided in the appendix.

CHAPTER 4

The JavaScript Objects

It might seem when looking at JavaScript examples that there are a great number of JavaScript objects. However, what you're really seeing are objects from four different domains:

- Those built into JavaScript
- Those from the Browser Object Model
- Those from the Document Object Model
- Custom objects from the developer

The JavaScript objects are those that are built into JavaScript as language-specific components regardless of the agent that implements the language engine. As such, they'll always be available, whether JavaScript is implemented in a traditional web browser or in a cell-phone interface.

Among these basic JavaScript objects are those that parallel our data types, discussed in Chapter 2: String for strings, Boolean for booleans, and, of course, Number for numbers. Each of these objects encapsulates our basic types; they manage conversion tasks, as well as provide additional functionality.

There are also several special-purpose objects, such as Math, Date, and RegExp. That last object provides regular-expression functionality to JavaScript. Regular expressions are powerful, though extremely cryptic, patterning capabilities that enable you to add very precise string matching to applications.

JavaScript also has one built-in aggregator object, the Array. All objects in JavaScript are inherently arrays, though they may not look as such when you work with them. All of these basic JavaScript objects are covered in this chapter.

The Object Constructor

Each JavaScript object is based on one object known as, appropriately enough, Object. Object is covered in Chapter 11, which goes into creating custom objects and libraries. JavaScript's approach to extensibility is a bit unusual. Though current versions of JS are not truly object-oriented, JavaScript does support the concept of a constructor and the ability to create instances of objects through the use of the new method.

All but one of the built-in objects have unique and useful methods and properties associated with the object type, some of which are accessible with object instances. Others are static, which means they're only accessible directly on the shared object.

The one object that doesn't have any unique properties or methods is the Boolean object. The only methods and properties it has are those associated with Object itself. I'll use it to demonstrate creating new instances of an object, and then move on to covering the other more complex objects.

To create a new instance of the Boolean object, use the new keyword and the following syntax:

```
var holdAnswer = new Boolean(true);
```

Once a Boolean is instantiated, you can access the primitive value it encapsulates (encloses) using another Object method, toValue:

```
if (holdAnwer.toValue) ...
```

You can also access it directly, as if it were a primitive data type:

```
if (holdAnswer) ...
```

If the Boolean object lacks new and exciting functionality, the other objects compensate for it.

The Number Object

The Number object's unique methods have to do with conversion—to string, to locale-specific string, to a given precision- or fixed-point representation, and to exponential notation. The object also has four constant numeric properties, directly accessible from the Number object.

Rather than list each Number object's methods and properties, Example 4-1 demonstrates how they work by calling each and printing out their results and/or values.

Example 4-1. The Number object methods

```
<!DOCTYPE html PUBLIC "-//W3C//DTD XHTML 1.0 Transitional//EN"
"http://www.w3.org/TR/xhtml1/DTD/xhtml1-transitional.dtd">
<html>
<head>
<title>The Number Object</title>
<meta http-equiv="Content-Type" content="text/html; charset=utf-8" />
</head>
<body>
<script type="text/javascript">
//<![CDATA[
```

Example 4-1. The Number object methods (continued)

```
// Number properties
document.writeln(Number.MAX_VALUE + "<br />");
document.writeln(Number.MIN_VALUE + "<br />");
document.writeln(Number.NEGATIVE_INFINITY + "<br />");
document.writeln(Number.POSITIVE_INFINITY + "<br />");

// Number specific methods
var newValue = new Number("34.8896");

document.writeln(newValue.toExponential(3) + "<br />");
document.writeln(newValue.toPrecision(3) + "<br />");
document.writeln(newValue.toFixed(6) + "<br />");


//]]>
</script>
</body>
</html>
```

Figure 4-1 shows the results of running this JavaScript application.

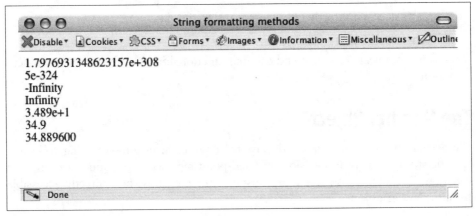

Figure 4-1. The Number object methods

In Example 4-1, two numeric constants—MAX_VALUE and MIN_VALUE—reflect the maximum and minimum numbers that can be represented in JavaScript. The other two infinity values represent specialized negative and positive infinity, returned when a math overflow happens or the minimum or maximum numbers are exceeded. In Chapter 2, we looked at the Infinity global constant in the section "The Number Data Type"; POSITIVE_INFINITY is equivalent to this value.

After printing out the numeric constants, the program creates an instance of a Number object. Either a string or a number can be used for the literal value, as long as the format is a proper number. If a string is used without a proper number, the value of the object is NaN.

The first method invoked is toExponential, which passes in the number of digits appearing after the decimal point—in this case, 3. The second method is toPrecision, which passes in a value of 3 also, representing the number of significant digits to include in the string transformation. The last method called, toFixed, is the number of digits to print out after the decimal—rounded if applicable. A method not included in the demonstration is toLocaleString, which prints out the number formatted for a given locale.

The String Object

The String object is probably the most used of the built-in JavaScript objects. A new String object can be explicitly created using the new String constructor, passing the literal string as a parameter:

```
var sObject = new String("Sample string");
```

The String object has several methods, some associated with working with HTML, and several not. One of the non-HTML-specific methods, concat, takes two strings and returns a result with the second string concatenated onto the first. Example 4-2 demonstrates how to create a String object and use the concat method.

Example 4-2. Creating a String object and calling the concat method

```
<!DOCTYPE html PUBLIC "-//W3C//DTD XHTML 1.0 Transitional//EN"
"http://www.w3.org/TR/xhtml1/DTD/xhtml1-transitional.dtd">
<html>
<head>
<title>Exploring String</title>
<meta http-equiv="Content-Type" content="text/html; charset=utf-8" />
</head>
<body>
<script type="text/javascript">
//<![CDATA[

var sObj = new String();
var sTxt = sObj.concat("This is a ", "new string");

document.writeln(sTxt);

//]]>
</script>
</body>
</html>
```

There is no known limit to the number of strings you can concatenate with the String concat method. However, I rarely use this myself; I prefer the String operators, such as the string concatenation operator (+).

The properties and methods available with the String object are listed in Table 4-1.

Table 4-1. String Object methods

Method	Description	Arguments
valueOf	Returns the string literal the String object is wrapping	None
length	Property, not method, with the length of the string literal	Use without parentheses
anchor	Creates HTML anchor	String with anchor title
big, blink, bold, italics, small, strike, sub, sup	Formats and returns String object's literal value as HTML	None
charAt, charCodeAt	Returns either character (charAt) or character code (charCodeAt) at given position	Integer representing position, starting at position zero (0)
indexOf	Returns starting position of first occurrence of substring	Search substring
lastIndexOf	Returns starting position of last occurrence of substring	Search substring
link	Returns HTML for link	URL for href attribute
concat	Concatenates strings together	Strings to concatenate onto the String's literal string
split	Splits string into tokens based on some separator	Separator and maximum number of splits
slice	Returns a slice from the string	Beginning and ending position of slice
substring, substr	Returns a substring	Beginning and ending location of string
match, replace, search	Regular expression match, replace, and search	String with regular expression
toLowerCase, toUpperCase	Converts case	None

The HTML formatting methods—anchor, link, big, blink, bold, italics, sub, sup, small, strike—generate strings that enclose the String's literal value within HTML element tags. Example 4-3 demonstrates this using one specific string and various String methods.

Example 4-3. Working with the String object's formatting functions

```
<!DOCTYPE html PUBLIC "-//W3C//DTD XHTML 1.0 Transitional//EN"
 "http://www.w3.org/TR/xhtml1/DTD/xhtml1-transitional.dtd">
<html>
<head>
<title>String formatting methods</title>
<meta http-equiv="Content-Type" content="text/html; charset=utf-8" />
</head>
<body>
<script type="text/javascript">
//<![CDATA[

var someString = new String("This is the test string");
```

```
document.writeln(someString.big( ));
document.writeln(someString.blink( ));
document.writeln(someString.sup( ));
document.writeln(someString.strike( ));
document.writeln(someString.bold( ));
document.writeln(someString.italics( ));
document.writeln(someString.small( ));

document.writeln(someString.link('http://www.oreilly.com'));
//]]>
</script>
</body>
</html>
```

One of the elements, `blink`, is deprecated HTML, and not supported at all in XHTML. However, if used with `document.writeln`, the results will validate because what the XHTML validators see is the proper use of JavaScript, not the generated results. If you copy the generated results into a new document and run these with any XHTML validator, you'll receive an error for the use of `blink`.

 Even if you don't receive an error directly, the use of the HTML format methods (other than `anchor` and `link`) should be avoided as much as possible, primarily because they don't use the more modern CSS styling. And whatever you do, avoid `blink`: it's an obnoxious holdover from the days when web designers believed the more animations in the page, the better. Nowadays, nothing will drive away a web-site reader faster than using `blink`.

The best way to try out the other `String` methods for yourself is to create a simple web page, such as that in Example 4-3, and then replace the working code with the code snippets associated with each method in the rest of this section.

The `charAt` and `charCodeAt` methods return the character and the Unicode character code, respectively, at a given location. The methods take one parameter—an index of the character to be returned:

```
var sObj = new String("This is a test string");
var sTxt = sObj.charAt(3);
document.writeln(sTxt);
```

The index values begin at zero; to return the character at the fourth position, pass in the value 3.

The `substr` and `substring` methods, as well as `slice`, return a substring given a starting location and length of string:

```
var sTxt = "This is a test string";
var ssTxt = sTxt.substr(0,4);

document.writeln(ssTxt);
```

As this example demonstrates, the String methods can be used with a string literal, as well as a String object. The JavaScript engine converts the variable to an object, calls the method, and then reconverts the object back to a primitive variable.

The indexOf and lastIndexOf methods return the index of a search string, with the former returning the first occurrence, and the latter returning the last:

```
var sTxt = "This is a test string";
var iVal = sTxt.indexOf("t");

document.writeln(iVal);
```

Example 4-2 demonstrated concatenating strings together. If you want the reverse—to split a string apart—use the split method. This method has two parameters. The first is the character that marks each break; you can also pass in the number of splits to perform in the second parameter. Example 4-4 takes a string and splits it on the comma (,)—performing a break only on the first three commas. The resulting values are then split on the equals sign (=).

Example 4-4. Using the String split function to break a string into tokens

```
<!DOCTYPE html PUBLIC "-//W3C//DTD XHTML 1.0 Transitional//EN"
 "http://www.w3.org/TR/xhtml1/DTD/xhtml1-transitional.dtd">
<html>
<head>
<title>The Split Method</title>
<meta http-equiv="Content-Type" content="text/html; charset=utf-8" />
</head>
<body>
<script type="text/javascript">
//<![CDATA[

var inputString = 'firstName=Shelley,lastName=Powers,state=Missouri,statement="This is a
test, of split"';
var arrayTokens = inputString.split(',',3);
for (var i in arrayTokens) {
   document.writeln(arrayTokens[i] + "<br />");
   var newTokens = arrayTokens[i].split('=');
   document.writeln(newTokens[1] + "<br />");
}
//]]>
</script>
</body>
</html>
```

The result of running this JS application is the following output to the web page:

```
firstName=Shelley
Shelley
lastName=Powers
Powers
state=Missouri
Missouri
```

In addition to demonstrating the `split` method, Example 4-4 also demonstrates an interesting aspect of JavaScript and how it automatically manages conversion between variable to literal to object and back. The input string is created as a variable and assigned a literal value. Yet the `split` method is called on the variable, just as if it were created as a `String` object:

```
var arrayTokens = inputString.split(',',3);
```

The JavaScript engine processes this code by first converting the literal variable to a `String` object, and then executing the function call. So technically, you never have to explicitly create a `String` object if you think you might be wanting to use `String` methods later in your project. You don't even have to create a variable; you can call `String` methods directly off of a string literal:

```
var tokens = 'firstname=Shelley'.split('=');
document.writeln(tokens[1]);
```

The same applies to all primitive types, and will be demonstrated later in the chapter with `RegExp`. These are perfectly legitimate uses of JavaScript but I don't recommend you use them often, because they can make a JS program difficult to read.

 The arrays used in Example 4-4 are covered later in this chapter.

Returning to the `String` object methods, `toUpperCase` and `toLowerCase` convert the string to all upper- or lowercase characters, respectively, and return the string:

```
var someString = new String("Mix of upper and lower");
var newString = someString.toUpperCase(); // uppercases all of the letters
```

This is a particularly useful function if case is going to be an issue, because you can convert the string to all upper- or lowercase before processing. There is also a static method on `String`: `fromCharCode`. A static method is called directly on the object, rather than an instance of an object. Here's an example that uses this method:

```
var s = String.fromCharCode(345,99,99,76);
document.writeln(s);
```

The `fromCharCode` method takes Unicode values separated by commas and returns a string. However, as discussed in Chapter 2, you can also embed Unicode characters directly in a string.

The last `String` methods are dependent on a concept known as regular expressions. There is also a JS object associated with regular expressions, `RegExp`. Because these are associated, we'll examine all of them in the next section.

Regular Expressions and RegExp

Regular expressions are arrangements of characters that form a pattern that can then be used against strings to find matches, make replacements, or locate specific substrings. Most programming languages support some form of regular expressions, and JavaScript is no exception.

Regular expressions can be created explicitly using the RegExp object, although you can also create one using a literal, as was demonstrated with the string literal in the last section. The following using the explicit option:

```
var searchPattern = new RegExp('+s');
```

While the next line of code demonstrates the literal RegExp option:

```
var searchPattern = /+s/;
```

In both cases, the plus sign(+) in the search pattern matches anything with one or more consecutive *s*'s in a string. The forward slashes with the literal, (/+s/), mark that the object being created is a regular expression and not some other type of object.

The RegExp Methods: test and exec

The RegExp object has only two unique methods of interest: test and exec. The test method determines whether a string passed in as a parameter matches with the regular expression. In the following example, the pattern /JavaScript rules/ is tested against the string to see whether a match is found:

```
var re = /JavaScript rules/;
var str = "JavaScript rules";
if (re.test(str)) document.writeln("I guess it does rule") ;
```

Matches are case-sensitive: if the pattern is instead /Javascript rules/, the result is false. To instruct the pattern-matching functions to ignore case, follow the second forward slash of the regular expression with the letter i:

```
var re =/Javascript rules/i;
```

The other flags are g for a global match and m to match over many lines. If using RegExp to generate the regular expression, pass these to the constructor as a second parameter:

```
var searchPattern = new RegExp('+s', 'g');
```

In the following snippet of code, the RegExp method, exec, searches for a specific pattern, /JS*/, across the entire string (g), ignoring case (i):

```
var re = /JS*/ig;
var str = "cfdsJS *(&YJSjs 888JS";
var resultArray = re.exec(str);
while (resultArray) {
    document.writeln(resultArray[0]);
    resultArray = re.exec(str);
}
```

The pattern described in the regular expression is the letter J, followed by any number of S's. Since the i flag is used, case is ignored, so the js substring is found. As the g flag is given, the last index is set to the location where the last pattern was found on each successive call, so each call to exec finds the next pattern. In all, the four items found are printed out, and when no others are found, a null value is assigned to the array. This ends the loop.

These code samples have demonstrated a couple of the special regular-expression characters. There are several regular-expression characters, such as the plus sign and asterisk in the previous example.

Typically, books and articles throw all such characters into a table, and then provide a couple of examples where several are used together in a long and complicated pattern, and that's the extent of the coverage. Because of this, there are many people who have a lot of trouble putting together regular expressions and, as a consequence, their applications don't work as they originally anticipated. I think that regular expressions are important enough to at least provide several examples, from simple to complex. If you have worked with regular expressions before, you might want to skip this section—unless you need the review.

Though the RegExp methods are used in applications, regular expressions and the RegExp object are used primarily with the String object's regex methods: replace, match, and search. The rest of the examples in this section demonstrate regular expressions using these methods.

Working with Regular Expressions

The first character is the backslash (\), usually called the escape character, because it's used to escape whatever character follows. In JavaScript regular expressions, this results in two behaviors. If the character is usually treated literally, such as the letter s, it's treated as a special character following the escape character—in this case, a whitespace (space, tab, form feed, line feed). If the backslash is used with a special character, such as the plus sign earlier, the character is treated as a literal.

Example 4-5 searches for instances of a space that's followed by an asterisk, and replaces them with a dash. Normally, the asterisk is used to match zero or more of the preceding characters in a regular expression, but in this case, we want to treat it as a literal.

Example 4-5. Escape character in regular expressions

```
<!DOCTYPE html PUBLIC "-//W3C//DTD XHTML 1.0 Transitional//EN"
"http://www.w3.org/TR/xhtml1/DTD/xhtml1-transitional.dtd">
<html>
<head>
<title>The Backslash in RegExp</title>
<meta http-equiv="Content-Type" content="text/html; charset=utf-8" />
</head>
```

Example 4-5. Escape character in regular expressions (continued)

```
<body>
<script type="text/javascript">
//<![CDATA[

var regExp = /\s\*/g;
var str = "This *is *a *test *string";
var resultString = str.replace(regExp,'-');
document.writeln(resultString);
//]]>
</script>
</body>
</html>
```

The result of applying the regular expression against the string is the following line:

```
This-is-a-test-string
```

This is a very handy expression to keep in mind. If you want to replace all occurrences of spaces in a string with dashes, regardless of what's following the spaces, use the following pattern: /\s/g in the replace method, passing in the hyphen as the replacement character.

Four of the regular-expression characters are used to match specific occurrences of characters: the asterisk (*) matches the character preceding it zero or more times, the plus/addition sign (+) matches the character preceding it one or more times, and the question mark (?) matches zero or one of the preceding characters. The dot (.) matches exactly one character.

Two patterns of interest are the greedy match (.*) and the lazy star (.*?). In the first, since a period can represent any character, the asterisk matches until the last occurrence of a pattern, rather than the first. If you're looking for anything within quotes, you might think of using /".*"/. If you use this with a string, such as:

```
test="one" or this is also a "test"
```

The match begins with the first double-quote and continues until the last one, not the second:

```
"one" or this is also a "test"
```

The lazy star forces the match to end on the second occurrence of the double quote, rather than the last:

```
"one"
```

In Example 4-6, the String search method looks for a date in the format of month name followed by space, day of month, and then year. The date begins after a colon.

Example 4-6. Patterns of repeating characters

```
<!DOCTYPE html PUBLIC "-//W3C//DTD XHTML 1.0 Transitional//EN"
  "http://www.w3.org/TR/xhtml1/DTD/xhtml1-transitional.dtd">
<html>
<head>
```

Example 4-6. Patterns of repeating characters (continued)

```
<title>Find Date</title>
<meta http-equiv="Content-Type" content="text/html; charset=utf-8" />
</head>
<body>
<script type="text/javascript">
//<![CDATA[

var regExp = /:\D*\s\d+\s\d+/;
var str = "This is a date: March 12 2005";
var resultString = str.match(regExp);
document.writeln("Date" + resultString);
//]]>
</script>
</body>
</html>
```

Looking more closely at the regular expression, the first character in the pattern is the colon, followed by the backslash with a capital letter D: \D. This sequence is one way of looking for any nondigit character; the asterisk following means that any number of nondigit characters will match. The next part in the regular expression is a whitespace character \s, followed by another new pattern: \d. Unlike the earlier sequence, \D, the lowercase letter means to match numbers only. The plus sign following it means one or more numbers. Another space follows \s in the pattern and then another sequence of numbers \d+.

When matched against the string using the String match method, the date preceded by the colon is found, returned, and printed out:

```
Date: March 12 2005
```

In the example, \D matches any nonnumber character. Another way to create this particular match is to use the square brackets with a number range, preceded by the caret character (^). If you want to match any character but numbers, use the following:

```
[^0-9]
```

The same holds true for \d, except now you want numbers, so leave off the caret:

```
[0-9]
```

If you wish to match on more than one character type, you can list each range of characters within the brackets. The following matches on any upper- or lowercase letters:

```
[A-Za-z]
```

Using these, the regular expression in Example 4-6 could also be given as:

```
var regExp = /:[^0-9]*\s[0-9]+\s[0-9]+/;
```

The caret is used in another pattern: it and the dollar sign are used to capture specific patterns relative to the beginning and end of a line. The caret, outside of brackets, matches any sequence beginning a line; the dollar sign matches any ending a line.

In the following code snippet, the match is not successful because the character searched did not occur at the beginning of the line:

```
var regExp = /^The/i;
var str = "This is the JavaScript example";
```

However, the following would be successful:

```
var regExp = /^The/i;
var str = "The example";
```

If the multiple line flag is given (m), the caret matches on the first character after the line break:

```
var regExp = /^The/im;
var str = "This is\nthe end";
```

The same positional pattern matching holds true for the end-of-line character. The following doesn't match:

```
var regExp = /end$/;
var str = "The end is near";
```

But this does:

```
var regExp = /end$/;
var str = "The end";
```

If the multiple line flag is used, it matches at the end of the string and just before the line break:

```
var regExp = /The$/im;
var str = "This is really the\nend";
```

The use of parentheses is significant in regular-expression pattern matching. Parentheses match and then remember the match. The remembered values are stored in the result array:

```
var rgExp = /(^\D*[0-9])/
var str = "This is fun 01 stuff";
var resultArray = str.match(rgExp);
document.writeln(resultArray);
```

With this example, the array prints out This is fun 0 twice, separated by a comma indicating two array entries. The first result is the match; the second, the stored value from the parentheses. If, instead of surrounding the entire pattern, you surround only a portion, such as /(^\D*)[0-9]/, this results:

```
This is fun 0,This is fun
```

Only the surrounded matched string is stored.

Parentheses can also help switch material around in a string. RegExp has special characters, labeled $1, $2, and so on to $9, that store substrings discovered through the use of the capturing parentheses. Example 4-7 finds pairs of strings separated by one or more dashes and switches the order of the strings.

Example 4-7. Swapping Strings using regular expressions

```
<!DOCTYPE html PUBLIC "-//W3C//DTD XHTML 1.0 Transitional//EN"
"http://www.w3.org/TR/xhtml1/DTD/xhtml1-transitional.dtd">
<html>
<head>
<title>Regular Expression Switch</title>
<meta http-equiv="Content-Type" content="text/html; charset=utf-8" />
</head>
<body>
<script type="text/javascript">
//<![CDATA[

var rgExp = /(\w*)-*(\w*)/
var str = "Java--Script";
var resultStrng = str.replace(rgExp,"$2-$1");
document.writeln(resultStrng);
//]]>
</script>
</body>
</html>
```

Here's the end result of this JavaScript:

```
Script-Java
```

Notice that the number of dashes is also stripped down to just one dash. This example also introduces another very popular pattern matching character sequence, \w. This sequence matches any alphanumeric character, including the underscore (underline). It's equivalent to [A-Za-z0-9_]. Its converse is \W, which is equivalent to any nonword character.

The last regular expression characters we'll examine in detail are the vertical bar (|) and curly braces. The vertical bar indicates optional matches. For instance, the following matches to either the letter a or the letter b:

```
a|b
```

You can use more than one character with vertical bars to provide more options:

```
a|b|c
```

The curly braces indicate repetition of the preceding character a set number of times. In the following, the pattern searched is two s characters together:

```
s{2}
```

Regular expressions are extremely useful when validating form contents, as demonstrated in Chapter 7.

Figure 4-2. The regular expression tool CocoaRegex

Purposeful Objects: Date and Math

The JavaScript Date and Math objects provide access to the type of functionality you might not think about—until the moment you need it and say to yourself, "I wonder how to…". They are created for specific purposes—to work with dates or math. No more, no less.

The Date

The Date object can create a date and then access any aspect of it—year, day, second, and so on. Creating a date without passing in any parameters produces a date based on the client machine's date and time:

```
var dtNow = new Date();
```

Right at the moment I'm reading this, in St. Louis, Missouri, at 9 p.m. on a Friday (authors have no lives), equals out to:

```
Fri Apr 07 2006 21:09:14 GMT-0500 (CDT)
```

You can also pass in parameters to create a specific date. You can enter the number of milliseconds since January 1, 1970 at 12:00:00:

```
var dtMilliseconds = new Date(5999000920);
document.writeln(dtMilliseconds.toUTCString());
```

This results in the following date written to the page:

```
Wed, 11 Mar 1970 10:23:20 GMT
```

You can also use a string to create a date, if you use the proper format:

```
var nowDt = new Date("March 12, 1980 12:20:25");
```

You can forgo the time and just get a date with times set to zeros. You can also pass in each value of the date as integers, in order of year, month (as 0 to 11), day, hour, minutes, seconds, and milliseconds:

```
var newDt = new Date(1977,12,23);
var newDt = new Date(1977,11,24,19,30,30,30);
```

Once you have a date, there are several methods you can access, including a few static methods and several that allow you to manipulate every last bit of the date.

Static methods are accessed directly off of the shared Date object, rather than an instance. Date.now returns the current date and time; Date.parse returns the number of milliseconds since January 1, 1970; and Date.UTC also returns the number of milliseconds given the longest form of the constructor, described earlier:

```
var numMs = Date.UTC(1977,16,24,30,30,30);
```

The Date object methods get and set specific components of the date, and there are several. Each of the following get specific values from the date according to local times:

- getFullYear
- getHours
- getMilliseconds
- getMinutes
- getMonth
- getSeconds
- getYear

The UTC equivalents are:

- getUTCFullYear
- getUTCHours
- getUTCMilliseconds
- getUTCMinutes
- getUTCMonth
- getUTCSeconds

Most of the get methods have equivalent set methods that set a component's value within a Date. An example would be setYear to set the year, or setUTCMonth to set a UTC month.

Of those methods that might not be quite as obvious, the getDate method returns the numeric day of the month for a date, while the getDay returns the day of week, starting with zero (0) for Sunday:

```
var dtNow = new Date();
alert(dtNow.getDay());
```

The getTimezoneOffset returns the number of minutes (+ or -) of the offset of the local computer from UTC. Because I'm writing this in St. Louis, which is UTC-5, I would get a value of 300 when calling this method against a local time date.

Six methods convert the date to a formatted string:

toString
: Outputs the string in local time

toGMTString
: Formats the string using GMT standards

toLocaleDateString *and* toLocaleTimeString
: Output the date and the time, respectively, using the locale

toLocaleString
: Converts the string using current locale

toUTCString
: Formats the string using UTC standards

Example 4-8 demonstrates these, as well as some of the other date methods already discussed.

Example 4-8. Several string setting and formatting Date methods

```
<!DOCTYPE html PUBLIC "-//W3C//DTD XHTML 1.0 Transitional//EN"
"http://www.w3.org/TR/xhtml1/DTD/xhtml1-transitional.dtd">
<html>
<head>
<title>A Dated Example</title>
<meta http-equiv="Content-Type" content="text/html; charset=utf-8" />
</head></body>
```

Example 4-8. Several string setting and formatting Date methods (continued)

```
<script type="text/javascript">
//<![CDATA[

var dtNow = new Date( );

// set day, month, year
dtNow.setDate(18);
dtNow.setMonth(10);
dtNow.setYear(1954);
dtNow.setHours(7);
dtNow.setMinutes(2);

// output formatted
document.writeln(dtNow.toString( ) + "<br />");
document.writeln(dtNow.toLocaleString( ) + "<br />");
document.writeln(dtNow.toLocaleDateString( ) + "<br />");
document.writeln(dtNow.toLocaleTimeString( ) + "<br />");
document.writeln(dtNow.toGMTString( ) + "<br />");
document.writeln(dtNow.toUTCString( ));

//]]>
</script>
</body>
</html>
```

Given so many date options, it might be puzzling to figure out which specific locale to use in an application. I've found a good rule of thumb is to reference everything in the web-page reader's local time if her actions are isolated—such as when placing an order at an online store. However, if the person's actions are in relation to others, especially within an international audience (such as a weblog for comments), I would recommend setting times to UTC in order to maintain a consistent framework for all of your readers.

> The Date object is managed the same between the major browsers except for one method: getYear. This method was not Y2K-compliant, and would return the year minus 1900 rather than the full year. The ECMA specification created a new method, getFullYear, that is Y2K-compliant, and Firefox and other ECMAScript Version 3 browsers support this. IE 6.x, though, has redefined getYear to be Y2K, making it functionally equivalent to getFullYear.

Math

Arithmetic isn't math, at least in JavaScript, where the operators for basic arithmetic described in Chapter 2 are not associated with the Math object. The Math object provides mathematical properties and methods, such as LN10, which is the logarithm of 10, and log(x), which returns the natural logarithm of x. It doesn't participate in simple arithmetic, such as addition and subtraction.

I'll provide examples of the properties and functions for the `Math` object—you'll need to supply the math skills.

Unlike the other JavaScript objects, all of `Math`'s properties and methods are static. What this means is that you don't create a new instance of `Math` to get access to the functionality; you access the methods and properties directly on the shared object itself:

```
var newValue = Math.SQRT1;
```

As with other object properties, `Math`'s properties are accessed by attaching the property to the object, using the period operator:

```
Math.property
```

The following are the `Math` properties, as numbers and listed in the order they're found in ECMA-262:

`E`
> Value of e, the base of the natural logarithms

`LN10`
> The natural logarithm of 10

`LN2`
> The natural logarithm of 2

`LOG2E`
> The approximate reciprocal of `LN2`—the base-2 logarithm of e

`LOG10E`
> The approximate reciprocal of `LN10`—the base-10 logarithm of e

`PI`
> The value of PI

`SQRT1_2`
> The square root of 1/2

`SQRT2`
> The square root of 2

Math in programming is somewhat dependent on the underlying architecture, and this includes how some of the math functions are implemented by each browser that provides a JavaScript engine, as well as the operating system, machine, and so on. As such, there may be minor variations in the results of the trigonometric functions, but hopefully not so many as to make the functions unusable within this context.

The Math Methods

The Math methods are relatively straightforward. Regardless of variable type, all arguments passed to the Math functions are converted to numbers first. You don't have to do any conversion in your code.

The abs function takes an argument representing a numeric value and returns the absolute value of that number. If the number is negative, the positive value is returned. The following two lines of code return a value of 3.45:

```
var nVal = -3.45;
var pVal = Math.abs(nVal);
```

There are several trigonometric methods available through Math: sin, cos, tan, acos, asin, atan, and atan2. These provide, respectively, the sine, cosine, tangent, arc cosine, arc sine, arc tangent, and the computation of the angle between an x-point and the origin. Each takes a specific type of numeric argument and returns a result meaningful to the method:

Math.sin(x)
> A specific angle, in radians

Math.cos(x)
> A specific angle, in radians

Math.tan(x)
> An angle, in radians

Math.acos(x)
> A number between −1 and 1

Math.asin(x)
> A number between −1 and 1

Math.atan(x)
> Any number

Math.atan2(py,px)
> The y- and x-coordinates of a point

The Math.ceil method rounds a number to the next highest whole number. The following two lines of JavaScript return a value of 4.00:

```
var nVal = 3.45;
var pVal = Math.ceil(nVal);
```

The following lines of JavaScript result in a value of −3:

```
var nVal = -3.45;
var pVal = Math.ceil(nVal);
```

The Math.floor method, on the other hand, rounds a number down—returning the next lowest whole number. The following JavaScript generates a value of 3:

```
var nVal = 3.45;
var pVal = Math.floor(nVal);
```

The following lines of JS results in a value of −4:

```
var nVal = -3.45;
var pVal = Math.floor(nVal);
```

The Math.round method rounds to the nearest integer; whether this is higher or lower depends on the value. A value of 3.45 rounds to 3, while a value of 3.85 rounds to 4. The result is the nearest integer regardless of whether the value is negative or positive.

Math.exp(x) calculates a number equivalent to e, the base of natural logarithms, raised to the value of the argument passed to the method:

```
var nVal = Math.exp(4) // equivalent to e⁴
```

Math.pow raises any number to a given power:

```
var nVal = Math.pow(3,2) // 3² or 9
```

Math.min and Math.max compare two or more numbers and return either the minimum or the maximum:

```
var nVal = 1.45;
var nVal2 = 4.5;
var nVal3 = -3.33;
var nResult = Math.min(nVal, nVal2, nVal3) // returns -3.33
var nResult2 = Math.max(nVal, nVal2, nVal3) // returns 4.5
```

The last method, Math.random, generates a number between 0 (inclusive) and 1 (exclusive):

```
var nValue = Math.random( );
```

The limitations on the method could discourage you from using Math.random. However, you can multiply this value by 10 or 100, or any value, to generate random numbers beyond a value of 1. Unfortunately, you can't set limits to generate a random number within a range of values. You can emulate this behavior, though, using a loop, as demonstrated in Example 4-9.

Example 4-9. A quirky but accurate random-number generator

```
<!DOCTYPE html PUBLIC "-//W3C//DTD XHTML 1.0 Transitional//EN"
"http://www.w3.org/TR/xhtml1/DTD/xhtml1-transitional.dtd">
<html>
<head>
<title>Random Quote</title>
<meta http-equiv="Content-Type" content="text/html; charset=utf-8" />
<script type="text/javascript">
```

Example 4-9. A quirky but accurate random-number generator (continued)

```
//<![CDATA[

var quoteArray = new Array(5);
quoteArray[0] = "Quote one";
quoteArray[1] = "Quote two";
quoteArray[2] = "Quote three";
quoteArray[3] = "Quote four";
quoteArray[4] = "Quote five";

function getQuote( ) {
   do {
     iValue = Math.random( ); // random number between 0 and 1
     alert(iValue);
     iValue *= 10; // multiply by 10 to move the decimal
     alert(iValue);
     iValue = Math.floor(iValue); // round to nearest integer
     alert(iValue);
     }
   while (iValue > 4)
   alert(quoteArray[iValue]);
}

//]]>
</script>
</head>
<body onload="getQuote( );">
</body>
</html>
```

An array is created with five quotes. A function is called when the page loads, which uses a loop and several `Number` and `Math` functions to generate an application number (between 0 and 4, inclusive). Once found, the number is used to access an array element, which is then printed out (as are the interim steps in the random-number generator, as demonstrated).

This isn't the prettiest approach to random-number generation (or the most efficient), but it is accurate and does the job. Sometimes that's enough—at least until you have time to explore other options.

Developing with JavaScript is a trade-off between finding the absolute best possible solution, and having to get the job finished within a specific period of time.

 JavaScript Best Practice: There are no perfect solutions in JavaScript, only the most accurate and best implementations that can be managed within a given time frame—allowing time for documentation, of course.

JavaScript Arrays

There's an interesting little fact about JavaScript: if there's an object, there's also a literal. As shown in the last few chapters, there's a `String` object and string literals; the same is true of `Boolean` and boolean, and `Number` and numbers. We also used this with regular expressions, and rarely referenced the `RegExp` object directly in the examples. This same object/literal relationship holds true with arrays.

Constructing Arrays

A JavaScript array is an object, just like `String` or `Math`. As such, it's created with a constructor:

```
var newArray = new Array('one','two');
```

An array is also a literal value, which doesn't require the explicit use of the `Array` object:

```
var newArray = ['one','two'];
```

In this latter case, the JS engine converts the literal to an object of type `Array`, assigning the result to the variable. Once created, array elements can be accessed by their index value—the number representing their location in the array:

```
alert(newArray[0]); // outputs one
```

Array indexes start at 0 and go up to the number of elements, minus 1. So an array of five elements would have indexes from 0 to 4.

Arrays don't have to be one-dimensional. It's not uncommon to have an array in which each element has multiple dimensions, and the way to manage this in JS is to create an array where each element is an array itself. In the following code snippet, an array of three-dimensional values is created:

```
var threedPoints = new Array();
threedPoints[0] = new Array(1.2,3.33,2.0);
threedPoints[1] = new Array(5.3,5.5,5.5);
threedPoints[2] = new Array(6.4,2.2,1.9);
```

If the inner array contains the x-, y-, and z-coordinates in order, then accessing the z-coordinate of the third point can be managed with the following code:

```
var newZPoint = threedPoints[2][2]; // remember, arrays start with 0
```

To add array dimensions, continue creating arrays in elements:

```
threedPoints[2][2] = new Array(4.4,4.6,44) // and so on
var newthreedZPoint = threedPoints[2][2][1];
```

The number of elements for an array doesn't have to be known ahead of time. As the examples demonstrate, you can create an array with so many elements in the array declaration, or just add elements as you go along. You can also set the size of an array by adding its nth or last element, first:

```
var testArray = new Array();
testArray[99] = 'some value'; // testArray is now an array with 100 elements
```

To find the length of an array (number of elements), use the Array property called length:

```
alert(testArray.length); // prints out 100
```

If you access the length of a multiple-dimension array, you'll get only the number of elements for a particular dimension:

```
alert(threedPoints[2][2].length); // prints out 3
alert(threedPoints[2].length); // prints out 3
alert(threedPoints.legnth); // prints out 3
```

In addition to length, there are a few other properties of interest and several methods on the Array object. One such is splice, which allows you to insert and/or remove from an array—a rather handy method to have. In the following code snippet, splice adds two elements and removes two, starting at index 2 (the third element):

```
var fruitArray = new Array('apple','peach','orange','lemon','lime','cherry');
var removed = fruitArray.splice(2,2,'melon,banana');
document.writeln(removed + "<br />");
document.writeln(fruitArray);
```

This code generates the following two lines:

```
orange,lemon
apple,peach,melon,banana,lime,cherry
```

The removed elements are returned as an array from the splice method call.

The slice method slices an array and returns the result:

```
fruitArray.slice(2,4); // returns an array of 3 elements: melon, banana, and lime
```

The concat concatenates one array onto the end of the other:

```
var newFruit = fruitArray.concat(removed) // returns an array of
apple,peach,melon,banana,lime,cherry,orange,lemon
```

Neither concat nor slice alter the original array. Instead, they return an array containing the results of the operation.

In the examples, I've been printing out the arrays directly. What the JavaScript engine does is convert the arrays to a string, using a default separator of a comma (,). If you want to designate a different separator, use the join method to generate a string:

```
var strng = fruitArray.join()
```

You can also reverse the order of the elements in an Array using the reverse method:

```
fruitArray.reverse();
```

In many cases, the exact order of the elements in an array is unimportant. There are times, though, when you want to have the order preserved, such as when the array serves as a queue. There are also several methods useful for maintaining arrays as queues or lists, which we'll look at next.

FIFO Queues

Arrays can be used to track a queue of items, where each is added FIFO (first in first out). There are four handy `Array` methods that can maintain queues, lists, and the like: push, pop, shift, and unshift.

The push method adds elements to the end of an array, while the unshift method adds elements to the beginning of the array. Both return the new length of the array.

The pop method removes the last element of the array, while the shift returns the first element. Both return the element retrieved from the array.

All four methods modify the array—either adding or removing elements, permanently, from the array. Example 4-10 demonstrates how a FIFO queue can be maintained in JavaScript.

Example 4-10. FIFO queue using Array methods

```
<!DOCTYPE html PUBLIC "-//W3C//DTD XHTML 1.0 Transitional//EN"
"http://www.w3.org/TR/xhtml1/DTD/xhtml1-transitional.dtd">
<html>
<head>
<title>FIFO</title>
<meta http-equiv="Content-Type" content="text/html; charset=utf-8" />
</head>
<body>
<script type="text/javascript">
//<![CDATA[
//create FIFO queue and add items using push
var fifoArray = new Array();
fifoArray.push("Apple");
fifoArray.push("Banana");
var ln = fifoArray.push("Cherry");

// print out length and array
document.writeln("length is " + ln + " and array is " + fifoArray + "<br />");

// use pop to pop the items off the array
for (var i = 0; i < ln; i++) {
   document.writeln(fifoArray.shift() + "<br />");
}

// print out length
document.writeln("length now is " + fifoArray.length + "<br /><br />");

// now, same with shift and unshift
var fifoNewArray = new Array();

fifoNewArray.unshift("Learning");
fifoNewArray.unshift("Java");
ln = fifoNewArray.unshift("Script");

document.writeln("length is " + ln + " and array is " + fifoNewArray + "<br />");
```

Example 4-10. FIFO queue using Array methods (continued)

```
// unshift
for (i = 0; i < ln; i++) {
  document.writeln(fifoNewArray.pop( ) + "<br />");
}
document.writeln("new length is " + fifoNewArray.length );i
//]]>
</script>
</body>
</html>
```

The first thing to notice in this example is that I've paired shift and push, and unshift and pop. The reason for this is the order in which these methods work. The push method adds an element to the end of an array, and as each new element is added, it pushes the first elements to the front of the array. The pop method removes the items from the end of the array first, creating a LIFO list (last in first out)—a perfectly legitimate queue, but not what we're after with the program. We want the first element added to be the first element retrieved. The shift method removes elements from the top of the array, which does suit our needs.

The same applies to unshift and pop. The unshift method adds items to the top of an array, each new item pushing the older ones further down the list, while pop removes them from the bottom of the queue first. This again maintains the order of items, and this is what we're after—not the order of the array elements themselves, but the order in which they're added.

The result of running this JavaScript is:

```
length is 3 and array is Apple,Banana,Cherry
Apple
Banana
Cherry
length now is 0

length is 3 and array is Script,Java,Learning
Learning
Java
Script
new length is 0
```

Example 4-10 also demonstrates how for loops can traverse an array. Rather than have to individually write out each shift or pop method call, I iterated through the same call the same number of times as elements in the array. This example is small, but you can imagine how much of a timesaver this can be with a larger array.

Typically when traversing an array with a for loop, the variable that's adjusted with each loop is incremented (or decremented when counting down) and used as an array index:

```
for (var i = 0; i < someArray.length; i++) {
    alert(someArray[i]);
}
```

However, there's no requirement that you must use the index; it's there if you need it. And as implied, you count down with a for loop as well as count up:

```
for (var i = someArray.length; i >= 0; i--) ...
```

As an alternative, you can use the for . . . in loop to access each array element:

```
var programLanguages = new Array
('C++','Pascal','FORTRAN','BASIC','C#','Java','Perl','JavaScript');
for (var itemIndex in programLanguages) {
    document.writeln(programLanguages[itemIndex] + "<br />");
}
```

There are other methods associated with the array that require the use of a callback function, which will be covered in Chapter 5. First though, let's look at associative arrays.

Associative Arrays: The Arrays That Aren't

I introduced associative arrays in Chapter 3. Unlike those just described, an associate array doesn't have a numeric index, so you can't access associative array elements using the following syntax:

```
assocArray[1]
```

Associative arrays can be created using the Array constructor, but this is considered bad form—primarily because you can't access the array using numeric indexes. Instead, Object is normally used, and the array is automatically extended as new members are added:

```
var assocArray = new Object();
assocArray["one"] = "one";
assocArray["two"] = "two";
```

Unlike the traditional numeric arrays, associative array members can also be accessed directly on the object, as seen in many of the examples with the document, Math or Date objects, and so on:

```
document.writeln...
Math.ceil...
```

Associative arrays are used in the last few chapters, so I won't get much further into the concept in this chapter. However, it is important to remember that when referencing a JavaScript Array, we usually mean the array that supports numeric indexing. Otherwise, we'll usually use object or associative array to reference the object type.

Questions

1. Comma-separated strings are a common data format. How would you create an array of elements when given one?

2. The \b special character can define a word boundary, and \B matches on a nonword boundary. Define a regular expression that will find all occurrences of the word "fun" in the string and replace them with "power":

   "The fun of functions is that they are functional."

3. Create code to get today's date, modify it by a week, and print out the new date.

4. Given a number of 34.44, how would you round the number down? Round it up?

5. Given a string like the following, use pattern match and replace to turn all punctuation into commas, and then load as an array and print out each value:

   ```
   var str = "apple.orange-strawberry,lemon-.lime";
   ```

Answers are provided in the appendix.

CHAPTER 5
Functions

JavaScript functions are a key part of the language, but they're not quite what they seem. They look like they would belong in the family of statements, but in actuality, they're objects just like all the others we've covered in the last chapter. You can define a function, create a new one, even print one out.

Thanks to this functionality, you can assign a function to a variable, an array element, or even pass one as an argument to another function call. This makes using functions a very handy and flexible beastie, but also a confusing one.

It's easy to get lost in discussions of anonymous functions as compared to function statements, function expressions, and references to literal functions. Add in concerns about function closure and memory leaks, as well as properties inherited by all functions, and you can see they are not a trivial JavaScript construct.

Defining a Function: Let Me Count the Ways

There are three primary approaches to creating functions in JavaScript: declarative/static, dynamic/anonymous, and literal. It's important to understand the impact of each type of declaration before using it.

 Many programming tasks can be accomplished with the simple declarative/static approach. You may not want to use anonymous or literal functions while getting started, but it's useful to know what they are if you have to read someone else's code. (And eventually, of course, you'll probably want to use them!)

Declarative Functions

The most common type of function uses the declarative/static format. This approach begins with the function keyword, followed by function name, parentheses containing zero or more arguments, and then the function body:

```
function functionname (param1, param2, ..., paramn) {
    function statements
}
```

Unless I'm creating a new library with new objects, or defining functions on the fly based on events, this tends to be the syntax I use the most.

The declarative/static function is parsed once, when the page is loaded, and the parsed result is used each time the function is called. It's easy to spot in the code, simple to read and understand, and has no negative consequences (usually), such as memory leaks. It's also more familiar to developers who have worked with other programming languages.

This type of function has been demonstrated extensively in the previous chapters, so I won't provide a full example of its use here. The following snippet of code creates a function that uses this function format, which is called immediately after it's declared:

```
function sayHi(toWhom) {
    alert("Hi " + toWhom);
}
sayHi("World!");
```

In this code, calling the function results in a dialog window with "Hi World!". Barring JavaScript errors, no matter what string is passed to the function or how many times it's called, the same function object is used, and the same result happens: a dialog window opens with a message.

A reminder on function naming conventions

Functions do actions. As such, you'll want to incorporate a verb summarizing the activity of the function as much as possible. If you have a hard time naming the function because it's doing more than one task, you may want to consider splitting the function into smaller units, which tends to also encourage reusability.

In fact, the rule should be to keep functions small, specific to a task, and as general as possible. This makes up this chapter's best practice.

 JavaScript Best Practice: Keep your functions small, specific to a task, and try to generalize the contained code so that the function can be as reusable as possible.

Function Returns and Arguments

Functions communicate with the calling program through the arguments passed to it and the values returned from it.

Variables based on primitives, such as a string, boolean, or number are passed to a function by value. This means that if you change the actual argument in the function, the change is not reflected in the calling program.

Objects passed to a function, on the other hand, are passed by reference. Changes in the function to the object are reflected in the calling program.

In Example 5-1, two arguments are passed to a function: one is a string variable, the other an array. Both are modified in the function, and then their contents output in the calling program. The string is unchanged, but the array object now has a new value among its members.

Example 5-1. Function arguments, passed as value and by reference

```
<!DOCTYPE html PUBLIC "-//W3C//DTD XHTML 1.0 Transitional//EN"
"http://www.w3.org/TR/xhtml1/DTD/xhtml1-transitional.dtd">
<html>
<head>
<title>Pass Me</title>
<meta http-equiv="Content-Type" content="text/html; charset=utf-8" />
</head>
<body>
<script type="text/javascript">
//<![CDATA[

function alterArgs(strLiteral, aryObject) {

    // overwrite original string
    strLiteral = "Override";
    aryObject[aryObject.length] = "three";
}

var str = "Original Literal";
var ary = new Array("one","two");

alterArgs(str,ary);

document.writeln("string literal is " + str + "<br /> ");
document.writeln("Array object is " + ary);

//]]>
</script>
</body>
</html>
```

Communication to and from the function is simple: data is passed to a function through one or more arguments; a return statement returns a value from a function to the calling program.

A function may or may not return a value. If it does, the return statement can occur anywhere in the function code, and there could even be more than one return statement. When it encounters a return statement, the JS engine stops processing the function code at that point and returns control to the calling statement.

One reason you might have more than one return statement is if you want to terminate and exit the function when a condition is met. In the following snippet of code, if a condition isn't met in the function, it's terminated immediately; otherwise, processing continues:

```
function testValues(numValue) {
if (isNan(numValue) {
    return "error -- not a number";
}
...
return ...
```

Functions don't require return values, though they may be useful in error handling—returning a value of `false` if the function isn't successful. (More sophisticated methods of error handling are covered in Chapter 11.)

Opposite in behavior to the declarative function is the dynamic/anonymous function, discussed next.

Anonymous Functions

Functions are objects. As such, they can be created—just like a `String` or other type—by using a constructor and assigning the function to a variable. In the following code, a new function is created using the function constructor, function body, and argument passed in as arguments:

```
var sayHi = new Function("toWhom","alert('Hi ' + toWhom);");
sayHi("World!");
```

This type of function is often referred to as an *anonymous function* because the function itself isn't directly declared or named. I know, they are strange-looking—but that's understandable if you remember that a JavaScript function is an object, and any object can be created dynamically at runtime.

Unlike the declarative function, the JavaScript engine creates the anonymous function dynamically, and each time it's invoked, the function is dynamically reconstructed. If the function is used in a loop, this means it's created with each iteration; a declarative/static function is only created once. As such, you might think anonymous functions aren't too useful. However, a dynamic function is a great way to define the functionality necessary to meet a need that's only determined at runtime.

Here's the syntax of an anonymous function using a constructor:

```
var variable = new Function ("param1", "param2", ... , "paramn", "function body");
```

The first parameters are the arguments to the function as they would be defined in a declarative function. The last parameter is the function body. The whole is assigned to a variable:

```
var func = new Function("x", "y", "return x * y")
```

This is equivalent to the following using a declarative/static function:

```
function func (x, y) {
   return x * y;
}
```

Example 5-2 takes the dynamic nature of an anonymous function to its extreme. The function body and the value of the two parameters defined for the function are provided by the user via a prompt dialog window. The whole is invoked, and the result is printed out to the page.

Example 5-2. A dynamic/anonymous function

```
<!DOCTYPE html PUBLIC "-//W3C//DTD XHTML 1.0 Transitional//EN"
"http://www.w3.org/TR/xhtml1/DTD/xhtml1-transitional.dtd">
<html>
<head>
<title>Build a Function</title>
<meta http-equiv="Content-Type" content="text/html; charset=utf-8" />
</head>
<body>
<script type="text/javascript">
//<![CDATA[

// prompt for function and args
var func = prompt("Enter function body:");
var x = prompt("Enter value of x:");
var y = prompt("Enter value of y:");

// invoke anonymous function
var op = new Function("x", "y", func);
var theAnswer = op(x, y);

// print out results
document.writeln("Function is: " + func + "<br />");
document.writeln( "x is: " + x +
                  " y is: " + y + "<br />");
document.writeln("The answer is: " + theAnswer);

//]]>
</script>
</body>
</html>
```

Because JavaScript is loosely typed, the function can work with number values:

```
Function is: return x * y
x is: 33 y is: 11
The answer is: 363
```

It can also work with strings:

```
Function is: return x + y
x is: This is y is: the string
The answer is: This is the string
```

The only requirement is that the operation has to be meaningful for the data type. Even then, a JavaScript error won't happen because the browser doesn't see the error; it happens at runtime. What you'll end up with is something like the following:

```
Function is: return x * y
x is: this is y is: the answers
The answer is: NaN
```

Needless to say, this functionality must be used with caution. I don't recommend allowing your web-page readers to define the functions used within your pages. However, dynamic functions can be an interesting way of dealing with user input, as long as you strip out anything in that input that can cause problems: embedded links, messing around with cookies, calling server-side functionality, creating new functions, etc.

There is another hybrid approach to creating functions that combines the static capabilities of the declarative function with some of the anonymity of the anonymous functions: the function literal, discussed next.

Function Literals

Before introducing the next—and potentially confusing—type of function, a little refresher on objects and literals might be helpful. As demonstrated in earlier chapters, JavaScript objects can have a literal form. Rather than have to use a constructor and the object, you can use a representation. A string can be constructed using the String constructor, and the String methods accessed:

```
var str = new String("Learning Java");
document.writeln(str.replace(/Java/,"JavaScript"));
```

You can also use a variable based on the primitive string type and still access the String object's methods; the JavaScript engine implicitly wraps the literal in an object:

```
var str2 = "Learning Java";
document.writeln(str2.replace(/Java/,"JavaScript"));
```

In fact, you don't even need a variable:

```
document.writeln("Learning Java".replace(/Java/,"JavaScript"));
```

What works for strings also works for functions, which means that you don't have to use a function constructor to create a function and assign it to a variable; it literally becomes a function literal:

```
var func = (params) {
statements;
}
```

Function literals are also known as *function expressions* because the function is created as part of an expression, rather than as a distinct statement type. They resemble anonymous functions in that they don't have a specific function name. However, unlike anonymous functions, function literals are parsed only once. In fact, other than the fact that the function is assigned to a variable, function literals resemble declarative functions:

```
var func = function (x, y) {
    return x * y;
}
alert(func(3,3));
```

Their uniqueness stands out when you extend the concept to do something such as passing a function as a parameter to a function. In Example 5-3, a function, funcObject, is defined, and passes the first two arguments to the third, which is, itself, a function.

Example 5-3. Passing a function to a function

```
<!DOCTYPE html PUBLIC "-//W3C//DTD XHTML 1.0 Transitional//EN"
"http://www.w3.org/TR/xhtml1/DTD/xhtml1-transitional.dtd">
<html>
<head>
<title>Pass Me</title>
<meta http-equiv="Content-Type" content="text/html; charset=utf-8" />
</head>
<body>
<script type="text/javascript">
//<![CDATA[

// invoking third argument as function
function funcObject(x,y,z) {
    alert(z(x,y));
}

// third parameter is function
funcObject(1,2,function(x,y) { return x * y});

//]]>
</script>
</body>
</html>
```

If a function is used within an expression in another statement, it's an example of a function literal—no matter what the expression is.

A second form of the function literal isn't anonymous, in that the function is given a name:

```
var func = function multiply(x,y) {
    return x * y;
}
```

However, the name is accessible only from within the function itself. This isn't all that handy, unless you're implementing a recursive function (covered in a later section).

Function Type Summary

To summarize, there are three different function types:

Declarative function
> A function in a statement of its own, beginning with the keyword function. Declarative functions are parsed once, static, and given a name for access.

Anonymous function
> A function created using a constructor. It's parsed each time it's accessed and is not given a name specifically.

Function literal or function expression
> A function created within another statement as part of an expression. It is parsed once, is static, and may or may not be given a specific name. If it is named, the name is accessible only from within the function itself.

Declarative functions are available in all forms of JavaScript, in all browsers. Anonymous functions based on the function constructors are dynamic, memory-intensive, and based on later versions of JS; as such, they may not be available with older browsers. Function literals are later innovations, based in JavaScript 1.5. Only the most modern browsers support these, though the most common—such as Mozilla, Firefox, IE, Safari, and others—do. However, how each of these work with function literals can lead to interesting complications in memory usage, as is examined later in the section on closure.

Function literals also form the basis for most advanced Ajax libraries, as you'll see when we take a closer look at Prototype, Dojo, and other libraries in the last chapters of the book. In addition, function literals, as just demonstrated, are what's used with object event handlers that require *callback functions*, such as those associated with the Array object.

Callback Functions

In Chapter 4's section on the Array object, I wrote that there are some methods dependent on functions that are invoked automatically based on some event. The Array methods are filter, forEach, every, map, and some, and the functions used are function literals, though when used in this manner, they're usually referred to as *callback functions*.

Returning to the Array methods, the filter method ensures that elements are not added to any element unless they pass certain criteria. Rather than have to test a value and then add to an array, you can just toss everything at the array and let filter take care of the work for you. The forEach method takes a function that's then processed against each element. Unlike filter, the array is not impacted by the function.

The every method runs the callback function against every element in the array until one returns a false value. The map method runs the callback function against all the array elements and creates a new array from the results. Finally, the some method is the opposite of every, in that it runs the callback function against every element until one returns a true value.

Each callback function has three parameters: element, index, and array. Some return a value, others don't. None impact the original array.

Example 5-4 demonstrates how to use a callback function with an Array. In this example, the original array contains elements that are themselves an array containing color values in a range of 0–255. After the array is built, one function is attached, checkColor, which checks each array element for proper range. A second then checks to make sure all three RGB values are present.

Example 5-4. Using callback functions with Array filter method

```
<!DOCTYPE html PUBLIC "-//W3C//DTD XHTML 1.0 Transitional//EN" "http://www.w3.org/TR/
xhtml1/DTD/xhtml1-transitional.dtd">
<html>
<head>
<title>Array filter and callback functions</title>
<meta http-equiv="Content-Type" content="text/html; charset=utf-8" />
</head>
<body>
<script type="text/javascript">
//<![CDATA[

// check color range callback function
function checkColor(element,index,array) {
  return (element >= 0 && element < 256);
}

// check to ensure you have three RGB colors
function checkCount(element,index,array) {
  return (element.length == 3);
}

// color array
var colors = new Array( );
colors[0] = [0,262,255];
colors[1] = [255,255,255];
colors[2] = [255,0,0];
colors[3] = [0,255,0];
colors[4] = [0,0,255];
colors[5] = [-5,999,255];

// filter on color range
var testedColors = new Array( );
for (var i in colors) {
      testedColors[i] = colors[i].filter(checkColor);
}

// filter on three values
var newTested = testedColors.filter(checkCount);
for (i in newTested) {
  document.writeln(newTested[i] + "<br />");
}
//]]>
</script>
</body>
</html>
```

In the end, only four of the color points survive both checks—the middle four.

Functions and Recursion

 Recursion is not a commonly occurring functionality in most Java-Script applications. It's also a fairly advanced form of programming. As such, you may want to skip this section for now and return to it after you've finished the rest of the book.

A function that calls itself is known as a *recursive* function. Typically, it's used when a process must be performed more than once, with each new iteration of the process performed on the previously processed result. The use of recursion isn't common in JavaScript, but it can be useful when dealing with data that's in a tree-line structure, such as the Document Object Model. However, it can also be memory- and resource-intensive, as well as complicated to implement and maintain. As such, use recursion sparingly.

Previously in the chapter I wrote about named function literals, in which the function is given a name but only the function itself can access that name. This is an ideal setup for recursion.

In Example 5-5, a recursive function is used to traverse a numeric array, add the numbers in the array, and add the numbers to a string.

Example 5-5. JavaScript function recursion

```
<!DOCTYPE html PUBLIC "-//W3C//DTD XHTML 1.0 Transitional//EN"
"http://www.w3.org/TR/xhtml1/DTD/xhtml1-transitional.dtd">
<html>
<head>
<title>Recursion</title>
<meta http-equiv="Content-Type" content="text/html; charset=utf-8" />
</head>
<body>
<script type="text/javascript">
//<![CDATA[

var addNumbers = function sumNumbers(numArray,indexVal,resultArray) {

    // recursion test
    if (indexVal == numArray.length)
       return resultArray;

    // perform numeric addition
    resultArray[0] += Number(numArray[indexVal]);

    // perform string addition
    if (resultArray[1].length > 0)
      resultArray[1] += " and ";
    resultArray[1] += numArray[indexVal].toString();

    // increment index
    indexVal++;
```

Example 5-5. JavaScript function recursion (continued)

```
    // call function again, return results
    return sumNumbers(numArray,indexVal,resultArray);
}

// create numeric array, and the result array
var numArray = ['1','35.4','-14','44','0.5'];
var resultArray = new Array(0,''); // necessary for the initial case

// call function
var result = addNumbers(numArray,0, resultArray);

// output
document.writeln(result[0] + "<br />");
document.writeln(result[1]);
//]]>
</script>
</body>
</html>
```

In this application, the function calls itself using its internal name repeatedly until the array index is equivalent to the length of the numeric array. The result is then returned and passed up via each recursive call until it's returned to the statement that first invokes the function. Think of each iteration of the function call as pushing the string and numeric sum onto a stack, and when the numeric array has been traversed, the string and number have to be popped up through the stack to the top.

Of course, with this example, a while loop could be used to create the same results. However, as I mentioned earlier, when we're working with tree-structured data such as the DOM, recursion is extremely valuable, as is the function literal used to implement this process. However, not all uses of function literals in all browsers are without potential negative side effects. One area of risk is with nested functions, and possible memory leaks from an item called closure.

Nested Functions, Function Closure, and Memory Leaks

 Again, this is fairly advanced JavaScript programming, but because it occurs quite frequently in Ajax programming, I felt it best to include in the book. However, as with recursion, you may want to finish the book and then return to this section.

Another interesting aspect of function literals in JavaScript is their use as nested functions. Consider the following:

```
function outer (args) {
    function inner (args) {
        inner statements;
    }
}
```

With a nested function, the inner function operates within the scope of the outer function, including having access to the outer function's variables and arguments. The outer function, though, does not have access to the inner function's variables, nor does the calling application have access to the inner function. (Well, not unless it's created as a function literal and returned to the calling application, which then adds its own complication.)

Example 5-6 demonstrates creating a nested, inner-function literal, which is then returned to the calling application. The inner function uses the outer function's one argument, as well as its one variable. When the inner function is returned to the calling application and invoked directly, it concatenates the string passed as a parameter to the original outer-function call to the string passed to it directly as an argument. The inner function concatenates this string with that created as the local variable in the outer function, and then returns the result. Changing the argument to the inner function changes the string, as does calling the outer function again, to get another instance of the inner function.

Example 5-6. Nested functions and closure

```
<!DOCTYPE html PUBLIC "-//W3C//DTD XHTML 1.0 Transitional//EN"
"http://www.w3.org/TR/xhtml1/DTD/xhtml1-transitional.dtd">
<html>
<head>
<title>Getting Closure</title>
<meta http-equiv="Content-Type" content="text/html; charset=utf-8" />
</head>
<body>
<script type="text/javascript">
//<![CDATA[

// outer function
function outerFunc(base) {

   var punc = "!";

   // inner function
   function returnString(ext) {
     return base + ext + punc;
   }

   return returnString;
}

// create access to inner function
var baseString = outerFunc("Hello ");

// inner function still has access to outer function argument
var newString = baseString("World");
document.writeln(newString);
```

Example 5-6. Nested functions and closure (continued)

```
// and still
var notherString = baseString("Reader");
document.writeln(notherString);

// create another instance of inner function
var anotherBase = outerFunc("Hiya, Hey ");

// another local string
var lastString = anotherBase("you");
document.writeln(lastString);

//]]>
</script>
</body>
</html>
```

The result is this line in the web page:

```
Hello World! Hello Reader! Hiya, Hey you!
```

Pretty nifty stuff. The only question is, how does this work? Isn't this in violation of scoping rules, which state that when a function terminates, all of the memory for its local variables gets released via automatic garbage collection?

Not quite.

Each time a new scope is created in a JavaScript application, an associated scoping bubble, if you will, is created to enclose it. This applies to functions, which operate in their own scope.

Normally, when the function terminates, the scope is released because it's no longer necessary. However, in the case of an inner function that's returned to the outer application and assigned to an external variable, the scope of the inner function is attached to the outer, which is in turn attached to the calling application—just enough to maintain the integrity of the function literal and the outer-function argument and variable. Returning a function literal created as an internal object within another function, and assigning it to a variable in the calling application, is known as *closure* in JavaScript. And it is the scope chaining that ensures that the data necessary for this to work is in place.

This is very neat stuff, and you can see intriguing uses of closure in creating new objects or extending existing ones. We'll explore these further later in the book; however, there's another problem associated with closure.

Closures can be created accidentally or used unintentionally. In Example 5-6, if a new reference to the inner function is created for each string created, rather than reusing the variable referencing the inner function, there will be a lot of instances of that object over time.

Accidental closure can also occur when a circular reference is created, such as the following from the Mozilla documentation site:

```
function leakMemory( ) {
    var el = document.getElementById('el');
    var o = { 'el': el };
    el.o = o;
}
```

We'll get into the Document Object Model in Chapter 10, but in this case, the DOM is accessed to get an element identified by el. This is used to create a new object reference using a very abbreviated form of a function literal. That object creates an unnamed object that assigns the retrieved DOM object to a property identified by a property name of el.

Then comes the kicker: we assign this to the variable referencing the original object, which literally means we've assigned the object as a property of itself. This is not something I want to encourage, but most browsers can manage to terminate the closure and reclaim the memory—except Internet Explorer.

IE provides its own memory management for DOM objects, in addition to memory management for JavaScript objects. In the case of accidental closures caused from such circular references as this and the crossover between JS and DOM objects, the memory is allocated and never freed—not even when the page is closed. In fact, the only time the memory is freed is when the browser is closed.

The memory leak that results is usually small, unless you put all of this into a loop, in which case the memory loss could quickly build. This explains why you should use the power of closure with caution.

 For an excellent overview of closures, see the paper by Jim Ley on the topic at *http://jibbering.com/faq/faq_notes/closures.html*.

Function As Object

Whatever can be created using a constructor has properties and methods above and beyond the obvious, and functions are no exception.

The Function object seems to be the JavaScript object that's had the most changes over time. Originally, the arity property provided the number of arguments. This has been replaced by calling the length method off of the function name—or by accessing length on the arguments array. This, itself, used to be accessible via the function name, but now is accessible just as "arguments" within the function call. Example 5-7 demonstrates accessing both Function object properties.

Example 5-7. Examining Function object properties of length and arguments

```
<!DOCTYPE html PUBLIC "-//W3C//DTD XHTML 1.0 Transitional//EN"
"http://www.w3.org/TR/xhtml1/DTD/xhtml1-transitional.dtd">
<html>
<head>
<title>Function Object</title>
<meta http-equiv="Content-Type" content="text/html; charset=utf-8" />
</head>
<body>
<script type="text/javascript">
//<![CDATA[

// invoking third argument as function
function funcObject(x,y,z) {

    for (var i = 0; i < funcObject.length; i++) {
      document.writeln("argument " + i + ": " + arguments[i] + "<br />");
    }
}

funcObject(1,2,3);

//]]>
</script>
</body>
</html>
```

In addition, as you'll see in Chapter 11, when building custom objects, it's the function's ability to reference its own scope through the keyword this that's important for building classes of new objects.

In 1997, I started a set of class objects to manage cross-browser differences. Eventually, I managed these differences by creating objects for the primary browser types at that time: one for IE, one for Netscape, and one for the ongoing efforts with the DOM at the W3C—an approach that the Mozilla foundation and eventually most other browsers (including Netscape and IE) would adopt. Using this, I then attached methods to these objects. These objects were then used to wrap every DIV object in the page, which gave me a set of page components with which I could do most things. Remarkably enough, these objects survived various new generations of browsers for several years and still work today, though I am updating them to be more efficient and take advantage of some of the newer specifications.

These objects worked by defining a model-specific object, such as the following abbreviated example from the DOM (Mozilla/W3C) object function:

```
function dom_object(obj) {
        this.css1 = obj;
        this.name = obj.id;
        this.objResizeBy = domResizeBy;
```

```
    this.objHide = ieobjHide;
    this.objShow = ieobjShow;
    this.objGetLeft = domGetLeft;
    this.objGetTop = domGetTop;
    this.objSetTop = domSetTop;
    this.objSetLeft = domSetLeft;
...
}
```

The same properties can be added to each model implementation, which allows you to hide the browser differences, because each custom object method is assigned a different browser or model-specific function. Handy thing, this. Almost as handy as a JavaScript function.

Questions

1. What are the three main types of functions and when would you use each type?

2. How can a function modify variables outside its scope?

3. How can you dynamically alter the number of arguments to a function?

4. What property allows a function to access its own scope?

5. Create a function that takes a data object and a function as parameters and invokes the function using the data object.

Answers are provided in the appendix.

CHAPTER 6

Catching Events

Events let you know when a user is doing something or when a page has loaded. Catching and handling events lets your code do the right thing at the right time, serving the users of your programs.

Regardless of why they happen or how they're implemented, events in JavaScript are associated with objects and are not intrinsic to the language itself. Typically, when working with browsers, events are related to the DOM implemented in each browser.

There is a default behavior associated with each event, but events can be used to modify functionality or add additional functionality. Extending the event behavior can be managed within the (X)HTML tag for the object, or in a separate JavaScript code block or file.

The events themselves are fairly intuitive. The W3C (World Wide Web Consortium) categorizes events into three distinct areas: user interface (mouse, keyboard), logical (result of a process), and mutation (action that modifies a document). The basic events, affected objects, and descriptions are listed in Table 6-1.

Table 6-1. Events and affected objects

Event	Description	Object(s)
abort	When image is prevented from loading	An image element
blur, focus	When object loses or receives focus	Applicable to window and form elements
change	When selection changes	Applicable to form elements where value changes and after element loses focus
click, doubleclick (dblclick)	Clicking or double clicking (two clicks in rapid succession) with mouse	Most page elements
contextmenu	Clicking with the right mouse button (bringing up context menu)	Web-page document
error	When page or image can't load	Web-page document and image

Table 6-1. Events and affected objects (continued)

Event	Description	Object(s)
keydown, keyup, keypress	Pressing key or releasing, and act of doing both	Web-page document and certain form elements
load, unload	When image or page is finished loading, or page loses focus	Web-page document and image (load only)
mousedown, mouseup	Pressing down on mouse button, releasing	Most page elements
mouseover, mouseout	Moving mouse over element, moving mouse away from element	Most page elements
mousemove	Mouse moves	Most page elements
reset	Form is reset	Form
resize	Resize of window or frame	Window or frame
select	Selecting text	Form text area or input
scroll	When object is scrolled	Window, frame, or element with overflow set to auto (presence of scrollbar)
submit	Form is submitted	Form

There are some proprietary events that aren't listed; they'll be covered in the text. Also, up to this point, most of the examples and material we've covered have been cross-browser-safe. By this I mean that most modern browsers (Netscape and IE 4.x and up, or 2002 and later) support what's been covered, and the examples work as detailed in this book. Events are the first topic we'll cover that differs between browsers and browser generations. Not just differ—differ with a vengeance.

Event handling in JavaScript has gone through more than one generation, as well as undergoing proprietary extensions. Many older iterations are still supported for reasons of backward compatibility, and many of the newer event models are not universally implemented across all popular browsers.

In this section, we'll start by looking at event systems from oldest to newest. At the end of each, browser compatibilities and quirky behaviors are listed.

The Event Handler at DOM Level 0

The earliest event system is often labeled Events or DOM Level 0. This earliest, and still most common, approach to assigning new or modified functionality to an object event is through an event handler.

An *event handler* is a property of an object that has the syntax of:

```
onevent
```

Where the event handler starts with "on-", and the event can be load, click, etc.

The syntax for adding a JavaScript event handler directly to an object is to attach the event handler name as an attribute of the object tag and assign the code to run when the event occurs. The code can be implemented directly in the handler:

```
<body onload="var i = 23; i *= 3; alert(i);">
```

More frequently, though, a function is called:

```
<body onload="calcNumber( );">
```

Adding events as an attribute to an HTML element is sometimes known as an *inline model* or inline registration model.

Unlike most functions in JavaScript, event handlers are all lowercase, though if your web page is defined with an HTML DOCTYPE, your browser may accept a Hungarian/Camel notation (mixed upper- and lowercase). However, the mixed-case approach works if, and only if, you invoke the event handler as an attribute on an HTML element:

```
<body onload="calcNumber( );">
<body onLoad="calcNumber( );">
```

XHTML demands that all attributes be lowercase. As such, you'll want to use the lowercase notation for all of your JavaScript applications.

Event handlers can also be accessed directly, as a property, on each object. The following assigns a function to the onload event property of the window object:

```
window.onload=calcNumber;
```

To remove the function, assign the event handler to null. This approach of assigning a function to an event handler that is an object property is sometimes called the *traditional model* or traditional registration model.

Example 6-1 demonstrates both the traditional and inline event models, based on the page load onload event. These are the same events, and you would expect the pop-up window with the message to open twice.

Example 6-1. Both traditional and inline event handlers are used to capture load event

```
<!DOCTYPE html PUBLIC "-//W3C//DTD XHTML 1.0 Transitional//EN"
"http://www.w3.org/TR/xhtml1/DTD/xhtml1-transitional.dtd">
<html>
<head>
<title>Traditional and Inline DOM 0 Event Registration</title>
<meta http-equiv="Content-Type" content="text/html; charset=utf-8" />
<script type="text/javascript">
//<![CDATA[

// handle keyboard events
//if (navigator.appName != "Microsoft Internet Explorer") {
//    document.captureEvents(Event.KEYDOWN);
//    }
```

Example 6-1. Both traditional and inline event handlers are used to capture load event (continued)

```
function helloMsg( ) {
var helloString = "hello there";
alert(helloString);
}

function helloTwice( ) {
var helloString = "hi again";
alert(helloString);
}

window.onload=helloTwice;

//]]>
</script>

</head>
<body onload="helloMsg( );">
</body>
</html>
```

The pop-up message of "hello there" displays for the first method but not for the second message. The reason only one pop-up window opened is that only one event handler is allowed for any given event and object. The function assignments are not cumulative. If you want more than one function to be processed based on an event for a specific object, you need to list them in the event-handler code—either inline or called from one function using the traditional method:

```
<body onload="helloMsg( ); helloTwice( )">
```

Or from within the code:

```
function helloMsg( ) {
var helloString = "hello there";
alert(helloString);
helloTwice( );
}
```

The inline events work with all browsers; however, you should restrict their use. The reason is that if you add events to HTML elements, and you change the function name that's called or want to change the behavior of the JavaScript in a bunch of pages, you then have to go into each and manually make the changes. For anything but the simplest sites, this is prohibitive. A better approach would be to use the traditional method, which works with all modern browsers. The best approach is to use the newer event-handling procedures, for reasons detailed later in the chapter.

 JavaScript Best Practice: Limit use of inline event registration, which embeds JavaScript into HTML elements rather than within a JS code block. A better approach is to use the traditional event registration. The best approach is to use the newer event-management techniques.

With some events, such as submit, that are based on the results of running the Java-Script code, you may not want the event to continue its default process. In such cases, you can return a value of false from the event-handler function:

```
function doSomething( ) {
    // does some code
    return false;
}
```

This signals the browser to terminate the event at that point. You'll see this in action later in the chapter when we move into form processing.

For many events, knowing that an event happened is enough, but for others, such as click or mousedown and so on, you might want additional information about the event, such as page location. So the question is, how is this information accessed? That's the next bit of cross-browser event irregularity—albeit fixable—we'll look at next.

The Event Object

DOM Level 0 events can be split into two camps: the old Netscape camp, which is now subsumed by Mozilla/Firefox, and Internet Explorer. For the most part, getting an interactive page to work with both can be done, but you might have to use a few tricks. One trick is how to get access to the Event object.

The Event object is associated with all events. It has properties that provide information about the event, such as location of a mouse click and so on. The Event object actually looks quite similar to both Internet Explorer and Mozilla; a couple of methods differ. However, getting access to the object is drastically different.

IE attaches Event as a property of the window object. When accessed as part of event processing, the data it contains is populated accordingly. In Example 6-2, the IE Event object is accessed from Windows when the mouse button is depressed, and the screen X and Y location are printed out in a pop-up window.

Example 6-2. Accessing IE Event object

```
<!DOCTYPE html PUBLIC "-//W3C//DTD XHTML 1.0 Transitional//EN"
"http://www.w3.org/TR/xhtml1/DTD/xhtml1-transitional.dtd">
<html>
<head>
<title>X/Y Marks the Spot</title>
<meta http-equiv="Content-Type" content="text/html; charset=utf-8" />
<script type="text/javascript">
//<![CDATA[

function mouseDown( ) {
    var locString = "X = " + window.event.screenX + " Y = " + window.event.screenY;
    alert(locString);
}
```

Example 6-2. Accessing IE Event object (continued)

```
document.onmousedown=mouseDown;
//]]>
</script>

</head>
<body>
</body>
</html>
```

This method of capturing the Event object persists into Internet Explorer 7, as well as the older versions. The Netscape-based browsers—such as Netscape, Firefox, Mozilla, Opera, and Camino—obtain the Event object differently: it's passed as part of the function. In this case, the function to work with a browser such as Firefox looks like:

```
function mouseDown (theEvent) {
    var locString = "X = " + theEvent.screenX + " Y = " + theEvent.screenY;
    alert(locString);
}
```

A way to handle these cross-browser differences is to test whether an object passed into the function is instantiated. If it is, assign this to a local variable; otherwise, assume the window.event is the event, and assign it to the variable. Example 6-3 shows a cross-browser-compatible version of Example 6-2.

Example 6-3. Cross-browser-compatible version of Event object

```
<!DOCTYPE html PUBLIC "-//W3C//DTD XHTML 1.0 Transitional//EN"
"http://www.w3.org/TR/xhtml1/DTD/xhtml1-transitional.dtd">
<html>
<head>
<title>X/Y Marks the Spot</title>
<meta http-equiv="Content-Type" content="text/html; charset=utf-8" />
<script type="text/javascript">
//<![CDATA[

function mouseDown(nsEvent) {
  var theEvent = nsEvent ? nsEvent : window.event;
  var locString = "X = " + theEvent.screenX + " Y = " + theEvent.screenY;
  alert(locString);
}

document.onmousedown=mouseDown;
//]]>
</script>

</head>
<body>
</body>
</html>
```

(Remember a few chapters back how I wrote that the ternary operator is handy for dealing with cross-browser differences? Well, Example 6-3 just demonstrated its usefulness.)

The following Event properties are compatible across browsers:

altKey
: Boolean if the Alt key is pressed at time of event

clientX
: The client X-coordinate of the event

clientY
: The client Y-coordinate of the event

ctrlKey
: Boolean if the Ctrl key is pressed at time of event

keyCode
: The code (number) of the key pressed

screenX
: The screen X-coordinate of the event

screenY
: The screen Y-coordinate of the event

shiftKey
: Boolean if the Shift key is pressed at time of event

type
: Type of event

I'll cover the client and screen system in more detail later in the book when we start creating dynamic pages. Testing the control keys is a good way to determine if a certain sequence of keys are pressed—each perhaps leading to a different set of actions. In addition, the key number is handy if you're creating something like a slide show, where you might want to intercept N or P for next or previous slide.

Among the properties that aren't compatible across browsers are fromElement, which is IE, and relatedTarget, which is equivalent for Netscape. These properties capture the object the mouse moved away from with mouse events. Comparable properties are toElement and currentTarget (IE and Netscape, respectively)—noting the element to which the mouse moved. These sets of properties are useful when doing drag and drop.

The srcElement and target are properties that represent the object receiving the event. One way to grab this information is to use the same cross-browser trick shown in Example 6-3:

```
var theSrc = theEvent.target ? theEvent.target : theEvent.srcElement;
alert(theSrc);
```

Another pair of properties that aren't cross-browser compatible are cancelBubble and stopPropagation. These have to do with event bubbling, which is covered next.

Event Bubbling

When you click a web page, you're not just clicking the document, you're also clicking on a link, or perhaps a DIV element, and so on. In most cases, you don't have to worry about it because you've most likely set an event handler for only one element. What happens, though, if you set the same event handler for multiple elements? In what order do they fire, and how do you keep the event from triggering the event handler if you want only one element to be impacted at a time?

In Example 6-4, the web page has two DIV elements, one inside the other. They and the document object are all assigned event-handler functionality for the `mousedown` event.

Example 6-4. Bubble-up behavior with multiple elements

```
<!DOCTYPE html PUBLIC "-//W3C//DTD XHTML 1.0 Transitional//EN"
"http://www.w3.org/TR/xhtml1/DTD/xhtml1-transitional.dtd">
<html>
<head>
<title>Event Bubbling`</title>
<meta http-equiv="Content-Type" content="text/html; charset=utf-8" />
<script type="text/javascript">
//<![CDATA[

function mouseDown(nsEvent) {
  var theEvent = nsEvent ? nsEvent : window.event;
  var locString = "X = " + theEvent.screenX + " Y = " + theEvent.screenY;
  var theSrc = theEvent.target ? theEvent.target : theEvent.srcElement;
  alert(locString + " " + theSrc);
}

document.onmousedown=function (evnt) {
    var theEvnt = evnt? evnt : window.event;
    alert(theEvnt.type);
}

window.onload=setupEvents;

function setupEvents( ) {

    document.getElementById("first").onmousedown=mouseDown;
    document.getElementById("second").onmousedown=function ( ) {
       alert("Second event handler");
    }
}
//]]>
</script>

</head>
<body>
<div id="first" style="padding: 20px; background-color: #ff0; width: 150px">
<div id="second" style="background-color: #f00; width: 100px; height: 100px">
```

Example 6-4. Bubble-up behavior with multiple elements (continued)

```
</div>
</div>
</body>
</html>
```

Figure 6-1 demonstrates what can happen with a stack of elements—page objects who share the same location in the page, differing in their order from top to bottom. In the figure, the top DIV element is clicked by the mouse, but the DIV element it's contained in, as well as the document object, also receive the event, and the event handler's triggered.

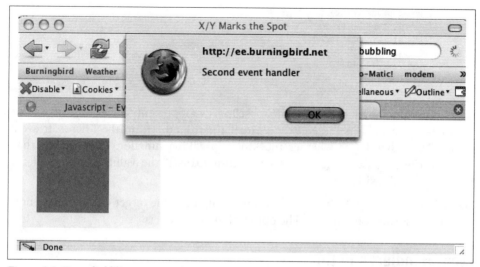

Figure 6-1. Event bubbling

With Firefox, the event handlers for the elements fire from top to bottom; in IE, it's the reverse. Even in this, we're dealing with differences.

The concept of events and their propagation between elements in a stack is usually known as *event bubbling*, though Netscape once designed around the concept of *event capturing*.

Back in bad olden times, Netscape and IE had a worlds-apart view of events and objects and their relationship to one another. Netscape designed Navigator 4.x so that events moved down the stack of elements from top to bottom. The event would fire with each element, unless you captured the event to prevent it from continuing. Netscape provided a function, captureEvent, just for this purpose.

Microsoft, though, designed IE to follow a bubble-up model. This means that an event fell through the stack of elements to the bottom-most element that had a handler, and then would bubble up from there.

Of course, you may not want an event to trigger other event handlers if a certain condition is met. You can then cancel the event propagation, whether it's on its way down, or on its way bubbling up. Unfortunately, canceling an event in this older event model is also cross-browser dependent.

To cancel an event within IE, use the IE event's cancelBubble *property*; for the Netscape/Mozilla model, you use the event's stopPropagation *method*. The way to determine which to use is to test for the existence of the stopPropagation method and, based on the result, use one or the other. In Example 6-4, you can add a stopEvent function to manage this, passing the cross-browser-compatible event object:

```
function stopEvent(evnt) {
   if (evnt.stopPropagation) {
     evnt.stopPropagation( );
   } else {
     evnt.cancelBubble = true;
   }
}
```

Calling this function at the end of the mouseDown event prevents document.onmousedown from being triggered in the Netscape/Mozilla path and within the Microsoft event model. Note that I test whether the stopPropagation function exists rather than cancelBubble because cancelBubble will return false if the value is false or if the property doesn't exist.

We've been accessing the event object, but what about the target of the event—how can we access this consistently? The object of interest here is this.

Event Handlers and this

Within an event-handler function or method on an object, one way to get code to access the properties of the containing element is to use this. For instance, in the following event handler function for the window onload event, this is used to access the function's object's property status:

```
window.onload=setupEvents;

function setupEvents( ) {
   alert(this.status);
}
```

The approach is a good shortcut to test form values, without having to follow the path of document to form name, to field name, and so on. In Example 6-5, the blur event for a form element is assigned to an onblur event handler, which then uses this to access the form element's value property.

Example 6-5. Use of this with event handlers

```
<!DOCTYPE html PUBLIC "-//W3C//DTD XHTML 1.0 Transitional//EN"
"http://www.w3.org/TR/xhtml1/DTD/xhtml1-transitional.dtd">
<html>
<head>
<title>Event Handlers and this</title>
<meta http-equiv="Content-Type" content="text/html; charset=utf-8" />
<script type="text/javascript">
//<![CDATA[

window.onload=setObjects;

function setObjects() {
    document.personData.firstName.onblur=testValue;
}

function testValue() {
    alert("Hi " + this.value); // form field value
}

//]]>
</script>
</head>
<body>
<form name="personData">
First Name: <input type="text" name="firstName" /><br /><br />
Second Name: <input type="text" name="secondName" />
</form>
</body>
</html>
```

When the input field is clicked, a pop-up window opens and displays its value. Chapter 7 provides more demonstrations of this element/event integrations.

This older event model described is still supported, more or less, with modern browsers. Though I don't cover the older Navigator 4.x or IE 4.x and 5.x browsers in the book, their legacy lives on in inline event handlers.

I've been splitting the two event models into Netscape/Mozilla and Microsoft/IE, but the actuality is that the Netscape/Mozilla path is also the one of open specification, which makes it the W3C path. Referring to the path as "Netscape" disregards that this event model is supported in browsers such as Apple's Safari and Opera.

As regards events, the W3C eventually came out more or less on the side of Microsoft and event bubbling, with a nod to event capturing. Within the W3C specifications and most modern browsers, the event proceeds down the stack of elements, each captured in turn. It then bubbles back up, firing the event handlers as it goes. This new event model is covered in the next section.

A major difference between the DOM 2 Event model and the earlier versions is that it isn't dependent on a specific event-handler property, which means you can register multiple event-handler functions for any one event on any one object. Instead of the event-handler property, each object has three methods: addEventListener, removeEventListener, and dispatchEvent. The first is to add an event listener, the second to remove an existing listener, and the third to dispatch a new event.

The syntax of the addEventListener is:

```
object.addEventListener('event',eventFunction,boolean);
```

The event, such as click or load, is the first parameter; the handler function is the second; and whether the event is treated as a cascade-down or bubble-up event is the third. If the third parameter is false, the event listener is treated as bubble up; otherwise, true turns the event listener into a cascade-down listener.

In Example 6-6, a form with one element, a submit button, is added to the page, and the click event is captured for both, as well as document. Handlers are attached to the event for both the cascade-down (writeY) and bubble-up (writeX) propagation. In the handler functions, the event object is accessed, and two properties, target and currentTarget, are printed out. We'll get to the new event properties in a moment.

Example 6-6. Trapping events with DOM Level 2 event handlers

```
<!DOCTYPE html PUBLIC "-//W3C//DTD XHTML 1.0 Transitional//EN"
"http://www.w3.org/TR/xhtml1/DTD/xhtml1-transitional.dtd">
<html>
<head>
<title>Capture/Bubble</title>
<meta http-equiv="Content-Type" content="text/html; charset=utf-8" />
<script type="text/javascript">
//<![CDATA[

function writeX(evnt) {
    alert("Capturing: " + evnt.target + " " + evnt.currentTarget);
    return true;
```

Example 6-6. Trapping events with DOM Level 2 event handlers (continued)

```
}

function writeY(evnt) {
   alert("Bubbling: " + evnt.target + " " + evnt.currentTarget);
   return true;
}

window.onload=setup;

function setup(evnt) {

   // capturing
   document.addEventListener('click',writeX,true);
   document.forms[0].addEventListener('click',writeX,true);
   document.forms[0].elements[0].addEventListener('click',writeX,true);

   // bubble up events
   document.addEventListener("click",writeY,false);
   document.forms[0].addEventListener("click",writeY,false);
   document.forms[0].elements[0].addEventListener("click",writeY,false);
}

//]]>
</script>
<body>
<form style="background-color: #f00; width: 100px; height: 100px; padding: 10px">
        <input type="submit" value="Submit" /><br>

</form>
</body>
</html>
```

Clicking the button causes six pop-up windows. In Firefox, these are the values that print, in order:

```
Capturing [object HTMLInputElement] [object HTMLDocument]
Capturing [object HTMLInputElement] [object HTMLFormElement]
Capturing [object HTMLInputElement] [object HTMLInputElement]
Bubbling: [object HTMLInputElement] [object HTMLInputElement]
Bubbling: [object HTMLInputElement] [object HTMLFormElement]
Bubbling: [object HTMLInputElement] [object HTMLDocument]
```

What's happened is that the capturing event is processed first, and the handlers for the document, the form, and then the element itself are processed in order. This makes sense, when you consider that cascade means that the lowest element in the stack of elements is processed first, then the next highest, and so on until the target element is reached. This sequence is reflected in the currentTarget property. However, the original element that received the event is always maintained in the target property.

Next, the bubbling phase occurs, and the order of process this time is from form element, to form, to document—bottom up. Again, the event's currentTarget reflects the event propagation, while the target reflects the actual element that received the event.

What happens if you want to stop the propagation? Use the `removeEventListener`. Example 6-6 is modified to add the following function:

```
function stopNow( ) {
    document.removeEventListener('click',writeX,true);
    document.forms[0].removeEventListener('click',writeY,true);
    document.forms[0].elements[0].removeEventListener('click',writeY,true);
}
```

For the sake of demonstration, the following hypertext link is added with an inline event handler below the form:

```
<p><a href="" onclick="stopNow( ); return false">Stop Now</a></p>
```

When you click this link, along with triggering the document's event handler, the capturing event handlers assigned to the click event for the form, form input, and document are all removed. When you click the button now, only the bubble-up event handlers are processed.

The concept and execution of `addEventListener` and `removeEventListener` are terrific, except for one thing: Microsoft supports only its own event-handler model. Even within the new IE7, the company supports only what it has created itself. At the Microsoft IE weblog, *IEBlog*, author Dave Massy wrote the following about AddEventListener:

> We are unlikely to get support for AddEventListener in IE7. It's definitely something we'll look into for a future release though.

Since it took several years for Microsoft to release IE7, it's unlikely that a Microsoft product will support the W3C event model any time soon, so we'll need to look at a workaround.

The comparable IE methods for `addEventListener` and `removeEventListener` are attachEvent and detachEvent, respectively. The syntax for attachEvent is:

```
object.attachEvent("eventhandler", function);
```

The syntax for detachEvent is the same as for attachEvent: the first parameter is the event handler, the second the function.

Though the ways to attach the events differ, it's relatively easy to compensate for this difference. Example 6-7 provides an example of a cross-browser web page that handles the click event for a specific document element.

Example 6-7. Cross-browser event handling

```
<!DOCTYPE html PUBLIC "-//W3C//DTD XHTML 1.0 Transitional//EN"
"http://www.w3.org/TR/xhtml1/DTD/xhtml1-transitional.dtd">
<html>
<head>
<title>Capture/Bubble</title>
<meta http-equiv="Content-Type" content="text/html; charset=utf-8" />
<script type="text/javascript">
```

Example 6-7. Cross-browser event handling (continued)

```
//<![CDATA[
function clickMe(evnt) {
  alert(evnt.target + " " + evnt.type);
  alert("Can be canceled? " + evnt.cancelable);
  alert("Bubbling? " + evnt.bubbles);
  alert(evnt.timeStamp);
}

window.onload=setup;
window.onunload=cleanup;

function setup(evnt) {
    var evtObject = document.getElementById("clickme");

    // test for object model
    if (evtObject.addEventListener) {
       document.addEventListener("click",clickMe,false);
    } else if (evtObject.attachEvent) {
       evtObject.attachEvent("onclick", clickMe);
    } else if (evtObject.onclick) {
       evtObject.onclick=clickMe;
    }
}

// cleanup
function cleanup( ) {
    var evtObject = document.getElementById("clickme");
    if (evtObject.detachEvent) {
        evtObject.detachEvent("onclick",clickMe);
    }
}
//]]>
</script>
<body>
<div id="clickme" style="background-color: #ff0; width: 200px; height: 200px; padding:
20px">
Click Me
</div>
</body>
</html>
```

The code tests to see if addEventListener is supported. If it is, it's used to attach the event. If it isn't, attachEvent is used.

Contrary to the event handlers in the traditional model, an event object does get passed with the attachEvent as it does with addEventListener. Unfortunately, though, the contextual object, this, is associated with the window object regardless of object and event. With the W3C model, this is associated with the object that received the event. Again, though, testing for window.this, as compared to this, and assigning whichever is found to a variable should manage this difference.

Another concern with the Microsoft model is that memory is set aside for each event handler, and if you reload the page, additional memory continues to be set aside for each successive page loading—leading to significant memory usage after a while. To avoid excessive memory use, you can trap the window unload event and detach each event with detachEvent. This kick-starts the memory management system to unload that memory when the page is unloaded. In Example 6-7, the cleanup function is assigned to the window.onunload event handler and manages this activity.

As for the event object that gets passed, this isn't the same among event model implementations, either. Differences also exist in properties on the event object and the events supported.

The following is a list of properties on the event; whether they are set or not depends on the type of event. Not all browsers support all event properties; where a property is not supported, an undefined value is returned when the property is accessed:

altKey
> State of Alt key (pressed or not)

bubbles
> If the event bubbles through the document object model

button
> Mouse key

cancelBubble
> Whether bubbling has been canceled

cancelable
> Whether the event can be canceled

charCode
> Unicode value of the character key pressed

clientX
> Horizontal position of event

clientY
> Vertical position of event

ctrlKey
> State of Ctrl key (pressed or not)

currentTarget
> Reference to currently registered target

detail
> Detail about the event

eventPhase
> Which phase event is being evaluated

isChar
> Whether an event produces a character

keyCode
> Unicode value of noncharacter key pressed

layerX
> The x-position relative to current layer (element) if element is absolutely positioned

layerY
> The y-position relative to current layer (element) if element is absolutely positioned

metaKey
> Whether meta key was pressed

pageX
> The x-position relative to page

pageY
> The y-position relative to page

screenX
> The x-position relative to screen

screenY
> The y-position relative to screen

shiftKey
> State of Shift key

target
> Original object to receive the event

timeStamp
> Time when event was created

view
> AbstractView from which event was generated (the window object, based on an effort to standardize the window object across implementations; discussed with DOM in Chapter 10)

which
> Unicode value of key pressed, regardless of whether it was a character

As mentioned, not all browsers support all properties. In particular, Internet Explorer does not support many of these properties. If you try to access those it doesn't support, you'll get an undefined value. For example, accessing currentTarget returns an undefined value.

The events discussed earlier in this section are supported in the newer event system, as are additional ones relative to the DOM. These include keypress, click, the mouse events, window loading, and events specific to working with forms and form elements.

For more on the event models and all things JavaScript, a great resource is QuirksMode, maintained by Peter-Paul Koch and located at *http://www.quirksmode.org/*.

Generating Events

Events usually start when someone accesses the page. Either he pushes a button, clicks a link, makes a selection, etc. There are times, though, when you might want to trigger an event.

To trigger an event on a web page or page element, it has to be an event that's associated with the type of element. For instance, you can trigger a click on a form button, but not a form text-input field. In this case, the event is click, and the method called on the object is click:

```
<input type="button" name="someButton" value="Some Button" />
...
document.formname.someButton.click( );
```

One reason for directly invoking an event is to use the focus event on an input field in order to move the cursor to the field. In Example 6-8, when the page is loaded, the focus is set to the last-name field, rather than the first name, which is the first field.

Example 6-8. Using focus to move the cursor to a field

```
<!DOCTYPE html PUBLIC "-//W3C//DTD XHTML 1.0 Transitional//EN"
"http://www.w3.org/TR/xhtml1/DTD/xhtml1-transitional.dtd">
<html>
<head>
<title>Focus</title>
<meta http-equiv="Content-Type" content="text/html; charset=utf-8" />
<script type="text/javascript">
//<![CDATA[

window.onload=setObjects;

function setObjects( ) {
    document.personData.lastName.focus( );
}

//]]>
</script>
</head>
<body>
<form name="personData">
First Name: <input type="text" name="firstName" /><br /><br />
Last Name: <input type="text" name="lastName" />
</form>
</body>
</html>
```

In Chapter 12, we'll use focus and a few other tricks to create a dynamic forms validation—moving the cursor to a field that's invalid and highlighting the errors directly in the page.

Two other methods based on events, reset and submit, are used with forms. You can use reset( ) to reset the form contents back to their initial values (as specified with the value attribute). You can also use submit( ) to submit the form for processing. In fact, this is probably one of these most common reasons for triggering an event directly:

```
document.formname.submit( );
```

Using submit( ) is equivalent to pushing a submit button on the form. More on forms, form elements, and Just-in-Time (JiT) validation using events in Chapter 7.

Questions

1. List three ways you can attach an event-handler function to a specific event.
2. Given an onclick event handler on the document object, how can you find the screen location for the click?
3. Using the DOM Level 2 event system, how would you stop an event from bubbling to other elements?
4. Convert the following DOM Level 0 event handler to a cross-browser DOM Level 2 approach:
   ```
   <body onload="functionCall( );">
   ```
5. Write JavaScript to capture the keydown event on the document and print out the key pressed using a document.writeln function call.

Answers are provided in the appendix.

CHAPTER 7
Forms and JiT Validation

The JiT in this chapter's title stands for Just-in-Time, an old manufacturing term that, in JavaScript lingo, represents timely forms validation that is triggered as the web-page reader makes her way through form fields. One of the most popular and useful JavaScript applications, JiT verifies form data before submitting it to the server, saving a round trip from page to server and back if the data is invalid or incomplete.

The hypertext link was the fuel, but forms were the matches that set the Web on fire. Web pages were, more or less, a curiosity—a way of putting information online— but the page interaction was one way: from the server to the reader. With the advent of forms and server-side processing, the whole concept of online shopping took off, and that's all she wrote.

I remember when Amazon was a new site and a relatively new concept. It was a really ugly site, but it could take your order online and send what you wanted, and it didn't need anything then except HTML and a little server-side processing. You still don't need JavaScript to create or process forms; you only need it when you want to create and process forms *well*.

Accessing the Form

In JavaScript, forms are accessed through the DOM via the document object using a couple of different approaches. The first is to access the form using the forms property on document. Forms are just one of the many page elements collected in arrays. If the page only has one form, access it at the array index zero (0):

```
var theForm = document.forms[0];
```

The forms are added to the collection in the order in which they appear in the web page. As you can imagine, if you modify the page, you may end up knocking your JavaScript out of whack. A better approach would be to name the form and access it from the document object by name:

```
<form name="someform" ...>
...
var theForm = document.someform;
```

As discussed in earlier chapters, there are also a couple of ways to intercept a form before submitting it to the server. The event you're going for is submit on the form. However, you can trap the submit event using an inline event handler, a traditional handler, or the addEventListener/attachEvent option. The key is that once you've validated the form contents, you need to be able to cancel the event if the contents fail. In the next section, we'll look at how to attach an event handler and cancel a form submittal, based on the different event-handling approaches.

Attaching Events to Forms: Different Approaches

The primary event associated with a form is submit, and the event handler is onsubmit. Attaching the event handler to the form using the traditional method takes the following form:

```
document.formname.onsubmit=formHandler;
```

When you attach an event handler to the form, incorporate it into a return statement:

```
<form name="someForm" onsubmit="return formHandler();">
```

To cancel the submission, just return false from the event-handler function; then return true or no explicit return value, and the form is submitted. In the code snippet, if the formHandler function returned false, the submittal is canceled; if true, the form contents are processed as usual.

For the newer event systems, which use either the attachMethod or addEventListener to assign a function to an event, within the submit event-handler function, you'll want to either set cancelBubble to true (for Microsoft), or use the preventDefault method call on the event object passed into the event handler to stop the form submission:

```
document.formname.addEventListener("submit",formFunction.false);
...
function formFunction(evnt) {
...
if (evnt.cancelable)
   evnt.preventDefault();
}
```

A typical validation procedure is to capture the submit event, access the individual form elements and check the data, and then provide a message to the web-page reader about what's missing or invalid. If the form is rather large, though, this means that several fields could have bad data, and listing all of them isn't a friendly response.

There are better or different approaches, especially with larger forms. For instance, you can validate each field as the person enters the data or makes a selection. Each of the following sections covers the different form input elements, how to get data from each, and what other tweaks you can perform using JavaScript.

Selection

The select element and its associated options provide a way to choose one or more items from a list. It's defined using the following syntax:

```
<select name="theSelection" multiple>
<option value="Opt1">Option 1</option>
<option value="Opt2">Option 2</option>
...
<option value="Optn">Option n</option>
</select>
```

The select element has the following properties that are accessible from JavaScript:

disabled
: Whether the element is disabled

form
: The containing form

length
: Number of options in options array

options
: Array of options

selectedIndex
: For single select, number of item selected; for multiple, first item selected

type
: Type of element

The select options are included in the options array. Each of these are objects, themselves with several properties. However, for forms validation, the properties of interest are selected, value, and text. The selected property is set to true if the option is selected; the option value is given in value, and the text that's visible to the web-page reader is given in text.

There are two ways to get the selected options from a selection, depending on whether multiple options can be selected or only one. If only one option can be selected at a time, using the select property of selectedIndex on the options array returns the selected object:

```
var slIdx= document.formname.theSelection.selectedIndex;
var opt = document.formname.theSelection.options[slIdx];
```

If multiple options can be selected, the code needs to iterate through the entire options array and check which options are selected. In Example 7-1, a multiple selection list is created with three options. When the form is submitted, the option text and value for each selected option is printed out in the pop-up window.

Example 7-1. Processing the results of a multiple-selection list

```
<!DOCTYPE html PUBLIC "-//W3C//DTD XHTML 1.0 Transitional//EN"
"http://www.w3.org/TR/xhtml1/DTD/xhtml1-transitional.dtd">
<html>
<head>
<title>Input form</title>
<meta http-equiv="Content-Type" content="text/html; charset=utf-8" />
<script type="text/javascript">
//<![CDATA[

if (window.addEventListener) {
    window.addEventListener("load",setupEvents,false);
  } else if (window.attachEvent) {
    window.attachEvent("onload", setupEvents);
  } else {
    window.onload=setupEvents;
}

function setupEvents(evnt) {
  document.someForm.onsubmit=checkForm;
}

function checkForm(evnt) {

  var opts = document.someForm.selectOpts.options;

  for (var i = 0; i < opts.length; i++) {
    if (opts[i].selected) {
      alert(opts[i].text + " " + opts[i].value);
    }
  }
  // no server side processing, cancel submit event
  return false;
}
//]]>
</script>
</head>
<body>
<form name="someForm">
<select name="selectOpts" multiple>
<option value="Opt1">Option One</option>
<option value="Opt2">Option Two</option>
<option value="Opt3">Option Three</option>
</select>
<input type="submit" value="Submit" />
</form>
</body>
</html>
```

Selection lists are normally used when you have a larger number of options—such as a list of states in the U.S. or cities in China. As such, you'll most likely want to limit your selection to one entry so that you can specifically access the option using selectedIndex, rather than have to iterate over a larger array. Still, the time to run through an array is short; the number of options picked is up to you.

You can also dynamically build a selection list based on real-time events.

In Example 7-1, DOM Level 2 event handling is used for the window load event, but traditional DOM Level 0 is used for the form submittal. Most of the examples in the rest of the book use the older event model because it's easier to implement, requires less code, and allows us to focus on those aspects of JavaScript currently being demonstrated. Example 7-3 provides a demonstration of DOM Level 2 for all functions.

For the most part, though, you'll want to use the newer event handling as much as possible—especially if you're using external libraries, as discussed in Chapter 14.

Dynamically Modifying the Selection

Using JavaScript, you can create and remove selection list items on the fly, perhaps based on some other user input. To add a new option in the code shown in Example 4-9, create a new Option element and add it to the options array:

```
opts[opts.length] = new Option("Option Four", "Opt 4");
```

Since arrays are zero-based, adding a new array element at the end can always be accomplished by using the array's length property as the index.

To remove an option, just set the option entry in the array to null. This resets the array so there is no gap in the numbering:

```
opts[2] = null;
```

To remove all options, set the array length to zero (0):

```
opts.length = 0;
```

It's not unusual to modify a selection list based on the answers given in other form elements—especially if you're using a drop-down listbox, in which the options don't show until the user clicks the arrow to open the list. Note, though, that the box may resize horizontally depending on the length of each option.

Selection and JiT Validation

In addition to processing the array elements during a form submit, you can capture when a change is made to the selection and perform instant or JiT validation. This is accomplished by capturing a change event for the form field, testing the value of the field, and then providing immediate feedback. This can be a lot less frustrating to the people filling out the forms; they won't have to wait until all the fields are filled in to validate the whole form.

I modified the code in Example 7-1 to create an example of JiT validation. In Example 7-2, two options are nested with two others so that if you select the parent option, you'll automatically get the nested option; however, the converse is not true—selecting the nested option does not give you the parent.

Example 7-2. Using JiT with a selection

```
<!DOCTYPE html PUBLIC "-//W3C//DTD XHTML 1.0 Transitional//EN"
"http://www.w3.org/TR/xhtml1/DTD/xhtml1-transitional.dtd">
<html>
<head>
<title>Input form</title>
<meta http-equiv="Content-Type" content="text/html; charset=utf-8" />
<script type="text/javascript">
//<![CDATA[

if (window.addEventListener) {
    window.addEventListener("load",setupEvents1,false);
  } else if (window.attachEvent) {
    window.attachEvent("onload", setupEvents);
  } else {
    window.onload=setupEvents;
}

function setupEvents(evnt) {
   document.someForm.selectOpts.onchange = checkSelect;
}

function checkSelect(evnt) {

   var opts = document.someForm.selectOpts.options;
   for (var i = 0; i < opts.length; i++) {
      if (opts[i].selected) {
         switch(opts[i].value) {
           case "Opt1" : opts[i + 1].selected = true;
                         break;
           case "Opt3" : opts[i + 1].selected = true;
                         break;
           case "Opt4" : opts[i + 1].selected = true;
                         break;
         }
      }
   }

   // no server side processing, cancel submit event
   return false;
}
//]]>
</script>
</head>
<body>
```

Example 7-2. Using JiT with a selection (continued)

```
<form name="someForm">
<select name="selectOpts" multiple>
<option value="Opt1">Option One</option>
<option value="Opt1a"> -- Option OneA</option>
<option value="Opt2">Option Two</option>
<option value="Opt3">Option Three</option>
<option value="Opt3a"> -- Option ThreeA</option>
<option value="Opt4">Option Four</option>
<option value="Opt4a"> -- Option FourA</option>
<option value="Opt5">Option Five</option>
</select>
<input type="submit" value="Submit" />
</form>
</body>
</html>
```

Having some options automatically selected can ensure the accuracy of the data. It's also rather impressive-looking without requiring a lot of effort.

How often you use JiT validation depends on the complexity of your form and the purpose for the form. Using JiT for every form element could irritate rather than help, but waiting to validate and providing a long list of needed changes could overwhelm. As always, the code can only do so much; you'll need to use your own judgment as to how and when to use it.

Radio Buttons and Checkboxes

Both radio buttons and checkboxes provide one-click option choosing, usually among a smaller number of options than a selection. They differ in that radio buttons allow one, and only one, choice; you can check as many checkboxes as you like.

Both types of form-input elements are grouped by name. Here's the syntax for a radio button:

```
<form name="someForm">
<input type="radio" value="Opt 1" name="radiogroup" />Option 1<br />
<input type="radio" value="Opt 2" name="radiogroup" />Option 2<br />
</form>
```

Notice that the name is the same for both options; that's how the buttons are grouped. The checkbox syntax is exactly the same, except the type is set to checkbox rather than radio.

To access the selected items, use the same functionality as selection, except that you check to see if the item is checked rather than selected:

```
        var buttons = document.someForm.radiogroup;

        for (var i = 0; i < buttons.length; i++) {
           if (buttons[i].checked) {
              alert(buttons[i].value);
           }
        }
```

The only difference in processing between the two types is that the radio buttons have only one checked item.

It's hard to screw up with radio or checkboxes, so JiT validation makes little sense. You could match the behavior of the buttons with other form options, but if you need to restrict one or more radio buttons or checkboxes, a better option would be to disable the option, rather than validate it post-event.

You can disable the option using the following JavaScript:

```
        document.someForm.radiogroup[1].disabled=true;
```

You can trap the click event for the group if you want to modify other form elements based on a radio button or checkbox selection. To attach an event handler, you attach it to the group:

```
        document.someForm.radiogroup.onclick=handleClick;
```

Unlike selection, you don't dynamically add or delete options from a radio group or set of checkboxes. You can use dynamic HTML (DHTML) to hide options, but you're better off using the disabled property to manage the dynamic nature of the control.

The textarea, text, hidden, and password Input Elements

The text, textarea, and password fields are probably the most used, as well as the input elements most likely to need validation. The hidden field usually doesn't have a problem with validation, but it is a text-based field, so I've thrown it in with the group to keep like controls together.

The single-row text-based input elements are defined in XHTML as:

```
        <input type="text|hidden|password" name="fieldName" value="Some value" />
```

Setting the type attribute defines the type of field. The text field is regular text, the hidden isn't visible to the person filling in the form, and the password field hides the text with asterisks—just in case someone is looking over your shoulder.

The textarea field is similar except that unlike the other input fields, it has an opening and closing tag, and you can set both column and row widths:

```
        <textarea name="fieldName" rows=10 cols=10>Initial text</textarea>
```

In JavaScript, the values of the fields for all text input types are accessible via the form element value property. In Example 7-3, a form with all four types is defined, and when the form is submitted, JavaScript is used to access all four and build a string, which is then added back to the textarea input element.

Example 7-3. Accessing text-based input fields from JavaScript

```
<!DOCTYPE html PUBLIC "-//W3C//DTD XHTML 1.0 Transitional//EN"
"http://www.w3.org/TR/xhtml1/DTD/xhtml1-transitional.dtd">
<html>
<head>
<title>Input form</title>
<meta http-equiv="Content-Type" content="text/html; charset=utf-8" />
<script type="text/javascript">
//<![CDATA[

if (window.addEventListener) {
    window.addEventListener("load",setupEvents,false);
  } else if (window.attachEvent) {
    window.attachEvent("onload", setupEvents);
  } else {
    window.onload=setupEvents;
}

function setupEvents(evnt) {
   if (document.someForm.addEventListener) {
       document.someForm.addEventListener("submit",validateForm,false);
     } else if (document.someForm..attachEvent) {
       document.someForm.attachEvent("submit", validateForm);
     } else {
       document.someForm.onsubmit=validateForm;;
   }
}

function validateForm(evnt) {

   var strResults = "";
   for (var i = 0; i < document.someForm.elements.length - 1; i++) {
      strResults += document.someForm.elements[i].value;
   }
   document.someForm.elements[3].value = strResults;

   if (evnt.preventDefault) {
      evnt.preventDefault();
   } else if (evnt.cancelBubble != null) {
      evnt.cancelBubble = true;
   }
  return false;
}

//]]>
</script>
</head>
```

Example 7-3. Accessing text-based input fields from JavaScript (continued)

```
<body>
<form name="someForm">
<input type="text" name="text1" /><br />
<input type="password" name="text2" /><br />
<input type="hidden" name="text3" value="hidden value" />
<textarea name="text4" cols="50" rows="10">The text area</textarea>
<input type="submit" value="Submit" />
</form>
</body>
</html>
```

In the example, the code accesses only the first four form elements because the fifth is the submit button. It does have a value, just not one we're interested in. Also notice in the code that the form submission is canceled. If we didn't cancel the submittal, the form fields would be reset, and we'd lose the string just created.

Also in the example, DOM Level event handling is used for all of the functionality, including canceling the form submission using `defaultPrevent` or `cancelBubble` in the form's validation code.

JiT Does Text

Text fields are the form elements most likely to have bad data resulting from a misunderstanding of what's required or typographical errors. As such, it is these fields you'll most likely want to implement with JiT validation.

The events of interest for JiT with text-input elements are change, focus, and blur. When the cursor moves into a text-input field, a focus event is fired; when the cursor leaves, the blur event is triggered. A change event happens when the cursor moves out of the field, and whatever contents were in the field are changed. Both are important because a user could click or tab into a field but not make any change, in which case the change event wouldn't fire. In these cases, you want to use the blur event to make sure the field has some value—if it's a required field, of course.

Modifying the application in Example 7-3, the blur event is trapped for the password field, and the value checked to make sure some entry is made in the new application in Example 7-4. In addition, when the first field is changed, the value is validated against a regular-expression pattern for a Social Security number with a pattern of: nnn-nn-nnnn.

Example 7-4. Applying Just-in-Time validation with text-based input fields

```
<!DOCTYPE html PUBLIC "-//W3C//DTD XHTML 1.0 Transitional//EN"
"http://www.w3.org/TR/xhtml1/DTD/xhtml1-transitional.dtd">
<html>
<head>
<title>JiT RegEx</title>
<meta http-equiv="Content-Type" content="text/html; charset=utf-8" />
```

Example 7-4. Applying Just-in-Time validation with text-based input fields (continued)

```
<script type="text/javascript">
//<![CDATA[

if (window.addEventListener) {
     window.addEventListener("load",setupEvents,false);
   } else if (window.attachEvent) {
     window.attachEvent("onload", setupEvents);
   } else {
     window.onload=setupEvents;
}

function setupEvents(evnt) {
   document.someForm.text2.onblur=checkRequired;
   document.someForm.text1.onchange = validateField;
}

function checkRequired (evnt) {
  var theEvent = evnt ? evnt : window.event;
  var target = evnt.target ? evnt.target : evnt.srcElement;

  var txtInput = target.value;
  if (txtInput == null || txtInput == "") {
     alert("value is required in field");
  }
}

function validateField(evnt) {
  var theEvent = evnt ? evnt : window.event;
  var target = evnt.target ? evnt.target : evnt.srcElement;
  var rgEx = /^\d{3}[-]?\d{2}[-]?\d{4}$/g;

  var OK = rgEx.exec(target.value);
  if (!OK) {
     alert("not an ssn");
  }

}
//]]>
</script>
</head>
<body>
<form name="someForm">
<input type="text" name="text1" /><br />
<input type="password" name="text2" /><br />
<input type="hidden" name="text3" value="hidden value" />
<textarea name="text4" cols=50 rows=10>The text area</textarea>
<input type="submit" value="Submit" />
</form>
</body>
</html>
```

Now, if the SSN doesn't have the proper format, you'll get notified as soon as you leave the field. In addition, if a password isn't provided, another pop up opens. Of course, pop ups get irritating over time, and later in the book we'll look at better ways of providing feedback.

This example also demonstrates how important regular expressions are with any form of user input. The last section of this chapter looks at applying regular expressions to text input.

Use extreme care if you decide to enforce a required field using the focus method to return the cursor to the field—especially in combination with a pop-up window giving an error. In some browsers, such as Opera, this can trigger a neverending loop. It can also irritate your users considerably. Bottom line, I would advise against enforcing a required field through the use of focus.

 JavaScript Best Practice: Don't enforce a required field using focus to force the person back to the field. It's better to provide a more passive approach.

Input Fields and JiT Regular Expressions

Most form fields just require some text without giving any concern to the format. However, certain types of fields may require a specific format. Rather than send the data across to the server to see if the data is valid, we'll use regular expressions to validate the format of the data, at a minimum, first.

Using regular expressions, as defined in Chapter 3, some of the more common validations are with the following fields:

- Warranty or purchase certificates
- Email addresses
- Phone numbers
- Social Security numbers or other forms of identification
- Dates
- State abbreviations
- Credit card numbers
- Web page URLs or other forms of URI (uniform resource identifiers)

Rather than try out various regular expressions directly in code, Example 7-5 contains a little application, the JiT RegEx Machine, that takes a regular expression typed in one field, a string in another, and then does a pattern match when the form is submitted. The results are output to a third field.

Example 7-5. The JiT RegEx Machine application

```
<!DOCTYPE html PUBLIC "-//W3C//DTD XHTML 1.0 Transitional//EN"
"http://www.w3.org/TR/xhtml1/DTD/xhtml1-transitional.dtd">
<html>
<head>
<title>The JiT RegEx Machine</title>
<meta http-equiv="Content-Type" content="text/html; charset=utf-8" />
<script type="text/javascript">
//<![CDATA[

if (window.addEventListener) {
    window.addEventListener("load",setupEvents,false);
  } else if (window.attachEvent) {
    window.attachEvent("onload", setupEvents);
  } else {
    window.onload=setupEvents;
}

function setupEvents(evnt) {
   document.someForm.onsubmit=validateField;
}

function validateField(evnt) {

  var rgEx = new RegExp(document.someForm.text1.value);
  var OK = rgEx.exec(document.someForm.text2.value);

  // result and print out
  if (!OK) {
     document.someForm.text3.value = "Not a match";
  } else {
     document.someForm.text3.value = "The Pattern matched!";
  }

  return false;

}
//]]>
</script>
</head>
<body>
<form name="someForm" style="padding: 10px">
Regular Expression: <input type="text" name="text1" /><br /><br />
<textarea name="text2" cols=50 rows=10></textarea><br />
Result: <input type="text" name="text3" /><br /><br />
<input type="submit" value="Check RegExp" />
</form>
</body>
</html>
```

Certificates of purchase and warranty numbers may have a pattern that requires certain letters and/or numbers to appear in certain positions. As an example, if you have a certificate identifier that is 13 characters long, with the characters BUS in the sixth through eighth position, and alphanumeric characters in the remaining spots, you might try the following regular expression:

```
^\w{5}BUS\w{5}
```

If you're validating an email address, which requires an amphora (at symbol), some form of domain, and little other restriction, the following should work:

```
^.+@[^\.].*\.[a-z]{2,}$
```

As for date, the following could work if you want a date in the format mm/dd/yyyy:

```
^\d{2}\/+\d{2}\/+\d{4}
```

Examples too simple so far? Well, check out the following for Social Security numbers:

```
^(?!000)([0-6]\d{2}|7([0-6]\d|7[012]))([ -]?)(?!00)\d\d\3(?!0000)\d{4}$
```

I'm so whizzy at regular expressions!

Well, actually, I'm not very good at regular expressions. When I need to have one that's more complicated than dates or perhaps email addresses, I go shopping online by searching for "regular expression" with whatever it is I'm trying to match against. In Example 7-4, the format validated against was my own (well, I devised; others have probably used the same pattern), and was a simple regular expression that ensures only that the appropriate number of digits are given, that the characters are only digits, and that each grouping is of the right size—all separated by dashes. Which, if you think about it, covers quite a bit.

Compare that, though, with the regular expression I just provided, created by Michael Ash and courtesy of the Regular Expression Library (an invaluable resource at *http://regexlib.com/*). This not only validates against the format, it also validates against what is known about Social Security numbers—the number groupings and so on. There are others at least as complex that can differentiate between a Visa credit card and a MasterCard.

If you want to become expert at regular expressions, spend some time at the Regular Expression Library, or you can also buy a copy of Friedl's *Mastering Regular Expressions*. This is the definitive guide on regular expressions.

On the other hand, do you need to differentiate between Visa and MasterCard? The important point to remember about regular expressions is that you can get carried away trying to find the perfect validation pattern, spending more time than the validation is worth. You have to weigh your time against how important it is to validate the entry before submitting it to the server.

Speaking of which, that's just about enough time on events, forms, and JiT validation. Time to move on to Chapter 8: JavaScript's roots, cookies, and evil things that go bump in the browser.

Forms Generation

I hate creating web-page forms; it's the most tedious part of web development. Luckily, there's plenty of web form-generation tools that are hosted online or that you can install on your site. They will not only generate your forms, they'll also start your server-side development for you. Though this technically isn't a JavaScript utility, it is a time-saving device, so I'm including it.

The one I've used the most is phpFormGenerator (*http://phpformgen.sourceforge.net/*). If your ISP provides cPanel for you to manage your account, it should be available as one of the many Fantastico-managed software applications.

This, and most other form generators, provide a way to specify the number and type of fields, give a name, and even associate a database field. Once the form is generated, you can add a script block to validate the entries once the form is submitted.

There's also an Eclipse plug-in that generates a form from XML. This tool is part of the Emerging Technologies Toolkit, a toolkit from IBM worth exploration even without the forms generator. Among the tools is the XForm Designer for forms generation and an Ajax Framework. Access the Toolkit at *http://www.alphaworks.ibm.com/ettk*.

Questions

1. How do you stop a form submittal if the form data is incomplete or invalid?
2. What event(s) do you want to capture on text-input fields to do JiT validation?
3. Given a selection list, how would you add options based on user input?
4. How do you ensure a name field has only characters and whitespace?
5. Create the JavaScript that captures an event when a radio button is checked and then disables a text-input field if one button is clicked, and enables it if another is clicked.

Answers are provided in the appendix.

CHAPTER 8

The Sandbox and Beyond: Cookies, Connectivity, and Piracy

JavaScript achieved its early popularity in part because of the assurances of the language's safety. After all, JavaScript in browsers operates within a sandbox—a protective environment that stringently restricts access to the client's machine. There are no mechanisms to open or create files; the language operates within a temporary environment, which is discarded as soon as the browser terminates or a web page is exited; if data is transmitted, the user is informed; and so on.

We learned over time that there is no way to completely protect the client machines, not when there are determined hackers ready to exploit even the smallest openings in browser or language. The only way to prevent this type of access is to completely close off the client machine from browser access, which makes the browser less than useful. After all, some of the more popular features of browsers are bookmarks, plug-ins and extensions, and remembering URLs and form-field entries. All of these require putting something on the client's machine; many require the use of cookies.

Cookies: hate them, love them. *Cookies* are bits of data storage on the client based on key information, provided by the server, that allows JavaScript developers to persist information either during a session (until a browser is closed), or between sessions (web accesses). The original concept was that only those requests to get or write cookies associated with the web page's domain would be given access, and therefore the information would be secure. Based on this premise, JavaScript was used to persist anything from a person's login name and password to shopping-cart contents. There's rarely a commercial site you can visit on the Web nowadays that doesn't have some form of cookie implemented—whether you want it or not.

Over time, breaks in the security of cookies, as well as concerns about privacy, have tarnished the JavaScript cookies' reputation. Concerns about privacy in particular have led to more people turning off cookie support in their browsers. Still, cookies are very popular and, if not abused, very helpful.

This chapter explores the JavaScript sandbox and the restrictions built into the language to prevent malicious activity. We'll also look at how cookies work within this environment, and some alternative cookie implementations using plug-ins and browser extensions.

Finally, we'll look at cross-site scripting (XSS) attacks—where modern-day pirates sail the Internet rather than the oceans, stealing sensitive data rather than gold and jewels. Arggh.

The Sandbox

Some security measures are browser-dependent or require deliberate action. One such uses digital signatures to sign a script. A signed script is allowed to bypass many of the sandbox security policies associated with JS, including the same-domain policy (depending on browser and access). For instance, this is an approach Ajax developers sometimes use to communicate with server applications located on domains different from the web page initiating the request.

The limitation with signed scripts is the lack of universal support for the concept. Mozilla/Firefox support signing the script, but Internet Explorer does not; IE supports only signing of controls. Other browsers don't support either. This limitation is enough to make the concept impractical for most Internet use.

Most JavaScript developers depend instead on the security policies inherent to all uses of JavaScript, rather than those specific to a particular browser. Among the key elements of the language, and unlike many other languages, JavaScript has no file-access functionality: there is no ability to open, create, or delete a file from the operating system. There are only low-level networking capabilities, such as loading a web page; none allow the language to initiate a connection to another site and transmit data silently.

Same-Origin Security Policy

Restricting the functionality of the language is only the start. As JavaScript has evolved over time—and through painful experience—other policies and procedures have been incorporated into the JavaScript engines to increase language security. One such policy is the same-origin security policy.

Since Netscape 2.0, JavaScript has operated under a policy called the *same-origin policy*. This policy, which is universally supported in browsers, ensures that there is no communication via script between pages that have different domains, protocols, or ports. The same-origin policy applies to communication between separate pages, or from a parent window to an embedded window, such as frames or iframes.

Why is this restriction so important? If a web site pops open a small window that ends up behind your main page, and you continue on to other sites, such as your bank, JavaScript in that pop-up window could listen in on your activities in that separate page. The same-origin policy prevents this type of snooping by preventing JavaScript in a page opened in one domain from having any access to a page opened in another.

As an example of same origin, if a page opened from a domain such as *http:// somecompany.com* tries to access information from a page accessed from any of the following domains, the JavaScript used would fail:

http://othercompany.com
> This would fail because the domain is different: *somecompany.com* is not the same as *othercompany.com*.

https://somecompany.com
> This would fail because the protocol is different: *http* is not the same protocol as *https*.

http://somecompany.com:8080
> This would fail because the port is different: the original request did not specify any port in the URL (falling back on the default port, usually 80).

http://other.somecompany.com
> This would fail because the host is different; the use of the other hostname (subdomain) changes the host.

Using document.domain

Unfortunately, same origin can work against a site developer's efforts. The use of alternative hostnames with the same domain, known as subdomains, such as *about. somecompany.com* and *help.somecompany.com*, is becoming increasingly popular and the last same-origin restriction can become prohibitive. To work around this restriction, there's a property on the document object, domain, which when set, allows subdomain pages to communicate with each other—but only subdomain pages, and only if the document property and the original host domain match.

If the page containing the JavaScript is accessed through the URL *http://admin. somecompany.com*, then *document.domain* can be set to the *somecompany.com*, which is the domain of the original access. It cannot be set to *othercompany.com*, which is a different domain.

The following will work:

```
document.domain = "somecompany.com";
```

This will not:

```
document.domain = "othercompany.com";
```

When set, JavaScript in a page at *admin.somecompany.com* could then communicate with a page opened at *help.somecompany.com*.

Luckily, the same origin policy does not apply when linking scripts in from other domains. Scripts can be linked from anywhere, and then are treated as if the Java-Script originates within the page—including the same domain for all further communication. Without this ability to link scripts in from other domains, functionality such as Google Maps (covered in Chapter 13) couldn't be implemented.

The policy of same origin does apply, however, to the implementation of cookies.

All About Cookies

Why cookie? The original name for a cookie came from the term "magic cookie"—a token passed between two programs. Though accessible from JavaScript, cookies aren't really script-based: they're a mechanism of the HTTP server. As such, they're accessible by both the client and the server.

Whatever the name, cookies are small key-value pairs associated with an expiration date and with a domain/path, both of which are meant to ensure that the right cookies are read by the right servers. The information they contain is transmitted as part of the web-page request, and thus the data is available to the server and to the browser.

Storing and Reading Cookies

Cookies are accessible, like most other browser elements, through the document object. To create a cookie, you'll need to provide a cookie name, or key, an associated value, a date when it expires, and a path associated with the cookie. To access it, you'll access the document cookie and then have to parse the cookie out.

Luckily there's a plethora of cookie functions out and about. To get a better idea of how they work, I'll provide a variation of functions for setting, getting, and erasing a cookie and explain what happens with each step in the process.

To create a cookie, just assign the document cookie value a string with the following format:

```
cookieName=cookieValue; expirationdate; path
```

The cookie name and value are whatever you want and need, as long as the value is a simple value. I've used cookie names starting with a dollar sign ($cookieName), with an underscore (_cookieName), and other characters. Regardless of what a browser will accept, you won't want to use the equals sign (=) or semicolon (;), or your cookie functions most likely won't work.

I've also experimented with different cookie values, and depending on the browser, what gets attached to the cookie name is the string conversion of whatever the object is—number, array, or object. However, this varies significantly between browsers. Figure 8-1 displays the *document.cookie* as printed out in Safari, Figure 8-2, as it's printed out in Firefox, and Figure 8-3 in Internet Explorer—all from the same Mac computer, run one right after another, and all setting the same cookie values.

Figure 8-1. document.cookie string in Safari

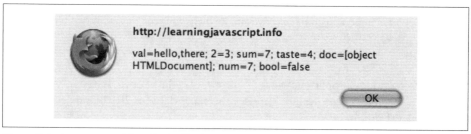

Figure 8-2. document.cookie string in Firefox

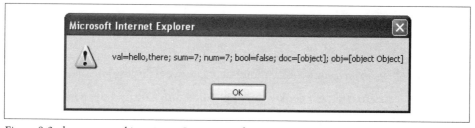

Figure 8-3. document.cookie string in Internet Explorer

To ensure consistent results, I would recommend that you use primitive types (string, boolean, and number), converted to string only.

 JavaScript Best Practice: Use simple types for cookie values.

As for the rest of the document cookie-setting string, the expiration date must be in a specific GMT (UTC) format. Creating a date object and then using the toGMTString is sufficient to ensure the date works. If no date is provided, the cookie is eliminated as soon as the browser closes.

The cookie path is especially important. The domain and path are compared with the page request, and if they don't sync up, the cookie can't be accessed or set. This prevents other sites from accessing any and all cookies set on your browser, though as you can see, this has been circumvented in the past.

A path setting of *path=/* sets the cookie's allowable path to the top-level directory at your domain. If you access the page at *http://somedomain.com*, this means that the cookie is accessible by any subdirectory off of *http://somedomain.com*. If you specify a subdirectory, such as *path=/images*, the cookie is accessible only from web pages in this subdirectory. Conversely, if you have many subdomains at your web site, such as *sub1.somedomain.com*, *sub2.somedomain.com*, and so on, you can make a cookie accessible at all of them by specifically giving the higher-level domain: *path=some-domain.com*.

 It's important to be selective about where your cookies are accessible. Be restrictive by setting your path to the topmost level essential for your application.

The following code snippet shows an example of a JavaScript function that sets a cookie to a specific key and value, but uses the same date (in 2010) and sets the path to the top-level subdirectory:

```
function setCookie(key,value) {
    var cookieDate = new Date(2010,11,10,19,30,30);
    document.cookie=key + "=" + escape(value) + "; expires=" + cookieDate.toGMTString(
) + "; path=/";
}
```

The escape function is used to escape any special characters that might be part of the cookie value. This makes your cookie more secure, as we'll discuss later in the chapter.

Other approaches to coding a cookie function adjust the date and the path, as well as the key and value. Note that there is one space, following the semicolons in the string.

 A fourth parameter for a cookie is a flag on whether the cookie is secure or not. A secure cookie can be requested only using SSL (HTTPS rather than HTTP).

Getting the cookie is not as easy because all cookies get concatenated into one string, separated by semicolons(;) on the cookie object. Following is an example of a cookie string:

```
var1=somevalue; var2=3.55; var3=true
```

I've seen several approaches used to get the keys. One uses the String split method to split on the semicolon; others use a variety of searches on substrings. The example function I've created uses a mix of both techniques:

```
function readCookie(key) {
  var cookie = document.cookie;

  var first = cookie.indexOf(key+"=");

  // cookie exists
  if (first >= 0) {
    var str = cookie.substring(first,cookie.length);
    var last = str.indexOf(";");

    // if last cookie
    if (last < 0) last = str.length;

    // get cookie value
    str = str.substring(0,last).split("=");
    return unescape(str[1]);
  } else {
    return null;
  }
}
```

In the code, the key is concatenated to the equals sign (=), and the whole is searched in the string. When found, its first position gets a substring of the rest of the string. Within this new string, then, the semicolon is searched and if found, the string is either shortened to the semicolon or accessed as a whole (key is last item). Finally, the string is split on the equals sign to get the key and the value, separately. The return value is unescaped to return the original value.

To erase the cookie, eliminate its value (set to nothing), set the date to a past date, or both, as the following JS function demonstrates:

```
function eraseCookie (key) {

  var cookieDate = new Date(2000,11,10,19,30,30);
  document.cookie=key + "=; expires=" + cookieDate.toGMTString() + "; path=/";
}
```

When the document cookie string is accessed next, the cookie will no longer exist.

Before any cookie functionality is used, it's best to first test to make sure cookies are implemented and enabled for the browser. It's not unusual for people to turn cookies off, and you'll want to account for this in your code. To check if cookies are enabled, use another built-in browser object, navigator, and the cookieEnabled property:

```
if (navigator.cookieEnabled) ...
```

Note that not all browsers return the correct value when testing the cookieEnabled property. For instance, IE 6.x does not set this property correctly. In these cases, there's little you can do other than set the cookie and see if you can find it.

Taking all of this together, Example 8-1 demonstrates an application that sets a value as a cookie that's accessed and incremented each time the page is loaded. When the value gets to 10, the cookie gets erased, and in the next iteration (page load), the cookie gets recreated.

Example 8-1. Setting, reading, and erasing cookies

```
<!DOCTYPE html PUBLIC "-//W3C//DTD XHTML 1.0 Transitional//EN"
"http://www.w3.org/TR/xhtml1/DTD/xhtml1-transitional.dtd">
<html>
<head>
<title>Cookies</title>
<meta http-equiv="Content-Type" content="text/html; charset=utf-8" />
<script type="text/javascript">
//<![CDATA[

// if cookie enabled
if (navigator.cookieEnabled) {

   var tst = new Array( );
   tst[0] = "hello"; tst[1]="there";
   setCookie("doc",document);
   alert(document.cookie);
   var sum = readCookie("sum");
   var iSum = 0;
   if (sum) {
      iSum = parseInt(sum) + 1;
      alert(iSum);
      if (iSum > 10) {
         eraseCookie("sum");
      } else {
         setCookie("sum",iSum);
      }
   } else {
      setCookie("sum", 0);
   }

}

// set cookie expiration date in year 2010
function setCookie(key,value) {

   var cookieDate = new Date(2010,11,10,19,30,30);
   document.cookie=key + "=" + escape(value) + "; expires=" + cookieDate.toGMTString( ) +
"; path=/";
}
// each cookie separated by semicolon;
function readCookie(key) {
  var cookie = document.cookie;

  var first = cookie.indexOf(key+"=");

  // cookie exists
  if (first >= 0) {
    var str = cookie.substring(first,cookie.length);
    var last = str.indexOf(";");

    // if last cookie
    if (last < 0) last = str.length;
```

Example 8-1. Setting, reading, and erasing cookies (continued)

```
      // get cookie value
      str = str.substring(0,last).split("=");
      return unescape(str[1]);
   } else {
     return null;
   }
}

// set cookie date to the past to erase
function eraseCookie (key) {

    var cookieDate = new Date(2000,11,10,19,30,30);
    document.cookie=key + "= ; expires="+cookieDate.toGMTString( )+"; path=/";
}

//]]>
</script>
</head>
<body>
</body>
</html>
```

Cookies are handy little buggers, but one of their limitations is that a domain can store only 20 cookies, up to 4 KB in total size. For most cases, this is more than satisfactory; in fact, you should use even this smaller client-side storage sparingly. Still, there might be times when you want to store larger amounts of data.

Alternative Storage Techniques

To store larger cookies or more complex objects, previous applications have used a variety of hacks, including a LiveConnect interface between JavaScript and Java applets, or ActiveX controls. Another approach is to use hidden elements in forms to persist the data from form submission to submission. An approach gaining increasing popularity, especially with the advent of Ajax technologies, has been to use the Flash built-in persistent mechanism.

Communicating Outside the Box

Learning JavaScript never ends. Just when you think you've worked with all aspects of the language, something else comes along. It might be fun, it might not be fun, but there is more to this little lightweight language than first meets the eye.

As I mentioned in Chapter 1, JavaScript was originally intended to be one half of a one-two punch put out by Netscape: functionality created on both the server and the client browser, with communication between the two through an integration plug-in known as LiveConnect. Through LiveConnect, developers working with the newfangled programming language Java could interface directly to JavaScript on the browser.

Nowadays, most server-client interaction happens through Ajax, which is described in Chapter 13. But in those early times of technological exploration, LiveConnect was one sexy concept.

Much of the Flash/JavaScript early integration was based on this LiveConnect interface, though Macromedia eventually created its own scripting language, ActionScript, for its side of the equation. You can still manipulate Flash functionality through JavaScript, and web-page objects and JS through Flash. There's even a Flash-to-JavaScript integration kit, though it looks rather cobwebby and untouched.

 The Flash JavaScript Integration Kit can be downloaded at *http://osflash. org/doku.php?id=flashjs*. Note, though, that the kit hasn't been touched in some time, and it's unknown how many browsers support it.

Through this open door between JavaScript and Flash, a new storage medium was discovered when those creating more sophisticated client applications needed something more in the way of persistent storage on the client. This new form of Flash-enabled cookie, or super cookie as it's sometimes called, can be up to 100 KB and can take any form of JS object, not just primitives. The storage is managed through a specific object: the Flash Shared Object.

The Flash SO and Dojo Storage

Shared Objects (SO) in Flash operate in a manner similar to HTTP cookies. They're stored and accessible based on a domain, and pages served from one domain cannot access shared objects created from another domain. This sandbox protection was incorporated as part of the design of Shared Objects from Flash Version 7 and up.

Unlike the HTTP cookie, with its 4 KB limit, SO storage is unlimited—but only silently up to the first 100 KB. What this means is that if a web page or web application from one domain tries to set a SO greater than 100 KB, a message box opens asking for permission to use this space. The client then has to provide explicit permission for the SO to be set.

Of course, a drawback to using the Flash SO is having to work with Flash in addition to JavaScript. However, others have been down this path and have kindly provided open source implementations of this technology. One such is Brad Neuberg's Dojo.Storage (described, demonstrated, and linked in this weblog post: *http://codinginparadise.org/ weblog/2006/04/now-in-browser-near-you-offline-access.html*). Dojo is an increasingly popular Ajax tookit, which I describe in Chapter 14. The Storage library is an interface to multiple storage techniques, including using XPCOM (for Firefox), and ActiveX (for IE), as well as Flash for cross-browser support.

Over time, other approaches that enable client-side storage beyond the limits of cookies will be developed. The question then becomes: should we use them?

Could You, Should You?

Could you, should you, though? Before getting into the mechanisms that allow you to load down the client, should you? And if you do, should you let the client know?

If you are providing a functionality that your client wants, by all means, load down the client machine. However, you should give upfront notice that this is going to happen, rather than sneaking the data in through a back door.

All the whizzy frontend functionality won't compensate for taking a significant amount of client space, leaving your client wondering what's going on. A good rule of thumb is never use so much client space that your clients will notice it, unless you give them a heads up first. Any other practice would be just plain rude.

Beyond taking client space, there are privacy concerns. Browser cookies are very visible. After all, they are just small text files locally stored on the client. You can see these cookies through your browser, as shown in Figure 8-4. You might not recognize all of them, but at least you can see what's there, and (depending on your browser) individually remove each.

Figure 8-4. Peering into the browser cookies

Other approaches may not give this option. As it is, several online ad companies have been exploring the use of Flash to track a person's movement through various sites. Additionally, wherever there's an opening, the bad folks will exploit it. Enough so that many people are turning off Flash, even as they contemplate turning Java-Script back on.

Cross-Site Scripting (XSS)

As popular and helpful as cookies are, it's becoming increasingly popular for people to turn off any cookie support. The reason is understandable: we store anything, from usernames and passwords to credit cards and other sensitive information, in stores of text that aren't all that difficult to access. (Well, depending on how vulnerable—or not—a web site is.) The reason, though, is also not necessarily well founded. One of the greatest areas of vulnerability associated with a web site is known as a cross-site scripting (XSS) attack.

Here's how an attack happens: you receive an email, or there's a link in a web site comment or such—anything that allows anonymous or semianonymous content. The link is to a legitimate site that takes cookies. Attached to the link is a set of characters, perhaps in hexadecimal format. We're used to long and unreadable URLs, so we don't make much of it. However, attached to that URL is a script that can trick the browser into bringing up whatever cookies are set between the person and the site. These, then, can be attached to the end of a *document.location* redirect, which basically sends this information to the new site.

This site then uses this information to emulate the site you're expecting to access. You'll continue to input valuable information, all the while the server site is gathering up your password, bank account, credit card information, etc.

This is what happens, more or less, with the email-phishing (pronounced "fishing") attacks you get that command you to log in or your account will be suspended. Even if the hacker doesn't steal the cookie, she can poison it by changing its value or corrupting it in some way. But vulnerabilities don't just exist with cookies: any opening into a web site is a potential doorway for bad people to do bad things.

The Injectors

XSS attacks are part of a group of attacks that take advantage of too many vulnerabilities in our software. Each uses some form of injection to insert malicious material. Among these are:

Cross-site scripting, or JavaScript/script injection
> Embeds user information in a URL and inserts JavaScript to access this information for theft or malicious modification. A common variation uses the information it gathers to recreate what looks like a legitimate page where you do transactions (such as your bank account) but with added functionality to steal your information.

Eclipse: The All-Purpose Development Tool

Here's something safe! It can't protect your web site, but it can help you create your pages. Eclipse is a tool long used in the Java community for development, but its use extends beyond any one language. Eclipse has been gaining popularity for development in other languages, including JavaScript. You'll need a Java runtime environment to use Eclipse, but installing Eclipse can also install this environment if it's not already there.

Eclipse is an open source project that can be downloaded, along with many plug-ins, from the Eclipse web site at *Eclipse.org*. I've used the tool in Windows and Mac OS X, and there are also installations available for Linux and most flavors of Unix.

The installation is simple: primarily, you double-click and answer a few questions. During the installation, you'll be asked where to locate a workspace environment; accepting the default doesn't permanently commit you to one spot.

There are several JS plug-ins, and even some Dojo-based Ajax plug-ins. Some of these are for sale; others are free. One of the more popular is the Web Tools Plugin environment, which is free and sets up your Eclipse to develop almost anything web-related.

To install the Web Tools plug-in, click the Help menu item, then Software Updates → Find and Install. From the window that opens, click the "Search for New Features to Install" option, and then click Next.

In the page that opens, there's a box that lists what remote sites to explore for new and updated software. Click New Remote Site, and in the dialog box that opens, add in:

```
Name: Web Tools
URL: http://download.eclipse.org/webtools/updates/
```

Click Finish, and when given a new dialog with a list of features to install, check the box next to the Web Tools option, and then click the Next button. Following a request to agree to the license terms, Eclipse not only downloads the tools, it also downloads all the prerequisites needed for the tools to operate. That's it: when it's finished, it asks to reboot, and when that's done, you're ready to use the new functionality.

To test, create a new project by selecting File → New → Project → Other. From the list that opens, select Simple, and then give the project a name: **test**. Based on whatever project type is picked, Eclipse adds any supportive libraries and generated files, listed underneath the project name in the left pane.

Create a new JavaScript file by again selecting File → New → Other. From the dialog that opens, click Web, and then select JavaScript. Name the JS file: **test.js**.

At this point, the new *test.js* file shows in the left pane, and the open file, ready for edits, is shown in the center panel. Type in whatever JavaScript you want. As new program objects such as variables, are added, they show in the outline panel on the right. If using a built-in object, such as Math or document, after typing the period to access an object property or method, you'll see a pop-up window that lists available options and even the browser icon associated with the option.

When ready to preview the page, click the Preview tab at the bottom of the center edit pane. Figure 8-5 illustrates Eclipse within a Mac environment.

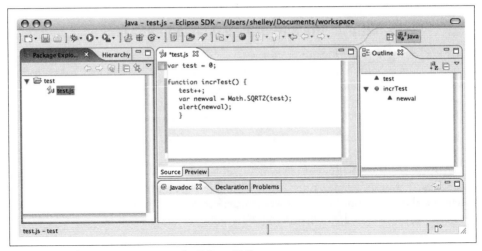

Figure 8-5. Editing JavaScript using the Eclipse IDE

SQL injection

> Potentially one of the most serious injection attacks. Many forms that take user input add the information the person provides directly to the database query. It's a simple matter to add SQL to emulate the end of one query and the beginning of another—getting information such as credit-card numbers in the database, or passwords in plain text. When this was discovered, many popular PHP-based applications were found vulnerable. Unfortunately, more SQL injection vulnerabilities are found weekly.

HTML embedding or bad-tag injection

> Embeds dangerous or malicious tags into data that's eventually going to be used to dynamically generate pages. One susceptible form involved weblog comments where hypertext links were allowed, and links to offensive pages could be added. The only skill required for this one was the ability to type and form a hypertext link.

Of course, add in holes in browsers and email programs, as well as web and email servers, and it can make you think fondly of days of log cabins, where you could see the bad guys coming from miles away.

What You Can Do

Things are not as bad as they seem—if you stay aware of the vulnerabilities of your site as you're creating your pages. If you have a form, especially one that is nonsecure and for general use, any field in that form is a potential vulnerability.

If you have a server-side application that processes parameters passed in a URL, then all of your web site URLs are also a point of vulnerability.

If you store cookies, they're points of vulnerability.

In particular, if you post content that is created by anonymous or semianonymous people, you're creating the potential for nefarious doings.

Other than taking the log-cabin approach, the simplest technique to ensure the safety of your site is to scrub all incoming data: remove all harmful or potentially harmful material. No web site URL or form needs to have the term javascript: embedded in it; this can open the door to malicious script injection. You'll also want to consider stripping all HTML from user input—especially images and hypertext links, and definitely script tags.

All HTML tags that are not allowed should be escaped, i.e., angle brackets converted to < and >, which prints them to the output but does not treat them as opening and closing brackets for HTML tags. As shown in earlier chapters, there are even encoding and escaping functions built into the JavaScript objects themselves that can aid this.

 Here are some helpful sites regarding this issue:

- CERT's Understanding Malicious Content Mitigation for Web Developers: *http://www.cert.org/tech_tips/malicious_code_mitigation.html*.
- Wikipedia entry on cross-site scripting at *http://en.wikipedia.org/wiki/XSS*
- If you dare, go into the lion's den: ha.ckers XSS Cheat Sheet for filter evasion at *http://ha.ckers.org/xss.html*.

There are many server-side approaches to securing a site using PHP or other language, and API functions such as htmlspecialchars, which escapes all HTML. However, you can make JavaScript the first line of defense in an attack by cleaning the incoming data before it's sent rather than cleaning up the mess after.

Questions

1. Name some ways to store material on the client machine.
2. What are the components of a script cookie?
3. How should a cookie be defined to be destroyed when the browser closes?
4. What type of data should be scrubbed on user input?
5. Think of a web site you have created or might create in the future. Now think of five different uses for script cookies. In all of these uses, could you see needing more space than is provided for cookies?

Answers are provided in the appendix.

CHAPTER 9

The Basic Browser Objects

The Browser Object Model (BOM) is a set of objects inherited from the browser context in which most JavaScript applications function. It's sometimes referred to as the Document Object Model Level 0, or even as the DOM, but it's a finite set of common web objects that have been accessible via JavaScript since earlier versions of Netscape Navigator and Microsoft's Internet Explorer.

We've worked with some of the objects—window, document, navigator, and form—in earlier chapters. This chapter looks at these in more detail, as well as the other objects that complete the set.

BOM at a Glance

The BOM forms a hierarchy of objects, with each object at each level accessible via a parent object above it. All of the elements of the BOM are accessible via the window, which is the topmost element. The next level below features document, which we've used extensively. The level also contains the navigator, frames, location, history, and screen objects. From the document, several collections of objects are accessible: forms, anchors, links, and images. As demonstrated in Chapter 3, the form itself has elements, but we'll stop at just the top three levels in this chapter.

Figure 9-1 shows the BOM at a glance, and how all of these elements relate to each other.

As can be quickly seen, window is the top dog in this bunch. We'll look at it first.

The window Object

The browser window encompasses the entire browser environment, including parts of the window "chrome" (the part of the browser that surrounds the document), the actual web page, and even the user's experiences.

The window object is global and always present even if its presence is implicitly, rather than explicitly, stated. In previous chapters we've used functions such as alert and

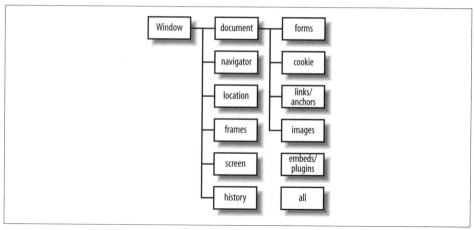

Figure 9-1. Hierarchy of the Browser Object Model

eval, and these functions may seem "independent" of any object model. However, they're implicitly a part of the window object—as is the document and other second-level objects, global variables, and other objects not associated with any other object within an object model.

The window has interest beyond being just a parent to all other elements. Through it you can manually set the status in the status bar of the browser, open a new window, resize one that's already open, and then close it again. This is handy if you're providing separate windows for help or additional information, though with the growing popularity of DHTML and Ajax, much of this now occurs within a document rather than a separate window.

The window object methods and properties fall into four categories: creating and managing new windows, manipulating the behavior of existing windows, serving as timers, and being the parent of the other objects in the BOM.

For the first category, creating new windows, three methods provide quick pop-up windows (each for a specific purpose), while a fourth can create a window with as much, or as little, window infrastructure included as you wish.

The Dialogs: Alert, Confirm, and Prompt

The three simple, pop-up window object methods create a window with minimal window chrome; each serves a specific purpose. These are usually referred to as the *dialog windows*.

We're familiar with the alert dialog, and it's a quick way to provide a message to the person accessing the page. The only parameter it takes is a message string, and it returns no value:

```
alert("This is the message");
```

The confirm method creates a dialog with a question and two buttons: Cancel and OK. The message is passed as a parameter, and depending on which button is pressed, either a true value is returned (OK) or a false (Cancel):

```
var result = confirm("Do you want fries with that?");
```

The prompt opens a window with a field for entering text, as well as the Cancel and OK buttons. It takes two parameters: a message providing the prompt for the response, and a default string, which is used to fill in the text field:

```
var response = prompt("What's your name?", "Wouldn't you like to know...");
```

Note that none of these methods are preceded by a reference to the window object; that object is global, and its presence is assumed.

I refer to these types of windows as pop ups because that's basically what they do: pop up. However, this phrase has normally been reserved for those windows that seem to take over your desktop every time you visit a web page. Yes, you know the type: the ones you instruct your browser to prevent.

However, not all windows that open are full of moving bunnies with an invitation to shoot one and win a Big Prize. Opening a separate window can be an effective way to provide additional information, without taking the person away from the current page.

Creating Custom Windows

There are many reasons to create a new window: accessing a help system, providing additional information, reviewing a shopping cart or other information, and yes, even displaying animated bunnies with roving bullseyes.

To open a window and control its contents, size, position, and so on, use the open method. This method takes several parameters, all of which are optional. The first parameter is the URL of the document to open, if any. The second is the name given to the window. This can be used for communication between the parent and child windows, or between siblings if many windows are opened.

The third parameter is a set of window options, all contained in one string and separated by commas. In the following lines of code, a window is created and named "test." It contains a link to the main O'Reilly web site, is 600×400 pixels, and doesn't have a location or toolbar:

```
window.open("http://oreilly.
com","test","width=600,height=400,toolbar=no,location=no");
```

Not all options can be set in all circumstances. Those that impact certain components of the window frame and layering position of the window can be modified from the default only if the script has a UniversalBrowserWrite privilege, usually granted with script signing. Since the support for this isn't universal, it's best to avoid any dependency on these options.

The common options supported by the majority of browsers, their default values, and their purpose are given in Table 9-1.

Table 9-1. Cross-browser compatible window.open options

Option	Purpose	Default value
alwaysLowered	Referred to as "pop under" window. Puts window under parent window unless parent window is minimized	Default is no; defined to work only with UniversalBrowserWrite
alwaysRaised	Opens window on top of parent window	Default is no; defined to work only with UniversalBrowserWrite
dependent	Opens a window dependent on parent window. When parent closes, all dependent windows close	Default is no
directories	Displays personal bookmarks or links bar in browser, depending on browser type	Default is yes; can be overridden by user in some browsers
height	Height of content area in pixels	Minimum of 100 pixels
width	Width of content area in pixels	Minimum of 100 pixels
outerHeight	Height of entire browser window, in pixels	Minimum of 100 pixels
outerWidth	Width of entire browser window, in pixels	Minimum of 100 pixels
top	Position of topmost edge of browser window	Must be positioned onscreen
left	Position of leftmost edge of browser window	Must be positioned onscreen
menubar	If yes, renders the menubar	Can be overridden by user in some browsers
toolbar	If yes, renders the toolbar	Can be overridden by user in some browsers
location	If yes, renders location or address bar	IE7 forces the location to always display
status	If yes, renders the status bar at bottom of browser window	Defaults to yes for some browsers
resizable	If yes, the window is resizable	Can be overridden by user in some browsers
scrollbars	If yes, the window has scrollbars (if the loaded document doesn't fit)	Can be overridden by user in some browsers
modal	Opens a window that must be closed before returning to the main window	Dialog windows are modal window; in some browsers, requires UniversalBrowserWrite
dialog	Opens a dialog window similar in appearance and behavior to alert window	
minimizable	Only when dialog is set to yes; inserts buttons to minimize window	
titlebar	Renders or removes titlebar	On by default; requires UniversalBrowserWrite; may be overridden by users in some browsers
close	Renders or removes close button (icon)	On by default; requires UniversalBrowserWrite; may be overridden by users in some browsers

As you can see, security is a real concern when it comes to pop-up windows. When I first started using JavaScript, anything went; back then, sites would use hidden windows to try out their deviltry, or size other windows and force them to the front so you couldn't work around them. Then there were the windows without a visible ability to close. It was an ugly time in JavaScript. Luckily, most of this is behind us.

Example 9-1 is an application that uses a prompt dialog to get a string to open a new window. Try out variations of the option string, and see the differences. Note that you'll be prompted to allow pop ups when you test the page.

Example 9-1. Using a prompt dialog to get window open options

```
<!DOCTYPE html PUBLIC "-//W3C//DTD XHTML 1.0 Transitional//EN"
"http://www.w3.org/TR/xhtml1/DTD/xhtml1-transitional.dtd">
<html>
<head>
<title>Windows</title>
<meta http-equiv="Content-Type" content="text/html; charset=utf-8" />
</head>
<body>
<script type="text/javascript">
//<![CDATA[

var optionString = prompt("Enter your option string");
optionString = optionString ? optionString : "";

document.writeln("Options are: " + optionString);
window.open("http://oreilly.com","test",optionString);

//]]>
</script>

</body>
</html>
```

If no option string is specified, the newly opened browser will, most likely, resemble the parent window. If some options are specified, others—such as toolbar, location, and menubar—may be off by default and dependent on the browser you're using.

 JavaScript Best Practice: Specify a value for all options when opening a window; avoid using any option that makes the window less accessible or that demonstrates a different behavior across browsers.

There are other options when opening a window, but many violate accessibility standards, and most are implemented only in older browsers, or one or two modern browsers. An example of this is fullscreen. This opens a browser to fill the screen, which is intimidating to users and a vile option. Mozilla/Firefox do not implement this. Other browsers might, but think carefully before trying it with your JavaScript applications.

Once you have a `window` object, you can adjust it from the parent window or have a window adjust itself. The methods to manage this are covered next.

 An excellent page covering the different options, the security associated with each, and which browsers they're implemented in, can be found at *http://developer.mozilla.org/en/docs/DOM:window.open*.

Cross-Window Communication

Once you have a window, you can have a little bit of fun. Among the methods that can manipulate a window are those that affect its size, focus, and position. This is true not just of windows that open, either. If you want to manipulate the window that contains the script containing the manipulating code, you can use `self` to refer to the window.

In the following code, the window containing the JavaScript being run is moved to a position of 0,0 for top and left:

```
self.moveTo(0,0);
```

If, instead, you want to reference a window you open from code, you'll need to capture the window reference, returned from the `window.open` call:

```
var newWindow = window.open("http://somecompany.com","NewWindow", "...options...");
newWindow.moveTo(0,0);
```

The opening window can reference any of those it opens using a reference to the window. This new window can also reference the window that opened it using the `opener` keyword:

```
opener.moveTo(0,0);
```

Each window can invoke the other window's methods, including getting access to the window objects, document, frames, location, and so on. There are few limitations to this cross-window communication, other than that most browsers do not let the opened window close the original window. Rightfully so, because closing the original window could lose the user's back-button history, opened tabs, half-filled fields, and so on. Those that do support this behavior provide a note to the user getting permission to close the window.

Once you have a reference to a window (either through an open window reference, through `self`, or through `opener`), each can be dynamically manipulated, as discussed in the next section.

Modifying the Window

Once you create a pop-up window, you can set the focus to that window, or reset it back to the opening window through the `focus` method. Using `blur`, you can also reset the focus to whatever next window would normally get the focus:

```
newWindow.focus();
...
newWindow.blur();
```

You can get an interesting effect by opening a window that's smaller than the opener and then resetting focus back to the opener. This effectively hides the pop-up window.

You can also resize a window using either the resizeBy or resizeTo methods. The resizeBy method works on the current window dimension, adjusting the current values by those specified as the parameters. The first is how much to adjust the width of the window; the second, the height:

```
newWindow.resizeBy(50,50);
```

The resizeTo method resizes the window to a specific width and height:

```
opener.resizeTo(100,100);
```

One of the more helpful methods is moveTo, which moves a window's upper-left corner to a given x-y dimension:

```
self.moveTo(x,y);
```

You can use this approach to open context-sensitive help windows that are positioned exactly where an event occurs. In Example 9-2, a page with a single form element is opened; a red-colored block underneath has the words "Push for Help." In script, an event listener is attached to this block to capture the click event. When the page opens, the focus is set to the form element in order for a person to type in his name. Of course there's no submit button, so it's not surprising that the user would then click the "Push for Help" button to get help.

Example 9-2. Opening a help window

```
<!DOCTYPE html PUBLIC "-//W3C//DTD XHTML 1.0 Transitional//EN"
"http://www.w3.org/TR/xhtml1/DTD/xhtml1-transitional.dtd">
<html>
<head>
<title>Cross-Window Communication</title>
<meta http-equiv="Content-Type" content="text/html; charset=utf-8" />
</head>
<body>
<script type="text/javascript">
//<![CDATA[

window.onload=setObjects;

function setObjects() {
   document.forms[0].elements[0].focus();

   var evtObject = document.getElementById("panicbutton");

   // test for object model
   if (evtObject.addEventListener) {
      evtObject.addEventListener("click",openHelp,false);
```

Example 9-2. Opening a help window (continued)

```
    } else if (evtObject.attachEvent) {
       evtObject.attachEvent("onclick", openHelp);
    } else if (evtObject.onclick) {
       evtObject.onclick=openHelp;
    }
}

function openHelp(x) {

    var optionString =
"width=200,height=100,menubar=no,toolbar=no,scrollbars=no,location=no,resizeable=no";
    var helpWindow = window.open("help.htm","test",optionString);
    helpWindow.focus();
    helpWindow.moveTo(x.screenX,x.screenY);
    return false;
}

//]]>
</script>

<form name="currentForm">
Your name: <input type="text" size="50">
</form>
<div id="panicbutton" style="width:100px;height:20px;background-color:#f00; padding:
5px;margin:10px auto">
Push for Help
</div>
</body>
</html>
```

A small window opens with minimum chrome, located just below and to the right of where the click has happened. The reason it's positioned based on the click event is that when the window is opened, it's moved to the screen location of the click event. Once opened, the focus is set to this window.

Example 9-3 contains the contents of the window that opens. It actually accesses the opener window, finds the form element, and copies whatever value it has. This provides a message in the window, which also has a link to close the window.

Example 9-3. Opened window

```
<!DOCTYPE html PUBLIC "-//W3C//DTD XHTML 1.0 Transitional//EN"
"http://www.w3.org/TR/xhtml1/DTD/xhtml1-transitional.dtd">
<html>
<head>
<meta http-equiv="Content-Type" content="text/html; charset=utf-8" />
</head>
<body>
<p>Helpful Information.</p>
<script type="text/javascript">
//<![CDATA[
```

Example 9-3. Opened window (continued)

```
var nmStr = opener.document.forms[0].elements[0].value;
document.writeln("Hello " +  nmStr + "!");

//]]>
</script>

<p><a href="javascript:self.close();opener.resizeTo('100','100')">close window</a></p>
</body>
</html>
```

This is an obnoxious little help window. When the window close link is clicked, an embedded script will close the window, yes, but it will also resize the opener to the minimum most browsers will allow within the JavaScript sandbox. A surprising number of browsers allow this behavior, including Firefox and Safari, though Opera is well behaved in this regard.

Of course, resizing the opener window to an unusable size isn't something I recommend. However, opening a help window, positioning it to where an event occurs, and communicating information between the windows can be very helpful. Later, when we get into Dynamic HTML, we'll create the same effect with hidden page elements, but for now, you have a way to provide context-sensitive help.

Another critical property associated with the window object is the JavaScript timer, covered next.

Timers

Timers are a way to add a dynamic aspect to your web pages. When we start working with DHTML, you'll see that timers are used to create any number of page animations. Even without DHTML, timers can open or close windows, pop up a message to the user, and even destroy a cookie for security purposes.

There are two types of timers: one that's set once, and one that reoccurs over an interval. Both can be canceled, though the one-time timer method fires just once.

To create a nonrepeating timer, use the setTimeout method. It takes a minimum of two parameters: the function literal or function name to run when the timer delay ends, and the length of the timer delay in milliseconds. If there are any parameters to send to the function, they are listed at the end of the call, separated by commas. The method returns the identifier of the timeout:

```
var tmOut = setTimeout(func, 5000,"param1",param2,...,paramn);
```

To clear the time out, use the clearTimeout method:

```
clearTimeout(tmOut);
```

If you want the timer delay to repeat over an interval, use the setInterval. This takes two parameters, the function name and the timer interval. As with setTimeout, it return an identifier:

```
Var tmOut = setInterval("functionName", 5000);
```

Again, to stop or cancel the interval timer, use the clearInterval method. If you want to have a repeating delay but still use a function literal or pass in parameters, you can use setTimeout and reset the timer when the previously set timer expires.

In Example 9-4, a timer is used to reset a document image at the end of each timer delay. We'll get into the document-images collection later, but for now, an image object in the page can be reset to another image, just by setting the image source. The images are from an old animation and game I created using the first versions of DHTML years ago. Changing the images forms a slow, crude animation.

Example 9-4. Using timer to change page image

```
<!DOCTYPE html PUBLIC "-//W3C//DTD XHTML 1.0 Transitional//EN"
"http://www.w3.org/TR/xhtml1/DTD/xhtml1-transitional.dtd">
<html>
<head>
<title>Timers</title>
<meta http-equiv="Content-Type" content="text/html; charset=utf-8" />
<script type="text/javascript">
//<![CDATA[

var ct = 0;
var imgs = new Array("impatient.gif","doomed.gif","upright.gif");
setTimeout("progress( )",3000);

function progress( ) {

    if (ct < 3) {
        document.images[0].src=imgs[ct];
        ct++;
        setTimeout("progress( )",3000);
    }
}
//]]>
</script>
</head>
<body>
<img src="mad.gif" />
</body>
</html>
```

Note that in the function, if all of the images haven't been displayed, the timer is reset to run again, using the function name. Another approach would be to use setInterval and then clear it once the last image has displayed.

 You want to avoid any type of timer operation that could generate a document.write or other method that alters the makeup of the document object. This leaves the page in an unstable state. Instead, modify components of the document rather than the entire document itself.

Up to this point, we've been working with one window and one document. However, with the use of frames, we can segment the page and give each segment a different URL and purpose. Frames are one of the several objects accessible through the main window object, and the first we'll cover.

Frames and Location

I must admit up front that I'm not fond of frames. Yes, they are extremely useful, and still a terrific way to manage applications in which an action in the left window (or top window) can trigger a change in the right (or bottom). Each can then scroll separately, without any effort on our part.

However, too many companies had (or still have) a habit of opening up other web sites into frames, which basically wrapped the other site's content in their own environment. Most of us didn't care for this. Luckily, thanks to JavaScript, we can defeat this technique using a second window object, location.

The location object stores information about the current location and provides a small set of routines to load a new document or replace whichever document is currently loaded.

The frame object has a few properties and methods, and is primarily a subset of the window object. This makes sense considering that each is a window, in miniature. Among the objects supported are frames, name, length, parent, and self. The methods supported are blur, focus, setInterval, clearInterval, setTimeout, and clearTimeout. Of these, the ones new to this example are parent, which would be the parent frameset, length for length of frame, and name, which is the frame name.

The name and parent are particularly important for cross-frame communication. A parent frameset can access each child frame through its name (or through the frames array using the number of the object as an index); each frame can access the frameset through the generic term, parent. Siblings can access each other by accessing parent and then the name of the sibling.

In Example 9-5, a frameset with two frames is loaded. The two frames are known as framea and frameb.

Example 9-5. Frameset loading two frames

```
<!DOCTYPE html PUBLIC "-//W3C//DTD XHTML 1.0 Transitional//EN"
"http://www.w3.org/TR/xhtml1/DTD/xhtml1-transitional.dtd">
<html>
<head>
<title>Frames</title>
<meta http-equiv="Content-Type" content="text/html; charset=utf-8" />
</head>
<frameset cols="300,*">
<frame name="framea" src="framea.htm" />
<frame name="frameb" src="frameb.htm" />
</frameset>
</html>
```

Into framea, a document, framea.htm, is loaded. It has one link that, when pressed, accesses its sibling through its parent and changes the frame location to itself. The page for this is shown in Example 9-6. The second frame document, frameb.htm, has the exact same page, except it steals framea's spot for itself.

Example 9-6. Each frame loading itself

```
<!DOCTYPE html PUBLIC "-//W3C//DTD XHTML 1.0 Transitional//EN"
"http://www.w3.org/TR/xhtml1/DTD/xhtml1-transitional.dtd">
<html>
<head>
<meta http-equiv="Content-Type" content="text/html; charset=utf-8" />
</head>
<body>
<h1>Frame A</h1>
<p><a href="" onclick="parent.frameb.location.replace"
('http://learningjavascript.info/framea.htm')">Change sibling</a></p>
</body>
</html>
```

The individual frame pages load themselves using the location's replace method.

More On Location

The location object's properties are all related to the page location. You've seen one of its functions, replace, used to replace the page for one of the frames. Another is reload, which instructs the browser to refresh the document. It also has properties associated with the page location, including the domain, port, and protocol, that are used with location; these are given in Table 9-2.

Table 9-2. Location object properties

Property	Purpose
hash	For URLS of the format *http://some.com/somepage#somehash*, this property contains "somehash"—the value after the hash mark
host	Hostname (domain) and port of URL

Table 9-2. Location object properties (continued)

Property	Purpose
hostname	The hostname (domain) only
href	The entire URL (read and write)
pathname	The pathname that follows the domain
port	The URL port
protocol	The protocol used with the URL, such as "http"
search	The query string, if one exists, that derives the page. This includes anything following the first question mark of the URL
target	If given, the URL's target name

Accessing a URL such as the following:

```
http://learningjavascript.info/ch09-01.htm?a=1
```

results in the following property values:

```
host/hostname: learningjavascript.info
protocol: http:
search: ?a=1
href: http://learningjavascript.info/ch09-01.htm?a=1
```

Returning to the initial issue about frames, and your pages being loaded into them without your permission, use the location object—in conjunction with a few other odds and ends—to defeat this technique.

Example 9-7 shows another frameset; this one loads frames named frameone and frametwo.

Example 9-7. Loading two frames

```
<!DOCTYPE html PUBLIC "-//W3C//DTD XHTML 1.0 Transitional//EN"
"http://www.w3.org/TR/xhtml1/DTD/xhtml1-transitional.dtd">
<html>
<head>
<title>Frames</title>
<meta http-equiv="Content-Type" content="text/html; charset=utf-8" />
</head>
<frameset cols="300,*">
<frame name="frameone" src="frame1.htm" />
<frame name="frametwo" src="frame2.htm" />
</frameset>
</html>
```

Neither frame1.htm nor frame2.htm is of much interest. The frametwo page has a link to another page, called noway.htm, which has the interesting bits, repeated in Example 9-8.

Example 9-8. Preventing opening in frameset

```
<!DOCTYPE html PUBLIC "-//W3C//DTD XHTML 1.0 Transitional//EN"
"http://www.w3.org/TR/xhtml1/DTD/xhtml1-transitional.dtd">
<html>
<head>
<meta http-equiv="Content-Type" content="text/html; charset=utf-8" />
<script type="text/javascript">
//<![CDATA[

if (self != top) {
if (window.location.href.replace)
        top.location.replace(self.location.href);
    else
        top.location.href=self.document.href;
}

//]]>
</script>

</head>
<body>
<h1>No Way</h1>
</body>
</html>
```

In the newly opened page, which normally opens into the frame, there's a script block that tests whether it is, itself, the top window. In framed windows, the frameset is the top window. In the code, if the window is not the top window (is loaded into a frame), it sets the top-window location href property to itself—effectively bumping the frameset out of the way.

Simple and clean. However, you'll find few pages that frame-protect themselves nowadays. Frames just aren't as popular as they once were, and most people don't want to add anything unnecessarily to their pages.

Not all frames require a frameset parent. The iframe can be embedded in a page, rather than a frameset.

Remote Scripting with the iframe

Ajax achieved almost instant fame through its promotion of in-page client/server interaction. This is a process in which data can be submitted to a server and a page updated without having to reload the page. This was all shiny new, though the technology had been around for a few years.

Even before Ajax and its MS precursor, there were ways to implement remote-server functionality. One popular method was to use the HTML element, the iframe, and a concept of *remote scripting*.

The concept of using the `iframe` for remote scripting was introduced at the Apple Developer Network in an article written by Eric Costello; it is available at *http://developer.apple.com/internet/webcontent/iframe.html*.

Unlike regular frames, an `iframe` is actually embedded within a page. It can be given both height and width to be displayed, or it can be hidden by setting both to zero. It considers the page it's embedded in as its parent, and that's how it communicates with the higher-level page. Normally, it can be accessed by using the document's `getElementById`; you can also load content into it using the target attribute in a link.

In Example 9-9, an `iframe` is embedded in the page, with text about making a choice between the red pill or the blue. Each of these is a link, which will load the choice page into the `iframe`.

Example 9-9. Communicating with an embedded iFrame

```
<!DOCTYPE html PUBLIC "-//W3C//DTD XHTML 1.0 Transitional//EN"
"http://www.w3.org/TR/xhtml1/DTD/xhtml1-transitional.dtd">
<html>
<head>
<title>iFrame</title>
<meta http-equiv="Content-Type" content="text/html; charset=utf-8" />
</head>
<body>
<script type="text/javascript">
//<![CDATA[

function handleResponse(choice) {
  var pick = frames["MyFrame"];
  pick.document.writeln(choice);
}

//]]>
</script>

<iframe id="MyFrame"
  name="MyFrame"
  style="width:100px; height:100px; border: 0px"
  src="blank.htm"></iframe>

<p>
<a href="" onclick="parent.MyFrame.location.replace('choice1.htm'); return false">Red
Pill</a><br />
<a href="" onclick="parent.MyFrame.location.replace('choice2.htm'); return false">Blue
Pill</a><br />
</p>
</body>
</html>
```

Note in the `onclick` event handlers that the last statement in the JavaScript is a return statement returning a value of `false`. This prevents the default behavior of the link—which is to load the page—from being initiated.

The page also includes a script block that writes the string passed as a parameter to the `iframe` page. This, in turn, is passed in from either of the choice pages, the first of which is shown in Example 9-10.

Example 9-10. One of the pages loaded into the iframe

```
<!DOCTYPE html PUBLIC "-//W3C//DTD XHTML 1.0 Transitional//EN"
"http://www.w3.org/TR/xhtml1/DTD/xhtml1-transitional.dtd">
<html>
<head>
<meta http-equiv="Content-Type" content="text/html; charset=utf-8" />
</head>
<body style="background-color: #f00">
<script type="text/javascript">
//<![CDATA[

  window.parent.handleResponse("You picked the red pill");

//]]>
</script>

</body>
</html>
```

Note that the page and the embedded page share the same parent.

One of the advantages to using the `iframe` for server communication is that it doesn't require any expertise with more esoteric communication mechanisms such as XML-RPC. The limitation is that there is no formalized API method for invoking services. All functionality is based more on pages loaded, and JS script processes.

Also, unlike other remote-scripting options, the history of options is maintained. In other words, the browser maintains state between choices.

history, screen, and navigator

The remaining three objects that are direct children to the `window` object are `history`, `screen`, and the `navigator`. Between these three, you'll have a good idea of what kind of browser is accessing the page, and how much space you have in which to work. You'll also be able to send your web-page readers on their way using the `history` object.

As these objects are fairly simple in functionality and single-purposed, I'll review each, in turn, and then provide one example for all three at the end of this section.

history

The history object is just as it sounds: it maintains a history of pages loaded into the browser. As such, its methods and properties have to do with navigation through these pages, including going forward and back.

You can traverse through history using relational properties, such as next and previous, or using the methods back and forward. You can find the current page with current, and get the length of history (number of pages stored in the history cache). You can also go to a specific page using the go method and passing in a page number—negative to go backward that many pages:

```
history.go(-3);
```

And positive to go forward:

```
history.go(3);
```

history, as they say, takes care of itself; you as page developer don't have to worry overmuch about it. About the only time when history becomes a concern is when using in-page techniques such as DHTML and Ajax, which work outside the normal patterns of page loading. However, we'll get into these issues later in the book. Returning to the BOM, the next object of interest accessible via the page hierarchy is the screen.

screen

The screen object contains information about the display screen, including width and height (both actual and available), as well as the color or pixel depth. Though not used very often, it is a good reference for any functionality that might change the size of the browser window or create colorful objects requiring a certain palette.

The exact properties supported can change from browser to browser, and version to version. At a minimum, most of the following are supported:

availTop (*or* top)
   The topmost pixel position where a window can be positioned

availLeft (*or* left)
   The leftmost pixel position where a window can be positioned

availWidth (*or* width)
   Width of screen in pixels

availHeight (*or* height)
   Height of screen in pixels

colorDepth
   Color depth of the screen

pixelDepth
   Bit depth of screen

The reason for the discrepancy between actual and available height and/or width is to accommodate the toolbar residing at the top, bottom, or side of many display screens.

In earlier DHTML implementations, developers would test the color depth of the screen and change to lower resolution images more appropriate to the configuration. However, even the more inexpensive monitors now support color depths greater than the older eight pixels, and most support true color. As such, the extra overhead to process the screen and return the images no longer has the payback it once had. Still, the color depth could alter your use of colors with style settings, so it's helpful information—as is the available width and height if you're working with a page layout.

navigator

Last, but not least, the navigator object provides information about the browser or other agent that accesses the page. This includes being able to check the operating system, the browser or browser family, security policy, language, and whether cookies are enabled. Some browsers also provide an array of installed plug-ins and other properties applicable to the specific user agent.

The navigator object usually supports the following:

appCodeName
    The name of the browser code base

appName
    The name of the browser

appMinorVersion
    The minor version number (such as 52 for Version 1.52) of the browser

appVersion
    The major version number (the 1.00 in 1.52) of the browser

cookieEnabled
    Whether cookies are enabled

mimeTypes
    An array of MIME types supported

onLine
    Whether the user is online

platform
    The platform on which the browser is operating

plugins
    Array of plug-ins supported in browser

userAgent
    Full agent description for browser (or other user agent)

userLanguage
    Language supported in browser

The `mimeTypes` collection consists of `mimeType` objects, which have properties of description, type, and `plugin`. The plugins collection consists of plug-in objects with properties of a `mimeType` array of its own: description, filename, length of `mimeType` array, and plug-in name.

There are also a small number of methods that are supported among several browsers: `javaEnabled`, to test for Java enabling in the browser; preference to get and set browser preferences; and `taintEnabled` to check if data taint checking (a security feature) is enabled.

One Page, Three Objects

Example 9-11 is a page that runs through all three of the objects just covered—history, screen, and navigator—printing out property values and providing a couple of options for testing history. Try it out in various browsers, in as many operating systems as you can, to see what's supported and what's not.

Example 9-11. Exploring the history, navigator, and screen objects

```
<!DOCTYPE html PUBLIC "-//W3C//DTD XHTML 1.0 Transitional//EN"
"http://www.w3.org/TR/xhtml1/DTD/xhtml1-transitional.dtd">
<html>
<head>
<title>History,Screen,Navigator</title>
<meta http-equiv="Content-Type" content="text/html; charset=utf-8" />
</head>
<body>
<h1>history object</h1>
<a href="" onclick="history.back();return false">history.back()</a><br />
<a href="" onclick="history.go(-2);return false">history.go(-2)</a><br /><br />
<a href="" onclick="history.forward();return false">history.forward()</a><br />

<h1>screen object</h1>
<script type="text/javascript">
//<![CDATA[

document.writeln("screen.availTop: " + screen.availTop + "<br />");
document.writeln("screen.availLeft: " + screen.availLeft + "<br />");
document.writeln("screen.availWidth: " + screen.availWidth + "<br />");
document.writeln("screen.availHeight: " + screen.availHeight + "<br />");
document.writeln("screen.colorDepth: " + screen.colorDepth + "<br />");
document.writeln("screen.pixelDepth: " + screen.pixelDepth + "<br />");

document.writeln("<h1>navigator object</h1>");

document.writeln("navigator.userAgent: " + navigator.userAgent + "<br />");
document.writeln("navigator.appName: " + navigator.appName + "<br />");
document.writeln("navigator.appCodeName: " + navigator.appCodeName + "<br />");
document.writeln("navigator.appVersion: " + navigator.appVersion + "<br />");
```

Example 9-11. Exploring the history, navigator, and screen objects (continued)

```
document.writeln("navigator.appMinorVersion: " + navigator.appMinorVersion + "<br />");
document.writeln("navigator.platform: " + navigator.platform + "<br />");
document.writeln("navigator.cookieEnabled: " + navigator.cookieEnabled + "<br />");
document.writeln("navigator.onLine: " + navigator.onLine + "<br />");
document.writeln("navigator.userLanguage: " + navigator.userLanguage + "<br />");
document.writeln("navigator.mimeTypes[1].description: " + navigator.mimeTypes[1].
description + "<br />");
document.writeln("navigator.mimeTypes[1].type: " + navigator.mimeTypes[1].type + "<br />
");
document.writeln("navigator.plugins[3].description: " + navigator.plugins[3].description +
"<br />");
//]]>
</script>
</body>
</html>
```

You might be surprised at what shows up in some of the collections, such as the plugins. I know I was surprised to see one that provided digital-rights management, when I don't remember having installed a plug-in of this nature.

As for the `mimeType` object, some browsers also support a suffix property on the object, such as *.html and so on.

These three objects just demonstrated are the last of the objects directly accessible via the `window` object, save one. The last object covered in this chapter is an old friend by now: the `document`. In a way, most of the rest of the book focuses on the `document` object. However, we'll take a little time to look at it from a BOM perspective before moving into covering its role in DOM, DHTML, and Ajax.

The Cross-Browser MouseOver DOM Inspector

In earlier chapters I mentioned Firefox's DOM Inspector, which allows you to discover information about each element in the browser. There is a cross-browser-compatible version of this functionality, the MouseOver DOM Inspector (MODI) by slayeroffice.com, that works with Firefox, Mozilla, Netscape, Opera, and IE 6.x. It's a bookmark-based application; you can access it at *http://slayeroffice.com/tools/modi/v2.0/modi_help.html*.

Once bookmarked, when you're at a page and want to investigate the properties of all the page elements, just click the bookmark. A little in-page box opens that provides information about whatever element currently has cursor focus. When you want to stop inspecting the elements, just click the Esc key.

It is listed as beta software, but I found it worked nicely in all my browsers except Safari and the newer IE 7.x. Figure 9-2 shows it in use with Opera on the Mac at the O'Reilly web site.

Figure 9-2. Slayeroffice.com's MouseOver DOM Inspector

document

Returning to Figure 9-1 at the beginning of the chapter, you can see that the document object is what provides access to any element contained within the browser page. This includes forms and form elements, as well as cookies, all covered earlier. This also includes the collection of page images, links, embedded objects; in fact, all elements contained within the page boundaries have document as parent. Older variations of document had another collection, called layers, and the newer browser versions all share a style property, but the figure gives you an idea of how important the document is to dynamic page development.

The previous chapters have covered the document object methods of getElementById, as well as writeln; the next chapter on the DOM provides information on accessing all page elements using generic methods. For now, I want to pull back to the older method of accessing page elements through the various document collections, focusing on links, images, and the all-purpose all collection.

Links

The difference between a link and an anchor is the type of anchor attributes used. Both are based on the anchor tag (`<a></a>`). However, if an `href` attribute is provided, it's a link to another site; if just the name attribute is provided, it acts just as an anchor, which can set focus to a specific point in the page.

The links collection off of the `document` object consists of all hypertext links in the page, accessible as an array, starting with the first link in the page and moving down and to the right. However, you can also add an identifier for each hypertext link and access it in the array through this identifier.

Each item in the collection is a link object, which has properties of its own. Some properties are similar to those found with `location`: `host`, `protocol`, `port`, `search`, and `hash`, each of which returns that specific piece of the hypertext link. You can also access the complete link through the `href` property, and the associated linked object (text), through `text`. This can be handy if you're pulling links from a document in a web page into a handy sidebar reference. Just make sure that you don't write the links out to the same page as the `document`, because you'll confuse the browser by adding new links at the same time as you're trying to process existing links.

In Example 9-12, the page contains text with three links. The links collection is accessed through the document object, and the links and associated text are extracted and printed just below the paragraphs.

Example 9-12. Pulling links from page

```
<!DOCTYPE html PUBLIC "-//W3C//DTD XHTML 1.0 Transitional//EN"
"http://www.w3.org/TR/xhtml1/DTD/xhtml1-transitional.dtd">
<html>
<head>
<title>Reference</title>
<meta http-equiv="Content-Type" content="text/html; charset=utf-8" />
</head>
<body>
<p>The <a href="http://msdn.microsoft.com/workshop/author/dhtml/reference/objects/link.
asp">links</a> collection off of the document <a href="http://www.w3.org/TR/html4/struct/
objects.html">object</a> consists of all hypertext links in the page, accessible as an
array, starting with the first link in the page and moving down and to the right. However,
you can also add an identifier for each hypertext link and access it in the array through
this identifier.</p><p>Each item in the collection is a <a href="http://www.devguru.com/
Technologies/ecmascript/quickref/link.html">link</a> object, which has properties of its
own. Among these are those similar to what we found with location: host, protocol, port,
search, and hash, each of which returns that specific piece of the hypertext link. You can
also access the complete link through the href property, and the associated linked object
(text) through text. This can be handy if you're pulling links from a document in a web
page, into a handy sidebar reference or other functionality such as this.
</p>
```

Example 9-12. Pulling links from page (continued)

```
<h5>References</h5>
<p>
<script type="text/javascript">
//<![CDATA[

for (var i = 0; i < document.links.length; i++) {
  var link = document.links[i];
  document.writeln(link.text + " : " + link.href + "<br />");
}
//]]>
</script>
</p>
</body>
</html>
```

A better approach might be to provide alternative text in the link, using the title attribute, and then printing this out:

```
<a href="http://somelink.com" title="A better description of link">than this</a>
...
document.writeln(link.title + " : " + link.href + "<br />");
```

However, this approach is sneaking into the higher-level DOMs where all attributes are accessible off an object. Still, regardless of level, most browsers support both.

Images

One of the earliest dynamic page-development techniques was to alter images within the document. This is still a popular technique for simple photo-slideshow types of applications, enabled through the document images collection.

As with links, images are objects in their own right, and you can set their attributes—such as src, the source URL for the image—directly. You can also create new instances of the images using the new constructor.

In Example 9-13, a slideshow is created of the first five images from Chapter 1, and a simple mechanism is put in place to traverse the list, replacing the current document image with the next one in the list. An array of images preloads the images when the page loads so that the transition happens more quickly.

Example 9-13. Creating a slideshow using the images collection

```
<!DOCTYPE html PUBLIC "-//W3C//DTD XHTML 1.0 Transitional//EN"
"http://www.w3.org/TR/xhtml1/DTD/xhtml1-transitional.dtd">
<html>
<head>
<title>Slideshow</title>
<meta http-equiv="Content-Type" content="text/html; charset=utf-8" />
<script type="text/javascript">
//<![CDATA[

var currentPhoto = 0;
```

Example 9-13. Creating a slideshow using the images collection (continued)

```
var pics = new Array( );
for (var i = 0; i < 5; i++) {
  pics[i] = new Image( );
}
pics[0].src = "fig01-1.jpg";
pics[1].src = "fig01-2.jpg";
pics[2].src = "fig01-3.jpg";
pics[3].src = "fig01-4.jpg";
pics[4].src = "fig01-5.jpg";

function changePhoto(photo) {
    document.images[0].src = pics[photo].src;
}

function nextPic( ) {
  currentPhoto++;
  if (currentPhoto < pics.length) {
    changePhoto(currentPhoto);
  } else {
    alert("at the end of the photo list");
  }
}

function prevPic( ) {
  if (currentPhoto > 0) {
    currentPhoto--;
    changePhoto(currentPhoto);
  } else {
    alert("at the beginning of the photo list");
  }
}

//]]>
</script>
<img src="fig01-1.jpg" />
<p>
<a href="" onclick="nextPic( );return false">Next picture</a> <a href="" onclick="prevPic(
); return false">Previous picture</a>
<p>
</head>
</body>
</html>
```

Again, like the previous example with links, this example tends to blur the line between DOM levels. However, it also works in all of the most popular web browsers, which is what's important for our purposes.

Also notice in Example 9-13 that, along with the images, the src attribute can be changed. This differs from Example 9-12, which just outputs the link attributes. The image source is an attribute that can be read or written, while the link attributes can only be read. There are ways, though, to adjust all page elements, and we'll look at them in the next section.

The all Collection, Inner/Outer HTML and Text, and Old and New Documents

The `all` collection on the document object contains references to all elements in the document page. It was a concept created by Microsoft as a way to collect all page elements into one array, before the W3C started work on standardizing the object hierarchy.

The `document.all` collection was one of the earlier methods that accessed individual elements; however, the actual collection itself is no longer supported in many modern browsers, such as Mozilla/Firefox. Still, the concept of being able to access any element in the document still remains; it's just the approach that has changed. Now, you can use `document.getElementById`, passing in the element's identifier to access the individual object.

 In Chapter 10, you'll see how other methods get all elements of a certain tag or, given a specific name, via the `document` object.

You'll see examples of `document.all` in many older scripts, when it was used to differentiate object support in cross-browser DHTML applications. It's not uncommon to see code like the following:

```
if (document.all)
    elem = document.all['elemid'];
else
    elem = document.getElementById['elemid'];
```

This actually works in most browsers. However, Internet Explorer is about the only browser that supports `document.all` now, so recognize it for what it was, but don't use it for modern applications. IE 6.x (5.x really) supports `getElementById`, just like other browsers.

Another interesting item you'll see in both older and newer dynamic JavaScript applications is the use of the following properties: `innerText`, `outerText`, `innerHTML`, and `outerHTML`.

These properties provided ways to change the content of the element, or both the content and the element. The `inner-` and `outerText` properties replace whatever is contained in the element, or the element itself, with text. The `inner-` and `outerHTML` properties replace the element's HTML or the element with HTML.

As noted in the last section, through the BOM, not all attributes of an element can be modified after the document is loaded. Using the inner/outer properties, this limitation could be worked around by actually replacing the contents of an element instead

---

of changing its attributes. This approach achieved a high level of success in its day because it provided a way to actually modify the page contents after the page was loaded—not just an attribute here or there. That was pretty heady stuff in its time.

Today, with the sophisticated DOM API, the only property still supported with the Mozilla line of browsers is innerHTML. In Example 9-14, the web page contains three DIV elements, each of which contains further markup. The first DIV contains a paragraph; the second, an unordered list; and the third, a hypertext link. When the page loads, these are accessed using the getElementsById document method, and their content is changed via innerHTML.

Example 9-14. Accessing named elements and changing their inner HTML

```
<!DOCTYPE html PUBLIC "-//W3C//DTD XHTML 1.0 Transitional//EN"
"http://www.w3.org/TR/xhtml1/DTD/xhtml1-transitional.dtd">
<html>
<head>
<meta http-equiv="Content-Type" content="text/html; charset=utf-8" />
<title>Modifying Elements after Page loads</title>
<script type="text/javascript">
//<![CDATA[

function changeDiv( ) {

    // get all elements idd 'elem1'
    var elem1 = document.getElementById("elem1");
    elem1.innerHTML = "<h1>Hello World</h1>";

    var elem2  = document.getElementById("elem2");
    elem2.innerHTML = "<ol><li>Option 1</li><li>Option 2</li></ol>";

    var elem3 = document.getElementById("elem3");
    elem3.innerHTML = "<img src='dotty.gif' alt='dotty' />";
}

//]]>
</script>

<body onload="changeDiv( );">
<div id="elem1">
<p>Paragraph text.</p>
</div>
<div>
<ul id="elem2">
<li>option 1</li>
<li>option 2</li>
</ul>
</div>
<div>
<a href="ch09-12.htm" id="elem3">Example 9-12</a>
</div>
</body>
</html>
```

The innerHTML property is all of the HTML that's contained within the identified element. It's a read/write property, which means it can be accessed, modified, or completely replaced, as shown in Figure 9-3. What's fascinating, though, is that this isn't reflected in the document source. If you look at view source, the HTML elements reflect the web page before the dynamic modification.

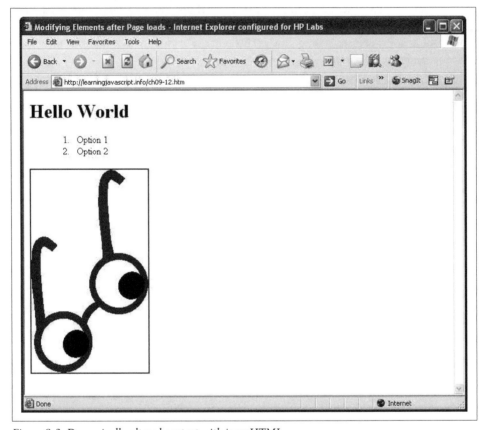

Figure 9-3. Dynamically altered content with innerHTML

All the major browsers support innerHTML, though each may have its own minor quirks in implementation (which is why you need to test your effects before putting them into production). The W3C has deprecated its use, but most browsers support it a) because of its widespread use, and b) because it's so easy to use compared to the DOM methods that accomplish the same task.

Something Old, Something New

The title of this section is from that old wedding rhyme about what a Western bride carries on her wedding day:

Something old, something new; something borrowed, something blue

Old, new, borrowed, and blue are all adjectives that can be used to describe the experience of creating applications that move between the different levels of the DOM, or from the BOM to the newer DOM.

Many of the existing JavaScript libraries or sample scripts still use technologies that worked with the old 4.x browsers popular in the late 1990s. With IE 4.x and Navigator 4.x, JavaScript and DHTML really took off, so it's not surprising that much of these older scripts are still easily available. Particularly since many of them still work.

Today, modern browsers such as IE, Firefox, Mozilla, Navigator, Opera, Safari, Camino, and others adhere to the W3C *as much as possible*. I emphasize the last phrase because it has a great deal of meaning in cross-browser and cross-version web-page development. The possibilities are limited by how widespread the use of some technologies are. For instance, Microsoft's newer IE 7 supports the newer DOM, up to the point where support would mean breaking older web pages. The company isn't necessarily ready to break backward compatibility, and though not doing so is a pain for web developers, it's also somewhat understandable.

So modern browsers borrow some of the older implementations, as well as support the newer. Developers use a variety of tests to see if one element or another is supported to provide functionality that works with as many browsers as possible. This tends to make the developers feel a little "blue"—if that's the right word—because the work can be rather extensive and difficult at times.

This demonstrates one of the major challenges with cross-browser JavaScript: having to, at times, compromise on what objects, properties, and methods you'll use to create content that works for all of your target browsers. For all of the criticism associated with Internet Explorer, Microsoft was the leader of the pack when it came to providing more features for dynamically changing a web page. As such, its unique properties and methods, though they may not be a part of any W3C specification, have had widespread use and continue to be used today.

The question then becomes: should you use them? I can't answer this for you. The more you use older objects, the quicker your pages will become obsolete. In addition, the more older browsers you support, the more work and the more limited the effects you can create. All I can do is point out some of the options, the older technologies as well as the newer, and how they can be compatible—or not.

The only people who can answer this question are your web-page readers. Know your audience and what tools they use, and adjust accordingly. No worries, though, that you'll be thrust out into the wild kingdom of the Web with only a stone axe and bearskin bikini. In the next several chapters, I'll show you how to use the old BOM with the new DOM and when to borrow between the models.

Questions

1. What kind of dialogue do you open if you want a text response?
2. Define a timer that invokes a function, `callFunction`, every 3,000 milliseconds passing in two parameters: `paramA` and `paramB`.
3. What object is used to change the web page in the browser?
4. What object and properties give you information about the browser?
5. Create a new window that is sized to 200×200 pixels, has no toolbar or status bar, and opens up the *help.htm* file.

Answers are provided in the appendix.

CHAPTER 10

DOM: The Document Object Model

One of the most significant changes associated with JavaScript was the W3C's work in conjunction with all browser vendors (including Netscape and Microsoft) to create a consistent underlying object model. All major browsers agreed to support this model, eliminating most, if not all, cross-browser compatibility issues. Though the default Browser Object Model discussed in the last chapter provided a great deal of functionality, much of the implementation of the model was based on influence of one browser, or browser company, over another. Over time, this led to a great deal of cross-browser incompatibility, hampering advanced uses of JavaScript until the last few years.

This changed with the release of the W3C's recommended Document Object Model (DOM). From the W3C comes this description:

> The Document Object Model is a platform- and language-neutral interface that will allow programs and scripts to dynamically access and update the content, structure, and style of documents. The document can be further processed, and the results of that processing can be incorporated back into the presented page.

The first release of the DOM was DOM Level 1, issued as a recommendation in 1998. This release helped define the infrastructure for the DOM—the schema and Application Programming Interface (API) that future versions of the DOM could use as a base of functionality. It also helped establish a core component of each recommendation that is required for a DOM-compliant user agent (such as a browser); all other specifications are issued as separate, but related, optional modules. This approach helped encourage early adoption, and maintain consistency with critical elements.

DOM Level 2 followed in 2000 and expanded on the earlier Level 1 release, while still maintaining consistency with the earlier release. You've already been exposed to one aspect of this release with the Level 2 event handling in Chapter 3. The DOM Level 2 added increased support for Cascading Style Sheets, improved access for document elements, and namespace support in the XML recommendation.

The DOM Level 3 was released in 2004 and at the time this book was written, had very little support in most major browsers. In addition to extensions and improvements to the previous releases, this version adds modules to extend support for web services, as well as increased support for XML. The DOM Level 3 is the last of the W3C levels—at least, the last planned W3C level release.

This chapter doesn't provide a complete reference for all of the objects in the DOM APIs. These are listed quite nicely at the W3C web site in a URL which should persist as long as the specification. Instead, I've focused on representative objects, how they interact with one another, and their impact within the browser page.

The W3C DOM Level 1 Recommendation can be seen at *http://www. w3.org/TR/REC-DOM-Level-1/*; DOM Level 2 recommendation at *http://www.w3.org/TR/DOM-Level-2-HTML/*; and the Level 3 Xpath Specification at *http://www.w3.org/TR/DOM-Level-3-XPath/*.

Of more interest is the ECMAScript *binding* (the implementation of the APIs you'll use with JavaScript) for each specification version. The Level 1 script binding for both HTML and Core is at *http://www.w3.org/ TR/REC-DOM-Level-1/ecma-script-language-binding.html*. The Level 2 script binding for the Core API is at *http://www.w3.org/TR/DOM-Level-2-Core/ecma-script-binding.html*, and the Level 2 script binding for the separate HTML module is at *http://www.w3.org/TR/2003/REC-DOM-Level-2-HTML-20030109/ecma-script-binding.html*. The ECMAScript binding for the third, and final, DOM Core API is at *http://www.w3. org/TR/DOM-Level-3-Core/ecma-script-binding.html*.

A Tale of Two Interfaces

When the W3C released the first version of the DOM, the organization also released two different APIs: the Core and the HTML API.

The DOM Core is a language- and model-neutral API that can be implemented in any language, not just JavaScript, and for any XML-based model, not just XHTML. As such, it literally is the core of the DOM.

Prior to the release of the DOM specification, though, browsers had already implemented the Browser Object Model in various forms, some proprietary and some not. To maintain a level of compatibility with previous work, the W3C also released a custom subset of the DOM API: The DOM HTML API.

The DOM HTML API is an object-oriented, hierarchical view of the web page, with objects mapped to HTML elements: `HTMLDocumentElement` for the document, `HTMLBodyElement` for the body, and so on. Using it is very similar to how we used the BOM in the last chapter. The primary difference between the two—BOM API and DOM HTML API—is that the W3C's is an attempt to formalize an approach that works with all browsers. The W3C also extended the API to make it more compatible with the underlying Core API.

The Core API is a generic API that, as I just mentioned, can work with any form of standard XML. It consists of objects such as Node and nodeLists, Attr, Element, and the all-important Document. The Core API also provides a basic set of data types and expected behaviors that agents such as browsers must support, though much of this support is not obvious when working with JavaScript.

The HTML API shows only in the first two W3C releases. The reason is that the additions and modifications documented in the W3C DOM Level 3 are specific to the Core API; the HTML API wasn't directly impacted. However, the HTML API is as valid as the Core. As such, you can use either the Core, HTML, or both as needed.

 A good source for an overview of the different DOM specifications is the OASIS Cover Pages article, at *http://xml.coverpages.org/dom.html*.

The DOM and Compliant Browsers

There is no such thing as complete cross-browser compatibility. I doubt there ever will be, even though the differences between browsers become smaller every year. The W3C DOM is responsible for much of this compatibility, and most browsers have implemented support for both the Core and HTML APIs. This includes Mozilla/Firefox, Netscape Navigator (6.0 and above), Internet Explorer (6.0 and above), Safari, Opera (7.0 and above), Camino, and others.

However, not all aspects of the DOM are implemented equally among all the browsers; as discussed in Chapter 6, Internet Explorer (neither 6.x nor 7+) does not support the DOM Level 2 event model. There are also individual differences in support for CSS, as well as object methods and properties that differ between the browsers.

Most of the compliance issues are subtle, with minor variations in support. They are enough, however, to require testing of any effect using the DOM APIs to ensure it looks good or works as expected with all of your target browsers.

As to the variations, one variation could be providing too much support, such as Firefox providing DOM-level access to the name attribute on all HTML elements, not just those for which it's valid. This is just as much an error, or lack of compliance, as no support for the event model—particularly if you develop in Firefox and build in an expectation for name to be JavaScript-accessible on all elements.

Another variation is more of a minor annoyance than anything. There are a set of constants built into the DOM so that you don't have to code in numeric references for something such as nodeType, which provides information about the type of DOM node you're working with when you access the page document as a whole. However, as shown later in the section discussing the Core model, and thanks to JavaScript's prototype nature (covered in the next chapter), you can work around this limitation by adding these constants where they don't exist.

Regardless of all the browser quirks, there are few noncompliance issues that can't be worked around. The only decisions that remain are how much time you want to spend on such effort, and how many browsers, browser versions, and operating systems you want to support. One key element of this is reviewing your web logfiles to see how your pages are accessed. Many ISPs provide access to your raw logfiles in some form or another, and each consists of lines that might look similar to the following (from one of my site's logfiles):

```
70.242.159.166 - - [30/May/2006:07:24:18 -0400] "GET / HTTP/1.1" 200 67510 "http://
weblog.burningbird.net/admin/edit.php" "Mozilla/5.0 (Macintosh; U; PPC Mac OS X Mach-
O; en-US; rv:1.8.0.3) Gecko/20060426 Firefox/1.5.0.3"
```

From left to right, the first field is usually the IP address of the person (or web bot) accessing the page; the fields represented by the dashes are the identity lookup and authenticated usernames that are found (if any); then follows the date, the page requested, the referrer, and finally information at the end that represents the operating system and user agent. With this example, the OS is Mac OS X, the language is English, and the user agent is Firefox 1.5.03. The order of fields may vary, but the user agents and operating system are usually fairly obvious:

```
"Mozilla/5.0 (Windows; U; Windows NT 5.1; en-US; rv:1.7.12) Gecko/20050915 Firefox/1.
0.7"
"Mozilla/5.0 (Macintosh; U; PPC Mac OS X; en) AppleWebKit/418 (KHTML, like Gecko)
Safari/417.9.2"
"Opera/9.00 (Windows NT 5.1; U; en)"
```

Note that browsers may claim to be Mozilla 5.0; the actual browser is a secondary piece of information.

As long as your pages degrade gracefully (i.e., don't force a certain type of browser on your web-page readers and ensure that it still works for nonsupported types), you don't have to support all browsers or browser versions for your DOM-specific effects.

 JavaScript Best Practice: Ensure your pages degrade gracefully when accessed by all browsers, including ones that don't have JavaScript enabled or that don't support specific DOM functionality.

The DOM HTML API

The core API works with any valid XML, including XHTML; the HTML API is specific to valid XHTML and HTML only. It consists of a set of HTML objects, each associated with a valid HTML element tag; all have properties and methods appropriate to the object.

Though a separate set of objects, the two models—core and HTML—overlap, with the HTML API objects incorporating methods and properties from both models. As such, HTML API objects inherit properties and methods of a basic HTML Element, as well as the core Node object (discussed in the next section).

The HTML Objects and Their Properties

The HTML API is a set of interfaces rather than actual classes. These interfaces can access existing or newly created page objects, and each is associated with a specific type of page object.

 I've introduced a new term, interface. For our purposes, an *interface* is an object representing the specific page element. It differs from a class in that there is no constructor; objects are created through other functions rather than directly.

Most HTML interface objects inherit the properties and methods of the Element and Node objects—both of which are part of the core model, and discussed later in the chapter. Most also inherit from HTMLElement, which has the following properties (based on the set of attributes of the same name allowed for all HTML elements): id, title, lang, dir, and className.

Each interface object takes its name from the HTML formal element name, not necessarily the element tag. As such, HTMLFormElement is the HTML form element's interface object, but HTMLParagraphElement is the object for the paragraph (P) tag. The objects provide access to all valid attributes for the elements, such as align for HTMLDivElement, and src for HTMLImageElement.

Most of these properties are read and write, which means they can be altered as well as accessed from JavaScript. To demonstrate, in Example 10-1, an image is accessed using the document images collection. The image attributes are concatenated to a string which is then output via an alert. Following the message, the image attributes are modified.

Example 10-1. Reading and modifying image element's properties

```
<!DOCTYPE html PUBLIC "-//W3C//DTD XHTML 1.0 Transitional//EN"
"http://www.w3.org/TR/xhtml1/DTD/xhtml1-transitional.dtd">
<html>
<head>
<meta http-equiv="Content-Type" content="text/html; charset=utf-8" />
<title>Accessing/Modifying HTML Elements</title>
<script type="text/javascript">
//<![CDATA[

function procImage( ) {

   var img = document.images[0];

   // get existing image attributes
   var imgAttr = img.align + " " + img.alt + " " + img.src
              + " " + img.width + " " + img.height;
   alert(imgAttr);
```

Example 10-1. Reading and modifying image element's properties (continued)

```
    // modify
    img.src="upright.gif";
    img.width="100";
    img.height="100";
    img.alt="Alternative";
    img.align="left";
    img.title="Upright";
    document.close( );
}
//]]>
</script>
<body onload="procImage( );">
<img src="dotty.gif" alt="Dotty" />
</body>
</html>
```

Several of the DOM HTML interface objects also provide methods to create, remove, or otherwise modify the associated page elements. The table elements, in particular, have a set of such methods and associated objects. However, the process is somewhat code-intensive, made more so because of the fact (as mentioned in a note earlier) that the API objects have no constructor. To create new objects, you'll need to use one of the factory methods, as demonstrated in Example 10-2.

 If you've not been exposed to programming languages that support interfaces, think of them as *code wrappers* that isolate the mechanics of the underlying objects. When working with an interface, the API provides methods, usually referred to as *factory* methods, that can create and return the objects they wrap.

In Example 10-2, an image and an empty HTML table are added to the document. When the document loads, a function is called that accesses the table and image using getElementById on the document object.

To add to the table, you call the insertRow method on the table element, passing in a value of –1, which appends the row to the end of the table. This method returns an object that implements the HTMLElement interface. Thanks to JavaScript's loose typing, this object also implements the HTMLTableRowElement interface.

Example 10-2. Outputting image properties to table using DOM HTML interfaces

```
<!DOCTYPE html PUBLIC "-//W3C//DTD XHTML 1.0 Transitional//EN"
"http://www.w3.org/TR/xhtml1/DTD/xhtml1-transitional.dtd">
<html>
<head>
<meta http-equiv="Content-Type" content="text/html; charset=utf-8" />
<title>Build-o-Table</title>
<script type="text/javascript">
//<![CDATA[
```

Example 10-2. Outputting image properties to table using DOM HTML interfaces (continued)

```
function procImage( ) {

    // get table and image
    var tbl = document.getElementById('table1');
    tbl.border="5px";
    tbl.cellPadding="5px";

    var img = document.getElementById("img1");
    img.vspace="10";

    // for each attribute, add table row
    var row1 = tbl.insertRow(-1);

    // create two table cells
    var cell1 = row1.insertCell(0);
    var cell2 = row1.insertCell(1);

    // create text values
    var txtAttr1 = document.createTextNode("src");
    var txtAttr1Val = document.createTextNode(img.src);

    // append to text values to cells
    cell1.appendChild(txtAttr1);
    cell2.appendChild(txtAttr1Val);

}
//]]>
</script>
<body onload="procImage( );">
<img id="img1" src="dotty.gif" />
<table id="table1">
</table>
</body>
</html>
```

There's a method on the `HTMLTableRowElement` interface, `insertCell`, which in turn creates another `HTMLElement` representing a specific table-row cell. Two such cells are created through `insertCell`: one for each TD (table data) element in the table.

To add text, the `createTextNode` factory object creates a text object consisting of a string passed to the method. The text object is appended to the table `cell` object using `appendChild`. (If you want to remove the row, use `removeRow`, passing in the row number.)

As you can see, adding and removing objects in the web page using the DOM HTML API isn't complicated, but it can be tedious.

There are other DOM HTML interfaces that don't directly represent specific HTML elements. The collections of objects that can be accessed through the `document` object are represented by the `HTMLCollection` interface. It has one property, `length`, and two methods: item, which takes a number index, and namedItem, which takes a string. Both return objects in the collection.

The HTMLOptionsCollections represents the list of options for a select element, itself represented by HTMLSelectElement. Accessing the options property on this later interface returns the HTMLOptionsCollections object with options. As with HTMLCollections, access the individual items with item and namedItem.

The last interface object I'll cover is HTMLDocumentElement. It inherits functionality from the Core model document object, and if you explored document in Chapter 9, you won't be surprised at the provided methods and properties. Images, applets, links, forms, and anchors are included as properties returning a collection. Other properties include cookie, title, referrer, domain, URL, and body (for the body object).

The methods HTMLDocumentElement exposes, again, will seem very familiar: open, close, write, and writeln. However, one that hasn't been demonstrated is getElementsByName, and we'll look at that next.

 This page (*http://www.w3.org/TR/DOM-Level-2-HTML/ecma-script-binding.html*) at the W3C provides a look at the ECMAScript binding (JavaScript implementation) of the Level 2 HTML API.

Accessing HTML Objects and Browser Differences

There are different techniques you can use to access the DOM HTML representation of a page element. The first gives it a specific identifier (id) and then uses the document's getElementById method:

```
<div id="div1">
...
var div1 = document.getElementById("div1");
```

You can also access the elements using their relationship with one another. For instance, in the following HTML:

```
<form>
<input type="text" />
</form>
```

Access the form field through the forms collection on the document object:

```
document.forms[0].fields[0];
```

We've looked at both approaches in previous examples. A third way to access an individual element is by using the document object's getElementsByName, and then passing in the element's name. This method returns a nodeList containing a collection of nodes of the same name. All browsers support document.getElementsByName, but not all browsers return the same nodeList.

Example 10-3 uses getElementsByName to access all elements with given names within the web page. There are several different types of HTML elements, each given a unique name: a DIV element, a link, an unordered list and one of its items, a form and a form field, and a paragraph. Once the named list is returned, the element's type—found in the tagName property of each node—is concatenated to a string and output via a dialog window at the end of the application.

Example 10-3. Finding elements by name and printing out their associated class name

```
<!DOCTYPE html PUBLIC "-//W3C//DTD XHTML 1.0 Transitional//EN"
"http://www.w3.org/TR/xhtml1/DTD/xhtml1-transitional.dtd">
<html>
<head>
<meta http-equiv="Content-Type" content="text/html; charset=utf-8" />
<title>Modifying Named Elements</title>
<script type="text/javascript">
//<![CDATA[

function findName() {

    // get all elements named 'elem' + number
    for (var i = 1; i <= 7; i++) {
        var nmStr = "elem" + i;
        var nmList = document.getElementsByName(nmStr);

        // create string of types
        var typeStr =   "";
        for (var j = 0; j < nmList.length; j++) {
            typeStr += nmList[j].tagName + " ";
        }

        // output string
        alert(typeStr);
    }
}

//]]>
</script>
</head>
<body onload="findName();">
<div name="elem1">
<ul name="elem2">
<li>option 1</li>
<li name="elem3">option 2</li>
</ul>
</div>
<a href="ch10-02.htm" name="elem4">Example 1</a>
<p name="elem5">Paragraph</p>
<form name="elem6">
<input type="text" name="elem7" />
</form>
</body>
</html>
```

As expected, this application works in Safari, Firefox, Netscape Navigator, Opera, and Internet Explorer, but the string returned differs.

Firefox, Safari, and Netscape Navigator return a string of:

```
DIV UL LI A P FORM INPUT
```

Opera and Internet Explorer return:

```
A FORM INPUT
```

Why the discrepancy? Well, in this case, Opera and Internet Explorer have it right. Running the page through the W3C validator, it doesn't validate as transitional XHTML (the current doctype), or when an override to HTML 4.01 is in effect. The reason is that the name attribute is not supported on DIV, UL, LI, and P tags—exactly the ones that IE and Opera did not list.

Another odd thing: valid HTML does not support multiple elements with the same name, though several browsers do. If I had given all the elements the same name, the example would still work with Firefox, Safari, and Navigator. This is a good example of how browser-specific JavaScript may forgive more than it should.

Internet Explorer has received a great deal of criticism in the last few years for its noncompliance to more universal norms. Much of it is deserved, as the industry struggled with cross-browser issues related to an old and outdated Internet Explorer 6.x. Many of the noncompliance issues still are not resolved with Internet Explorer 7+, though there is much improvement.

However, not all acts of noncompliance rest completely on IE. As this section demonstrated, sometimes a loose interpretation of a specification can be just as erroneous as a missing one.

One way around such browser differences is to avoid using the DOM HTML interfaces, code your web pages in compliant XHTML instead of HTML, and then use the Core API as much as possible.

Understanding the DOM: The Core API

The DOM HTML API was created specifically to bring in the many implementations of BOM that existed across browsers. However, over the last several years, there's been a move away from using HTML (with all the proprietary extensions) and toward the XML-based XHTML. The DOM HTML API is still valid for XHTML, but another set of interfaces—the DOM Core API—has gained popularity among current JavaScript developers.

The W3C specifications for the DOM describe a document's elements as a collection of nodes, connected in a hierarchical tree-like structure. If you use Firefox as a browser, and you've opened up the DOM Inspector to look at the page objects, you'll probably have noticed that the page contents strongly resemble a tree. A web page with a head and body tags, the body with a header (H1), as well as DIV elements containing paragraphs, would have a structure somewhat like this:

```
document -> HTML -> HEAD
                 -> BODY -> H1
                         -> DIV -> P
                                -> P
```

The DOM provides a specification that allows you to access the nodes of this content tree by looking for all of the tags of a certain type or traversing the different levels—literally walking the tree and exploring each node at each level. Not only can you read the nodes in the tree, but you can also create new nodes.

The DOM Tree

To better understand the document tree, consider a web page that has a head and body section, a page title, and a DIV element that itself contains an H1 header and two paragraphs. One of the paragraphs contains italicized text; the other has an image—not an uncommon web page:

```
<!DOCTYPE html PUBLIC "-//W3C//DTD XHTML 1.0 Transitional//EN"
"http://www.w3.org/TR/xhtml1/DTD/xhtml1-transitional.dtd">
<html>
<head>
<title>Document In</title>
<meta http-equiv="Content-Type" content="text/html; charset=utf-8" />
</head>
<body>
<div id="div1">
<h1>Header</h1>
<!-- paragraph one -->
<p>To better understand the document tree, consider a web page that has a head and
body section, has a page title, and contains a DIV element that itself contains an H1
header and two paragraphs. One of the paragraphs contains <i>italicized text</i>; the
other has an image--not an uncommon web page.</p>
<!-- paragraph two -->
<p>Second paragraph with image. <img src="dotty.gif" alt="dotty" /></p>
</div>
</body>
</html>
```

An element contained within another is considered a child node, other contained elements are siblings, and the containing element is the parent. Figure 10-1 provides a hierarchical description of this page, demonstrating the parent, child, and sibling relationships.

Information, such as the relationship each node has with the others, is accessible via each node's shared properties and methods, covered next.

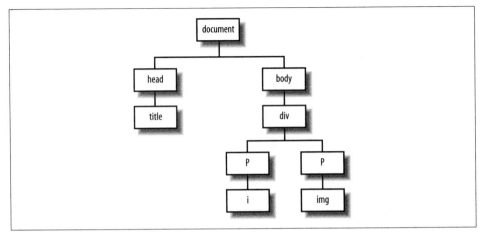

Figure 10-1. Hierarchy of elements in a web page

Node Properties and Methods

Regardless of its type, each node in the document tree has one thing in common with all the others: each has all of the basic set of properties and methods of the Node object. The Node object's properties record the relationships associated with the DOM content tree, including those of sibling elements, child, and the parent. It also has properties that provide other information about the node, including type, name, and if applicable, value. The following list gives this object's properties.

nodeName
> The object name, such as HEAD for the HEAD element

nodeValue
> If not an element, the value of the object

nodeType
> Numeric type of node

parentNode
> Node that is the parent to the current node

childNodes
> NodeList of children nodes, if any

firstChild
> First node in NodeList children

lastChild
> Last node in NodeList children

previousSibling
> If a node is a child in NodeList, it's the previous node in the list

`nextSibling`

If a node is a child in `NodeList`, it's the next node in the list

`attributes`

A `NamedNodeMap`, which is a list of key-value pairs of attributes of the element (not applicable to other objects)

`ownerDocument`

The owning document object

`namespaceURI`

The namespace URI, if any, for the node

`prefix`

The namespace prefix, if any, for the node

`localName`

The local name for the node if namespace URI is present

You can see the XML influence in the `Node` properties, especially with regard to namespaces. However, when accessing XHTML elements as nodes within a browser, the namespace properties are typically `null`. Also note that some properties are valid for node objects that are considered elements, such as those wrapping page elements like HTML and DIV; some are valid only for `Node` objects that are not, such as those of text objects associated with paragraphs or whatever element.

To better get a feel for this element/not element dichotomy, Example 10-4 is an application that accesses each `Node` object within a web page and pops up a dialog listing the node properties. The `nodeType` property provides the type of node as a numeric, and the `nodeName` is the actual object name currently being processed. If the node is not an element, its value is printed out with `nodeValue`; otherwise, this is null.

In addition, if the `Node` object is an element, it will have a `style` property (inherited as part of the element, and covered in much more detail in Chapter 12). This sets the background color of the object currently being processed (using a random-color generator), so that you can get visual feedback as the page processing progresses. (It also outputs this background color information to the message, as a secondary feedback method.)

Example 10-4. Accessing Node properties

```
<!DOCTYPE html PUBLIC "-//W3C//DTD XHTML 1.0 Transitional//EN"
"http://www.w3.org/TR/xhtml1/DTD/xhtml1-tran sitional.dtd">
<html>
<head>
<meta http-equiv="Content-Type" content="text/html; charset=utf-8" />
<title>The Node</title>
<script type="text/javascript">
//<![CDATA[

// random color generator
```

Example 10-4. Accessing Node properties (continued)

```
function randomColor( ) {
        r=Math.floor(Math.random( ) * 255).toString(16);
        g=Math.floor(Math.random( ) * 255).toString(16);
        b=Math.floor(Math.random( ) * 255).toString(16);
        return "#"+r+g+b;
}

// output some node properties
function outputNodeProps(nd) {

    var strNode = "Node Type: " + nd.nodeType;
    strNode += "\nNode Name: " + nd.nodeName;
    strNode += "\nNode Value: " + nd.nodeValue;

    // if style set (property of Element)
    if (nd.style) {
       var clr = randomColor( );
       nd.style.backgroundColor=clr;
       strNode += "\nbackgroundColor: " + clr;
    }

    // print out the node's properties
    alert(strNode);

    // now process node's children
    var children = nd.childNodes;
    for(var i=0; i < children.length; i++) {
       outputNodeProps(children[i]);
    }
}

//]]>
</script>
<body onload="outputNodeProps(document)">
<div id="div1">
<h1>Header</h1>
<!-- paragraph one -->
<p>To better understand the document tree, consider a web page that has a head and body
section, has a page title, and contains a DIV element that itself contains an H1 header
and two paragraphs. One of the paragraphs contains <i>italicized text</i>; the other has
an image--not an uncommon web page.</p>
<!-- paragraph two -->
<p>Second paragraph with image following.</p>
<img src="dotty.gif" alt="dotty" />
</div>
</body>
</html>
```

In the application, when the nodeValue property is not null, the style property is set—even for nonvisual elements such as those associated with the META tag. However, when the nodeValue property has a value (even if it's only a blank), the style property is not set.

Also note that elements containing text, such as a paragraph, actually contain a reference to a text node, which is what contains the text. In fact, you might be surprised at how many components go into this rather simple page.

Safari processes the onload event before the page finishes loading, so you'll lose the interactive effect of watching the objects change color as the application runs.

There is another aspect of this application that might surprise you, and that's the difference in what is printed out per browser. Firefox prints out the CDATA contents of the script tag, while Opera does not. Internet Explorer does not create text objects for whitespace outside of a tag, while other browsers do. IE also prints out the doctype definition while other browsers do not. Navigator doesn't color the entire page when processing the HTML element, but it does print out CDATA section for the script, and so on.

This one example demonstrates—probably more effectively than any other in the book—the fact that subtle differences in implementing even the exact same specification can cause behavioral and visual variations among the different browsers.

JavaScript Best Practice: Always test any CSS change or new JavaScript application with all supported browsers and within as many test environments as possible. Yes, it's obvious, but it can never be repeated too many times.

One property of node, nodeType, is a numeric. Rather than search for a specific node type using values of 3 or 8, the DOM specifies a group of constants you can access on the node prototype representing each type. These constants are:

- ELEMENT_NODE: value of 1
- ATTRIBUTE_NODE: value of 2
- TEXT_NODE: value of 3
- CDATA_SECTION_NODE: value of 4
- ENTITY_REFERENCE_NODE: value of 5
- ENTITY_NODE: value of 6
- PROCESSING_INSTRUCTION_CODE: value of 7
- COMMENT_NODE: value of 8
- DOCUMENT_NODE: value of 9
- DOCUMENT_TYPE_NODE: value of 10
- DOCUMENT_FRAGMENT_NODE: value of 11
- NOTATION_NODE: value of 12

These constants are helpful in maintaining more readable code, not to mention not having to memorize the individual values. Unfortunately, their implementation is not universal. Internet Explorer and Opera, at a minimum, don't implement these constants. Luckily, you can extend the Node object using the JavaScript prototype, covered in detail in Chapter 11. One of the examples is adding these constants to Node.

Traversing the Tree with the Node

The Node can be used to traverse a document's content, through its various parent, child, and sibling methods. Example 10-4 demonstrated this capability. The application uses the childNodes list to access a page element's children, and then uses recursion to traverse each child, in turn. The parent/child relationship isn't the only one that can be used to travel throughout a model; other properties can be used, including the sibling relationship.

The following three examples illustrate a frameset (Example 10-5), an input HTML page (Example 10-6), and a page with JavaScript to walk through the document in the first frame (Example 10-7). The script prints out the objects found, at what level, and if they have any children themselves. By level, I mean how deeply nested the HTML element is within the page.

Example 10-5 is the frameset page. I'm not using a frameset as a form of penance for not being fond of a perfectly good HTML construct. No, I'm using frames because I'll be printing to the document as I traverse it, and if I create new objects as I'm writing them out, I'll end up in a recursive loop that will never end.

Example 10-5. Frameset page

```
<!DOCTYPE html PUBLIC "-//W3C//DTD XHTML 1.0 Transitional//EN"
"http://www.w3.org/TR/xhtml1/DTD/xhtml1-transitional.dtd">
<html>
<head>
<title>Goin' for a walk</title>
<meta http-equiv="Content-Type" content="text/html; charset=utf-8" />
</head>
<frameset cols="40%,*">
<frame name="docin" src="docin.htm" />
<frame name="docout" src="docout.htm" />
</frameset>
</html>
```

Example 10-6 is the source page for the traversal. The frameset can be modified to use any page for the frame, and the JS will attempt to walk the tree. However, note that the function to process the tree is based on an onload event in the script page. If it loads before the source page, the results will not be as you expect.

Example 10-6. Source page

```
<!DOCTYPE html PUBLIC "-//W3C//DTD XHTML 1.0 Transitional//EN"
"http://www.w3.org/TR/xhtml1/DTD/xhtml1-transitional.dtd">
<html>
<head>
<title>Document In</title>
<meta http-equiv="Content-Type" content="text/html; charset=utf-8" />
</head>
<body>
<div id="div1">
<h1>Header</h1>
<!-- paragraph one -->
<p>To better understand the document tree, consider a web page that has a head and body
section, has a page title, and contains a DIV element that itself contains an H1 header
and two paragraphs. One of the paragraphs contains <i>italicized text</i>; the other has
an image--not an uncommon web page.</p>
<!-- paragraph two -->
<p>Second paragraph with image. <img src="dotty.gif" alt="dotty" /></p>
</div>
</body>
</html>
```

Example 10-7 is the web page with the script. Like Example 10-4, it uses recursion,
but before it digs deeper into the page nesting, the children nodes of the HTML element currently in the queue are accessed and printed out using the Node's relationship properties. Each child node is then processed in turn.

Example 10-7. Script page

```
<!DOCTYPE html PUBLIC "-//W3C//DTD XHTML 1.0 Transitional//EN"
"http://www.w3.org/TR/xhtml1/DTD/xhtml1-transitional.dtd">
<html>
<head>
<meta http-equiv="Content-Type" content="text/html; charset=utf-8" />
</head>
<body>
<script type="text/javascript">
//<![CDATA[

printTags(0,top.docin.document);

function printTags(domLevel,n) {
   document.writeln("<br /><br />Level " + domLevel + ":<br />");
   document.writeln(n.nodeName + " ");
   if (n.nodeType == 3) {
      document.writeln(n.nodeValue);
   }
   if (n.hasChildNodes()) {
      var child = n.firstChild;
      document.writeln(" { ");
      do {
         document.writeln(child.nodeName + " ");
         child = child.nextSibling;
```

Example 10-7. Script page (continued)

```
        } while(child);
        document.writeln(" } ");
        var children = n.childNodes;
        for(var i=0; i < children.length; i++) {
            printTags(domLevel+1,children[i]);
        }
    }
}
//]]>
</script>
</body>
</html>
```

This example is a fairly simple approach to walking the tree. A variation could be to store each level in an array and then print each level out, in turn. You could also traverse each tree branch in turn and print out the parent-child trail before going on to each sibling element.

 A better approach to traversing a document tree would be to use the W3C's optional Level 2 Traversal and Range Specification at *http://www.w3.org/TR/DOM-Level-2-Traversal-Range/*. This specification provides an API for objects that allow more sophisticated tree traversal, as well as the capability to deal with ranges of objects.

Other than its self-identification and navigation capabilities, the Node also has several methods that can be used to replace nodes or insert new nodes. These are used in association with document object methods that are used to create new elements.

The DOM Core Document Object

As you'd expect, the document object is the Core interface to the web-page document. It provides methods to create and remove page elements, as well as control where they occur in the page. It also provides two popular methods for accessing page elements: getElementById and getElementsByTagName.

The getElementsByTagName method returns a list of nodes (NodeList) representing all page elements of a specific tag:

```
    var list = document.getElementsByTagName("div");
```

The list can then be traversed, and each node processed for whatever reason.

 If the document has a DOCTYPE of HTML 4.01, all element references are in uppercase. If the document is XHTML 1.0 and up, the element tags are in lowercase. I've found that most browsers accept uppercase element tags regardless of doctype.

I've used getElementsByTagName to manage most of my DHTML effects, by encapsulating all dynamically accessible content within DIV tags and then loading all of these elements into a library of customized objects after the page loads.

To demonstrate getElementsByTagName, Example 10-8 also uses a frameset to load a source document in one pane and the script document in another.

Example 10-8. Frameset opening sample page and active page with script

```
<!DOCTYPE html PUBLIC "-//W3C//DTD XHTML 1.0 Transitional//EN"
"http://www.w3.org/TR/xhtml1/DTD/xhtml1-transitional.dtd">
<html>
<head>
<title>Highlighting</title>
<meta http-equiv="Content-Type" content="text/html; charset=utf-8" />
</head>
<frameset cols="80%,*">
<frame name="docin" src="docin.htm" />
<frame name="docout" src="findelem.htm" />
</frameset>
</html>
```

In this example, the findelem.htm page, shown in Example 10-9, has three page buttons that, when clicked, open prompts for three values: highlight color, source window to open, and element tag for which to search.

Example 10-9. Script page opening another document in a frame and highlighting all elements of a given type

```
<!DOCTYPE html PUBLIC "-//W3C//DTD XHTML 1.0 Transitional//EN"
"http://www.w3.org/TR/xhtml1/DTD/xhtml1-transitional.dtd">
<html>
<head>
<meta http-equiv="Content-Type" content="text/html; charset=utf-8" />
<style type="text/css">
div {
    border: 1px solid #000;
    padding: 5px;
}
</style>
<script type="text/javascript">
//<![CDATA[

var highlightColor = "#ffff00";
function changeColor() {
  highlightColor=prompt("Enter highlight color (hexidecimal format)");
}

function loadPage() {
    var pageURL = prompt("Enter page in this domain");
    top.docin.location.href=pageURL;
}
```

Example 10-9. Script page opening another document in a frame and highlighting all elements of a given type (continued)

```
function highlightElements( ) {
    var elemTag = prompt("Enter tag element name to highlight:");
    var nodes = top.docin.document.getElementsByTagName(elemTag);

    // highlight each
    for (var i = 0; i < nodes.length; i++) {
        nodes[i].style.backgroundColor=highlightColor;
    }
}
//]]>
</script>
</head>
<body>
<div onclick="changeColor( )">
<p>Click to change highlight color</p>
</div>
<div onclick="loadPage( )">
<p>Click to load source page</p>
</div>
<div onclick="highlightElements( )">
<p>Click to search for, and highlight, a specific tag</p>
</div>
</body>
</html>
```

The application opens the source document into the first pane and then finds all elements of a type and highlights them with the given color—in this case, the list item elements (LI), which are highlighted in gray, as shown in Figure 10-2.

 I can't load just any document with Example 10-9, though. The JavaScript sandbox prevents me from calling getElementsByTagName for a document that's outside the domain of the application page making this call. In other words, the application works with any page from the same domain as the script page, but no other.

The script can also work within the same document, which makes it effective if you want to highlight all like elements in a page based on some event, e.g., all text-input form elements or thumbnail images.

In addition to getElementsByTagName, the document object has several methods that can create new objects. These are demonstrated in the later section "Modifying the Tree." First, though, we'll look at the Element object and the concept of elements in context.

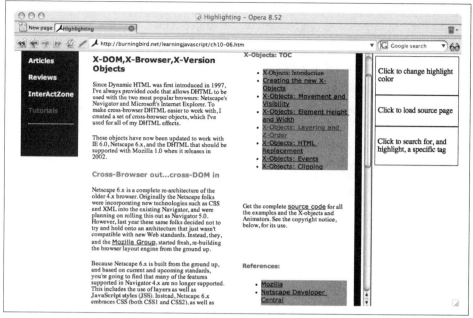

Figure 10-2. Highlighting same-tagged elements

Element and Access in Context

Another important element in the DOM Core is, appropriately enough, Element. All objects within a document inherit a basic set of functionality and properties from the Element. The majority of the functionality has to do with getting and setting the attributes, or checking for the existence of attributes:

- getAttribute(*name*)
- setAttribute(*name*, *value*)
- removeAttribute(*name*)
- getAttributeNode(*name*)
- setAttributeNode(*attr*)
- removeAttributeNode(*attr*)
- hasAttribute(*name*)

There are other methods, most having to do with the namespaces associated with the attributes, but these aren't methods you'll typically use with a web page.

Attributes are not always properties. Attributes change by element, with some elements having attributes such as width and align, while others don't. Properties are a component of the object class, rather than instances of the class. So properties would be associated with the document object, Element, Node, or even the HTML elements such as HTMLDocumentElement. But if you want to work with an element's attributes, and they're not exposed as a property on the object class, you'll need to use these Element methods.

Here's an image embedded in a web page:

```
<img src="dotty.gif" width="100" alt="an image" align="left" />
```

The following code accesses the image's attributes, concatenating them into a string, which is then printed in an alert:

```
var img = document.images[0];
var imgStr = img.getAttribute("src") + " " +
             img.getAttribute("width") + " " +
             img.getAttribute("alt") + " " +
             img.getAttribute("align");
alert(imgStr);
```

The following changes the value for the width and the alt:

```
img.setAttribute("width","200");
img.setAttribute("alt","This was an image");
```

Element also shares a method with the document, getElementsByTagName. Rather than work on all elements within the document, it operates on elements within context.

All the examples so far in the book have operated, more or less, within the context of the document object. For the most part, this is sufficient. However, there will be times when you'll want to work only with those elements nested within another element. Through the functionality inherited by the DOM Core, especially the Node and Element objects, any object in the page that can be accessed through a discrete access method such as getElementById can form a new context for working with content.

In the following HTML, two DIV blocks contain paragraphs: the first contains two; the second, one:

```
<div id='div1'>
<p>one</p>
<p>two</p>
</div>
<div id='div2'>
<p>three</p>
</div>
```

The paragraphs don't have identifiers to access each individually using getElementById. You can, instead, use getElementsByTagName by passing in the paragraph tag:

```
var ps = document.getElementsByTagName("p");
```

However, doing so, you'll get all paragraphs in the document. This might be what you want, but what if you want just the paragraphs within the first DIV block?

To access the paragraphs within this new context, you'll access the DIV element using getElementById (or whatever approach you wish):

```
var div = document.getElementById("div1");
```

Then, via inheritance from the `Element` object, you can use `getElementsByTagName` to get all paragraphs:

```
var ps = div.getElementsByTagName("p");
```

The only paragraphs in the node list returned are those nested within the first DIV block, identified by `div1`.

As more web pages are designed using CSS that are built in layers with elements nested within other layers, working with elements in context is a way to maintain some level of control over which components of the page are impacted by the Java-Script application. This is never more noticeable than when you use this approach to modify the document.

Modifying the Tree

The document is the owner/parent of all page elements. Because of this, most factory methods to create instances of new elements are methods on the Core document object. The `Node`, though, maintains the navigation within the Core API. This supports the hierarchical structure of the document tree, in which each node has a relationship to other nodes, and navigation follows this natural structure: parent/child, sibling/sibling. Finally, the `Element` provides a way to access elements within context in order to apply changes to nested elements. All three are essential objects when it comes to modifying the document tree.

The document factory methods, and the type of Core objects they create, are listed in Table 10-1. This also provides a brief introduction to several of the Core objects.

Table 10-1. Factory methods of the Document object

Method	Object created	Description
`createElement(tagname)`	`Element`	Creates an element that is cast to the specific tag
`createDocumentFragment`	`DocumentFragment`	The `DocumentFragment` is a lightweight document, used when extracting a section of the document tree
`createTextNode(data)`	`Text`	Holds any text in the page
`createComment(data)`	`Comment`	XML comment
`createCDATASection(data)`	`CDATASection`	CDATA section
`createProcessingInstructions (target,data)`	`ProcessingInstruction`	XML processing instruction
`createAttribute(name)`	`Attr`	Element attribute
`createEntityReference(name)`	`EntityReference`	Placeholder for an element to be placed later
`createElementNS (namespaceURI,qualifiedName)`	`Element`	Namespace for `Element`
`createAttributeNS (namespaceURI,qualifiedName)`	`Attr`	Namespace for `Element` attribute

It's simple to create a new node. Call the appropriate factory method on the document, and the node is returned:

```
var txtNode = document.createTextNode("This is a new text node");
```

The new operator is not used, as interfaces aren't classes; they have no constructors.

Once you have a new node, you can manipulate it as you would manipulate an existing page element of the same type. For instance, to add HTML to the object, you can use the innerHTML property:

```
var newDiv = document.createElement("div");
newDiv.innerHTML = "<p>New paragraph</p>";
```

Use the Node modification methods to add the new node once it's ready:

insertBefore(newChild,refChild)
>   Inserts new node before existing

replaceChild(newChild,oldChild)
>   Replaces existing node

removeChild(oldChild)
>   Removes existing child

appendChild(newChild)
>   Appends child node to document

Remember, though, that these methods have to be used within context to be effective. In other words, they have to operate on the element that contains the nodes that are being replaced or removed (or where the new node is being placed).

If the web page has a DIV element with a nested H1 header, and it's the header being replaced, you'll need to access the DIV element in order to modify its structure:

```
var div = document.getElementById("div1");
var hdr = document.getElementById("hdr1");
div.removeChild(hdr);
...
<div id="div1">
<h1 id="hdr1">Header</h1>
</div>
```

Demonstrating this more comprehensively, Example 10-10 is a variation of the static page that's used in previous examples in the chapter. It contains paragraphs, DIV blocks, an image, and a header. The script consists of a function, changeDoc, that's accessed when the page is clicked.

Example 10-10. Modifying a document

```
<!DOCTYPE html PUBLIC "-//W3C//DTD XHTML 1.0 Transitional//EN"
"http://www.w3.org/TR/xhtml1/DTD/xhtml1-transitional.dtd">
<html>
```

Example 10-10. Modifying a document (continued)

```
<head>
<title>Modifying Document</title>
<meta http-equiv="Content-Type" content="text/html; charset=utf-8" />
<script type="text/javascript">
//<![CDATA[

document.onclick=changeDoc;

function changeDoc( ) {

    // first, remove header
    var hdr = document.getElementById("hdr1");
    var div = document.getElementById("div1");
    div.removeChild(hdr);

    // replace the image with text
    var img = document.getElementById("img1");
    var p = document.getElementById("p2");
    var txt = document.createTextNode("New text node");
    p.replaceChild(txt,img);

    // add new element
    var div2= document.createElement("div");
    div2.innerHTML="<h1>The End</h1>";
    document.body.appendChild(div2);
}
//]]>
</script>

</head>
<body>
<div id="div1">
<h1 id="hdr1">Header</h1>
<!-- paragraph one -->
<p id="p1">To better understand the document tree, consider a web page that has a head and
body section, has a page title, and contains a DIV element that itself contains an H1
header and two paragraphs. One of the paragraphs contains <i>italicized text</i>; the
other has an image--not an uncommon web page.</p>
</div>
<!-- paragraph two -->
<p id="p2">Second paragraph with image. <img id="img1" src="dotty.gif" alt="dotty" /></p>
</body>
</html>
```

The first modification to the document is to remove the header from the DIV block.
To do this, the DIV is accessed using getElementById. The header element is also
accessed using this method, and once accessed, it's passed to the removeChild
method on the DIV block. This removes the element from the page—completely.

The next modification replaces the image contained in the last paragraph with text created using a text node. First, the image and paragraph are both loaded into JavaScript variables using getDocumentById (any method will do, as long as it's precise and returns the elements as nodes). A new text node is then created. It, and the image node, are passed to the replaceChild method on the paragraph node.

The last modification inserts a new DIV element, using innerHTML (discussed in Chapter 9) to create a new paragraph. This is appended to the body element, which results in a new header printed out at the end of the document that reads, "The End."

And it is the end—of this chapter, that is. There's plenty more still to come.

Questions

1. What attributes are supported for all HTML elements?
2. Using the HTML DOM when given a named element, how would you find its element type?
3. Given a node in the CORE DOM, how would you find the element types of each of its children?
4. How would you find out the IDs (identifiers) given all DIV elements in a page?
5. Rather than use innerHTML, how would you go about replacing the header element with a paragraph in the following DIV:

   ```
   <div id="elem1">
   <h1>This is a header</h1>
   </div>
   ```

Answers are provided in the appendix.

CHAPTER 11

Creating Custom JavaScript Objects

JavaScript is a wonderfully chaotic language. Some would say this is a good thing; others would say it's the biggest detriment to its use—so much so that there's a move to a new version of JavaScript, JavaScript 2.0, in order to tighten up some of the language's looser aspects. Proponents of a newer version say it's important to do so if JavaScript is to scale and be able to meet increasing demands.

After working with the previous examples, you might be scratching your head over the concept of JavaScript scaling. After all, the script tag is one of the most common found in web pages, and most sites use some form of JS. Any site that offers a shopping cart or other interactive element most likely uses JavaScript. Considering all of this, what could possibly be driving the concern about JavaScript and scaling?

The answer to that question—creating libraries of custom objects—is the core of this chapter. The new interest in Ajax and a renewed interest in Dynamic HTML has led to a growing number of fairly large JS libraries and even larger web-based applications, so it appears that scaling really has become an issue of concern.

Or does it? After all, most of us aren't going to be creating Ajax-based replacements for Microsoft Word or Adobe Photoshop. Most of what we need are smaller libraries of objects that manage some of the more esoteric elements of Ajaxian server-side access or DHTML's more complex effects.

It is an ongoing debate, and one that is taking place at the same time as efforts for JS 2.0 are progressing. At the heart of the debate are concerns about packaging, versioning, scope, collection generation and iteration, extensions, and most specifically, how objects are defined in JavaScript. For all that makes JavaScript an object-oriented language, it lacks one thing common to most OO implementations: it doesn't use classes.

I must admit to being one of those who appreciates how simple and straightforward JavaScript is to use despite its chaotic reputation. However, I can also understand the concerns of scaling. A bigger concern I have is whether this move to a newer, better JavaScript will lead to another decade of proprietary extensions and cross-browser differences. That's the type of chaos I could do without.

The JavaScript Object and Prototyping

An object in JavaScript is a complex construct usually consisting of a constructor as well as zero or more methods and/or properties. Additionally, all objects in JavaScript derive functionality from the standard JavaScript Object.

The Object itself is not particularly interesting. Originally it had several methods that have gradually been pulled out as global functions—such as eval, used earlier in this book—rather than Object methods.

What Object does provide is the framework for creating new objects; however, it doesn't do so via traditional object-oriented inheritance and the concept of classes. Instead, JavaScript derives its OO functionality from a concept called *prototyping*.

Prototyping

In a language such as Java or C++, to create a class as an extension of another, you define it in such a way that it inherits from the higher-level object. You then add your own functionality in addition to overriding any inherited functionality.

JavaScript, on the other hand, provides for a constructor, via Object, that allows developers to construct new objects. It is the Object constructor that then allocates the memory for the object, including all of its properties. The Object also provides a prototype property, which enables you to extend any object, including the built-in ones such as String and Number. It is this prototype that's used to derive new object methods and properties—not class inheritance.

This concept of extending objects via prototyping is best explained with an example. Example 11-1 demonstrates how to extend the built-in String object using the underlying Object prototype property, and then create an instance using the String constructor. The extension trim method trims leading and trailing whitespace from the string.

Example 11-1. First looks at JavaScript object creation and prototyping

```
<!DOCTYPE html PUBLIC "-//W3C//DTD XHTML 1.0 Transitional//EN"
"http://www.w3.org/TR/xhtml1/DTD/xhtml1-transitional.dtd">
<html>
<head>
<title>Adding trim function to String</title>
<meta http-equiv="Content-Type" content="text/html; charset=utf-8" />
</head>
<body>
<script type="text/javascript">
//<![CDATA[
```

Example 11-1. First looks at JavaScript object creation and prototyping (continued)

```
String.prototype.trim = function( ) {
return (this.replace(/^[\s\xA0]+/, "").replace(/[\s\xA0]+$/, ""));
}

var sObj = new String("  This is the string   ");
sTxt = sObj.trim( );

document.writeln("--" + sTxt + "--");

//]]>
</script>
</body>
</html>
```

Though browsers strip repeating spaces when a page is rendered, at least one space should have remained if all of them hadn't been trimmed.

With the prototype property, any use of String within the page or pages using this library now has access to this new trim function in addition to the older String object's methods and properties. We haven't created a new object class that's inherited from another, so much as we've taken an existing object and extended its functionality. That's the basic difference between a class-based OO system and one that uses prototyping.

Instead of using prototype, I could have added the trim function directly to a string instance (variable):

```
var str = " this is a string ";
str.trim = function( ) ...
```

However, only the instance would have access to the function, and I want to extend the actual String object itself; hence, the use of prototype. Every object in JavaScript, including those you create yourself, has a prototype property that allows the object to be extended.

How does the prototype work when the method is accessed? When the method is invoked on the object, the JavaScript engine first looks among those associated with the initial object implementation. If not found, it then looks within the prototype collection to see if the property/method exists. Only if the property or method is not found in the global object as part of the basic object or via the prototype collection, does the engine search for it locally, attached to the variable.

Of course, extending an existing object is only so helpful. Eventually, as you create increasingly sophisticated JavaScript applications, you're going to want to package your code into reusable components. The next section covers creating your own custom JavaScript objects and building reusable libraries.

Creating Your Own Custom JavaScript Objects

In the last few chapters of the book, which cover Ajax and the various code libraries you can download, you'll see how much improvisation was used to create objects using JavaScript. At times, these libraries look almost as if they're built in a language other than JS. In fact, many were built specifically to overlay the JavaScript language with other language characteristics, which has both advantages and disadvantages.

An advantage is that the library provides shortcuts for some of the more tedious operations, such as accessing page elements. Laying another language's flavor over JS may also make it easier if you use this language as the server-side component in an Ajax application.

The disadvantage is that this effort obfuscates the underlying JavaScript, making the library hard to read, hard to use, and confusing if you're not necessarily up on all the latest language advances.

One of the best essays I've seen written on the ambivalence associated with some of the clever and powerful, but obscuring, component libraries is "Painless JavaScript Using Prototype" by Dan Webb at Sitepoint (at *http://www.sitepoint.com/article/ painless-javascript-prototype*).

 JavaScript-library developers just can't seem to keep from trying to make JavaScript act like another language. The Mochikit guys want JavaScript to be Python, countless programmers have tried to make JavaScript like Java, and Prototype tries to make it like Ruby. Prototype makes extensions to the core of JavaScript that can (if you choose to use them) have a dramatic effect on your approach to coding JavaScript. Depending on your background and the way your brain works, this may or may not be helpful.

We'll get into the "make JavaScript be something else" approach to components and development later, but in this chapter, I'm focusing on how to make JavaScript work like JavaScript, but in a nice way.

Returning to the topic of creating objects, we find an old friend—the function—at the heart of the capability. It is the JavaScript function that's at the core when creating new objects.

Enter the Function

For close to a decade, when you created a custom object in JavaScript, you used functions. There have been some changes in how the functions are written, how private and public properties are defined, and even how those properties are packaged, but fundamentally if you want to create a new custom object in JavaScript, you start with the function.

In Example 11-2, JavaScript creates a very simple object, Tune, which takes one parameter, a song title. This is assigned to an object property, title. The object also incorporates an array of performers, which can be manipulated via two methods: addPerformer (which takes a string), and listPerformers, which takes no parameters.

Example 11-2. Creating a custom object

```
<!DOCTYPE html PUBLIC "-//W3C//DTD XHTML 1.0 Transitional//EN"
"http://www.w3.org/TR/xhtml1/DTD/xhtml1-transitional.dtd">
<html>
<head>
<title>First Object</title>
<meta http-equiv="Content-Type" content="text/html; charset=utf-8" />
<script type="text/javascript">
//<![CDATA[

var Tune = function(title) {
   this.title = title;
   var performedBy = new Array();
   this.addPerformer = function (performer) {
      var i = performedBy.length;
      performedBy[i] = performer;
   }
   this.listPerformers = function() {
      var singers = "";
      for (var i = 0; i < performedBy.length; i++ ) {
         singers += performedBy[i] + " ";
      }
      alert(singers);
   }
}

var song = new Tune("Hello");
song.addPerformer("Me");
song.addPerformer("You");
song.addPerformer("Us");
song.listPerformers();
alert(song.title);
//]]>
</script>

</head>
<body>
</body>
</html>
```

In the page, an instance of Tune is created using the Object constructor, passing in a song title, "Hello." The addPerformer method is called three times, passing in three performers: Me, You, and Us. The listPerformers method is then called to print out the performers and then the song title.

Going into greater detail, in the script I first create a function with the same name as the object, Tune. Remember from past chapters that all functions in JavaScript are also objects, so by creating this function we are, in effect, creating our custom object.

Within the function there are two properties and two methods. In this example, the code blocks to implement both methods are included as part of the object declaration. However, it doesn't have to be done this way. A set of objects I've used for years to manage my cross-browser DHTML efforts sets each object's properties to a method, which is then implemented outside the object constructor function:

```
function someObject() {
    this.method1 = objMethod1;
    ...
}
function objMethod1() {
    ...
}
```

A good reason for using this approach is to make the code easier to read. You could also attach the same method to different objects, though a better approach might be to use a form of JavaScript inheritance called chaining constructors (discussed later in the chapter).

Another approach to creating a custom object is to create an instance of the object, and then use the object's prototype to assign both properties and methods. Example 11-3 demonstrates this with a variation on the Tune object, but this time I'm using a prototype to assign a function to an object method.

Example 11-3. Using a prototype to assign properties and/or methods

```
<!DOCTYPE html PUBLIC "-//W3C//DTD XHTML 1.0 Transitional//EN"
"http://www.w3.org/TR/xhtml1/DTD/xhtml1-transitional.dtd">
<html>
<head>
<title>Second Object</title>
<meta http-equiv="Content-Type" content="text/html; charset=utf-8" />
<script type="text/javascript">
//<![CDATA[

function Tune (title) {
    this.title = title;
}
function printTitle() {
    alert(this.title);
}
var someTune = new Tune("Title");
Tune.prototype.print = printTitle;

var anotherTune = new Tune("Another Title");
anotherTune.print();

//]]>
</script>
```

Example 11-3. Using a prototype to assign properties and/or methods (continued)

```
</head>
<body>
</body>
</html>
```

The object has to be instantiated at least once in order for the JavaScript engine to generate the prototype on the new object. Once instantiated, though, it's just as usable, and in the same manner (as was demonstrated with the String object).

 Though perfectly acceptable, I'm not fond of using prototypes when I control how a custom object is derived. To me, it unnecessarily adds to the complexity of the object, as well as decreases its readability. They are, however, very handy as a way to extend objects defined elsewhere—including JavaScript's own basic set of objects.

The use of this associated with the title was demonstrated in both examples. It was also used with the methods in the first example, but not with the song array. The use of this signals a difference between a public and a private member within a JavaScript object, discussed next.

Public and Private Properties and Where this Enters the Picture

In Example 11-2, the this keyword is used to assign the value to the property of the object. It acts as a reference to the parent object, which is an instance of the new object we're creating. What this does (literally) is create a public property that is accessible outside the object, as was demonstrated when we printed the song title:

```
alert(song.title);
```

The use of this is also associated with the two methods. The array, though, is not assigned to the object using this; instead, it's created using the variable keyword var. This fact makes the property a private one—accessible internally to the object (including to its methods) but not outside of the object. Why have private rather than public variables? Primarily for data hiding—protecting data from direct application access.

There are times when you don't want application developers to directly access object data. They may end up making the object unusable or inadvertently cause an unwanted side effect. Usually you'll provide methods to get and set this data, rather than have it accessible as a property. To hide such data in JavaScript, you create it as a private member, with var, rather than a public member, with this.

The examples so far have passed basic JavaScript objects (Strings) as parameters. You can also use custom objects to wrap existing page elements in a form of encapsulation—an effective way to deal with browser differences. The next section covers this JavaScript object encapsulation, as well as cross-browser objects. We'll also look at how to detect when a certain functionality is supported or not.

Object Detection, Encapsulation, and Cross-Browser Objects

With the release of CSS and Netscape's Navigator 4.x, as well as Microsoft's Internet Explorer 4.x, web-page developers could finally create sophisticated page effects such as animated page contents, collapsing menus, and in-page notifications. The only problem was that not all of the browsers used the same object model when providing this capability.

One way around this cross-browser incompatibility was to access the agent string to determine what browser was accessing the page, and change the JavaScript accordingly. However, this approach, commonly called *browser sniffing*, was abandoned fairly quickly in favor of another approach: *object detection*.

Object Detection

With object detection, the JavaScript accesses the object being detected in a conditional statement. If the object doesn't exist, the condition evaluates to `false`. In Chapter 9, I mentioned one object that's commonly used in older scripts: `document.all`. Checking for `document.all` can detect a browser that supports the IE 4.x model. Another common object detection is to check for `document.layers`, which was supported by Netscape's Navigator 4.x:

```
if (document.layers) ...
```

Luckily, all modern browsers support a fairly consistent model. All support the `document.getElementById`, which is critical for accessing specific elements. All support the `style` property (covered in the next chapter), which allows you to change the CSS style properties of an element.

Still, even now, there are differences. Though I'll cover JavaScript manipulation of CSS properties in Chapter 12, we'll look at one specific property that differs between Internet Explorer and other browsers: `opacity`.

An element's transparency is determined by the percentage of its opacity. Microsoft was the first to provide a way to change an element's opacity dynamically, through a proprietary filter called the *alpha filter*. Later, the Mozilla group created a variation of the filter, called the *moz-opacity*. At about the same time, the KHTML effort (represented by the Safari browser and Konquerer on Linux) derived a property called *khtml-opacity*. With the release of CSS 3.0, a universal property was defined for opacity, simply named `opacity`.

The Mozilla line of browsers has moved to the new CSS3 standard, as has Safari. Oddly enough, Microsoft has decided not to support this property and still persists in using the alpha filter, even with the new IE 7. Object detection is necessary, then, to create an effect that works with IE as well as the other browsers that support the CSS3 opacity property.

In Example 11-4, object detection is used to determine which approach to use—the alpha filter or setting the CSS opacity. The target is an image embedded in the page. Its opacity is decreased 10 percent each time the page is clicked. Because the Microsoft alpha filter uses a percentage rather than a digital value, the variable used to hold the current opacity is multiplied by 100 when used with IE.

Example 11-4. Using object detection to determine how to adjust the opacity style

```
<!DOCTYPE html PUBLIC "-//W3C//DTD XHTML 1.0 Transitional//EN"
"http://www.w3.org/TR/xhtml1/DTD/xhtml1-transitional.dtd">
<html>
<head>
<title>Object Detection</title>
<meta http-equiv="Content-Type" content="text/html; charset=utf-8" />

<script type="text/javascript">
//<![CDATA[

var opacity = 1.0;
document.onclick=adjustOpacity;

function adjustOpacity( ) {
    opacity= opacity - 0.1;
    var img = document.getElementById("img1");
    if (img.style.filter) {
      opacity = opacity * 100;
      img.style.filter = "alpha(opacity:"+opacity+")";
    } else if (img.style.opacity) {
      img.style.opacity = opacity;
    } else {
      alert("Opacity not supported");
    }
}
//]]>
</script>

</head>
<body>
<img id="img1" src="fig01-1.jpg" style="opacity: 1.0; filter: alpha(opacity=100)"/>
</body>
</html>
```

In Mozilla, Navigator, Camino, Firefox, Safari, and IE, the image loses opacity with each click, fading away until it's completely transparent. With Opera, which doesn't support opacity, the message is given instead.

In Example 11-4, the initial opacity is set using an inline style setting. Without this initial setting, the `opacity` style setting returns `null` for any browser. The reason for this is that stylesheets and default settings aren't usually reflected with the style object when accessed by JavaScript. Stylesheets can be accessed as an array off the document object, and their individual rules accessed, using `document.stylesheets[0].cssRules[0]` (for W3C-complaint browsers), or `document.stylesheets[0].rules[0]` (for IE). You can also swap out an existing stylesheet using the stylesheets array.

This is an effective technique to work around cross-browser differences, but you might be asking yourself, what does this have to do with creating custom objects?

Encapsulating Objects

Earlier I touched on being able to pass page objects in as a parameter when constructing a new object. The custom object then wraps, or encapsulates, the page object, allowing you to create a set of functionality that hides most of the implementation details. When using a library that has this capability, instead of having to provide all of the JS yourself to change an object's opacity, you can just call a method that changes it for you.

If the underlying implementation changes because of what the browser supports, object encapsulation can hide all of the details for managing this alteration. The applications don't have to change because the underlying implementations have. This makes sophisticated interactive and dynamic applications so much easier to develop. If the browser's implementation is modified, you no longer have to worry about changing multiple applications.

Additionally, you no longer have to run a continuous set of operations that check whether the browser supports this functionality. Your code, or the JS library you're using, checks it up front when the objects are created (usually when the page loads).

Example 11-5 shows a self-contained application that demonstrates how object encapsulation can work in JavaScript, and how to manage cross-browser differences. The application includes a tiny object library that manages opacity. The page has two DIV elements, each of which contains an image. Both elements are positioned absolutely in the page: one is opaque, the other transparent. When the page loads, a function is called that creates an instance of the custom object, passing in each DIV element in turn. The first element's opacity is set to 1.0 (visible); the second to 0 (completely transparent). Clicking on the page decreases the opacity of the visible object and increases the opacity of the originally invisible object, creating a transformation effect between the two objects.

Example 11-5. Object encapsulation

```
<!DOCTYPE html PUBLIC "-//W3C//DTD XHTML 1.0 Transitional//EN"
"http://www.w3.org/TR/xhtml1/DTD/xhtml1-transitional.dtd">
<html>
<head>
<title>Object Detection</title>
<meta http-equiv="Content-Type" content="text/html; charset=utf-8" />

<style type="text/css">
div {
        position: absolute;
        top: 30px;
        left: 50px;
    }
</style>

<script type="text/javascript">
//<![CDATA[

var theobjs = new Array();

function alphaOpacity(value) {
   var opacity = value * 100;
   this.style.filter = "alpha(opacity:"+opacity+")";
}

function cssOpacity(value) {
   this.obj.style.opacity = value;
}

function getOpacity() {
   if (this.obj.style.filter) {
       return this.obj.style.filter.alpha;
   } else {
       return this.obj.style.opacity;
   }
}
function changeOpacity() {

   // div1
   var currentOpacity = parseFloat(theobjs["div1"].objGetOpacity());
   currentOpacity-=0.1;
   theobjs["div1"].objSetOpacity(currentOpacity);

   // div2
   currentOpacity = parseFloat(theobjs["div2"].objGetOpacity());
   currentOpacity+=0.1;
   theobjs["div2"].objSetOpacity(currentOpacity);
}

function DivObj(obj) {
   this.obj = obj;
   this.objGetOpacity = getOpacity;
```

Example 11-5. Object encapsulation (continued)

```
    this.objSetOpacity = obj.style.filter ? alphaOpacity : cssOpacity ;
}

function setup( ) {
  theelements = document.getElementsByTagName("DIV");
  for (i = 0; i < theelements.length; i++) {
      var obj = theelements[i];
      if (obj.id) {
          theobjs[obj.id] = new DivObj(obj);
      }
  }

  // set initial opacity
  theobjs["div1"].objSetOpacity(1.0);
  theobjs["div2"].objSetOpacity(0.0);

  // event handlers
  document.onclick=changeOpacity;
}

//]]>
</script>
</head>
<body onload="setup( )">
<div id="div1">
<img src="fig01-1.jpg" />
</div>
<div id="div2" style="opacity: 0.0; filter: alpha(opacity=0)">
<img src="fig01-3.jpg" />
</div>
</body>
</html>
```

In the example, rather than implementing the methods directly in the object, they're implemented outside as separate functions. You can use this approach if you're creating cross-browser objects where all versions of the objects can use some of the methods, such as the getOpacity function (which uses object detection each time it's called), but some methods are specific to types of support (such as the two methods for changing the opacity of the object, set by object detection when the object is created). It also, in my opinion, can make the code a little easier to read as you document each function, and you don't have an excessive amount of nesting.

 The example also used parseFloat to ensure that the numbers are accessed as numbers, not strings. Later, in the section on exception handling, I'll demonstrate what happens when you don't use this function.

The use of object detection, custom objects, and encapsulation is not as important today as it was in the past when browser DHTML support varied rather significantly.

However, it's still a great way to hide browser differences, not to mention enforce the old "code once, use many times" philosophy of application development.

Note the DOM Level 2 functionality of getElementsByTagName to access all DIV elements, which are then passed to the custom-object constructor to be wrapped in all that cross-browser goodness. For allover page effects, wrapping the page elements in DIV elements and then encapsulating each as a custom object is an approach that simplifies the development of more sophisticated functionality. We'll look at this in more detail in the next two chapters.

Chaining Constructors and JS Inheritance

JavaScript is not a typical OO language, and shouldn't be pushed, pummeled, or constrained into one. It has its own strengths, which should be used to advantage. Still, there are pieces of traditional object-oriented design that would be nice to use in applications. In the last section we saw one type of OO-based design: encapsulation. This section covers another: inheritance.

Inheritance incorporates, or inherits, another object's methods and properties in a new object. It's the fundamental power of class-oriented development because one class can inherit from another class, choosing to override whatever functions that have a new behavior in the new class. Something similar can be used in JS to emulate this behavior, starting with JavaScript 1.3—the function methods of apply and call.

Returning to previous examples, when a function defining a new object is written, it becomes the object constructor and is invoked when the new keyword is used with the function:

```
theobj = new DivObj(params);
```

Both the function apply and call methods allow you to apply or invoke a method within the context of another object. If used with an object constructor, it chains the constructors in such a way that all properties and methods of the one object are inherited by the containing object. The only difference between the two is the parameters passed; the behavior is the same. The call method takes the containing object as the first parameter, identified using this, and each of the arguments you want to pass to the constructor of the contained object:

```
obj.call(this,arg1,arg2,..., argn);
```

The apply method takes a reference to the containing object and the arguments array of the container. If the contained object has two parameters, and the container three, only the first two arguments of the arguments array are passed to the contained object:

```
obj.apply(this,arguments);
```

If you're sharing a set of arguments, use apply. Otherwise, use call.

Example 11-6 uses apply and chained constructors to demonstrate inheritance. The first object created, tune, stores information about a song's title and type. It also has a method that returns a string containing both. The second object, artist_tune, also contains a property for the artist, as well as a function to create a string of all properties. The apply method is called directly off of the tune function/object. In addition, once both objects are defined, the artist_tune prototype is assigned the tune constructor.

Example 11-6. Chained constructors and inheritance through the function method apply

```
<!DOCTYPE html PUBLIC "-//W3C//DTD XHTML 1.0 Transitional//EN"
"http://www.w3.org/TR/xhtml1/DTD/xhtml1-transitional.dtd">
<html>
<head>
<title>Inheritance</title>
<meta http-equiv="Content-Type" content="text/html; charset=utf-8" />
<script type="text/javascript">
//<![CDATA[

function tune(title,type) {
    this.title = title;
    this.type = type;
    this.getTitle=function() {
      return "Song: " + this.title + " Type: " + this.type;
    }
}

function artist_tune(title,type,artist) {
    this.artist = artist;
    this.toString("Artist is " + artist);
    tune.apply(this,arguments);
    this.toString = function () {
      return "Artist: " + this.artist + " " + this.getTitle();
    }
}

artist_tune.prototype = new tune();

var song = new artist_tune("I want to hold your hand", "rock", "Beatles");
alert(song.toString());
//]]>
</script>

</head>
<body>
</body>
</html>
```

Handy little methods, call and apply. Sometimes, though, you don't need inheritance, or even a class, when creating custom objects. Sometimes all you need is one object.

This is all going to be a bit much if you've never worked with a programming language prior to this book. Or even if you have, because JavaScript has some pretty unusual concepts. Some of the functionality described in this chapter, such as chained constructors, is pretty rare, so don't worry if you find your eyes glazing over on that one. However, creating custom objects and the use of prototype are common, so you may want to go over the other sections a couple of times until you feel more comfortable. Experiment with the examples, and try out some of your own.

One-Off Objects

In most cases, the power of OO-based development is being able to create instances of an object for various purposes. However, sometimes all you need is one object. The Prototype Ajax library uses these one-off objects quite a bit.

One way to create a one-off object is to create an associative array of properties and methods and assign the lot to a variable. Any of the following create the same object, with the same behavior; each just uses a different syntax:

```
var oneOff = {
    variablea : "valuea",
    variableb : "valueb".
    method : function () {
        return this["variablea"] + " " + this["variableb"];
    }
}
```

All objects are functions, and all functions are objects in JavaScript. In this case, the object is an associative array with two properties and a method. Because the method is a function and an object, it can be added to the array just like any other static item. To access the members, the method uses named-array notation, but outside the object, it uses standard property access:

```
alert(oneOff.variablea);
alert(oneOff.method());
```

Another approach is the following:

```
var oneOff = new Object();
oneOff.variablea = "valuea";
oneOff.variableb = "valueb";
oneOff.method = function () {
                    return this.variablea + " " + this.variableb;
                };
```

You can construct a new object from the actual Object, and then add properties and methods to the object instance. You don't use prototype, because you're not adding new properties or methods to an underlying object. You're adding them to an object instance directly. The method accesses the parent object's other properties using this and just provides a named property.

Here's how to access the properties:

```
alert(oneOff2.variableb);
alert(oneOff2.method());
```

The last approach we'll investigate uses our old function to create an object, but this time, we're assigning it directly to a variable and using it as a one-off:

```
var oneOff = new function() {
            this.variablea = "variablea";
            this.variableb = "variableb";
            this.method = function () {
                        return this.variablea + " " + this.variableb;
                    }
        }
```

Again, there's no difference in how the object properties are accessed.

You can use a one-off object when you need to encapsulate a group of methods and properties into one object, and then reuse this object throughout your entire application. You don't need many instances of the object—just one.

Object Libraries: Packaging Your Objects for Reuse

Most of the examples in the book are contained within one file, and this includes the JavaScript, the CSS, and so on. The reason is to make the examples as easy to replicate as possible, and also to make the functionality currently being demonstrated easier to see.

For your applications, though, you're going to want to put your JavaScript into a separate file or files, each with a *.js* extension. You'll also put your CSS into a stylesheet with a *.css* extension, as well as restrict any script or event handlers attached directly to objects within the page.

Using this approach, it's a lot easier to make code changes, and to see what's happening in the code (as well as the CSS, because they are, for the most part, connected).

The next question then is: how many JavaScript files do you want to create? After all, each adds to the overhead of the page.

A good rule of thumb to follow when packaging your JavaScript is to isolate your objects into different layers of access, processes, or business methods. As an example, I have a set of cross-browser DHTML objects that are then used for a set of animation objects I created. The DHTML objects are in one file, the animation objects in another. With this, if you're not interested in an animation, you can just include the DHTML objects.

You can break the objects into separate files even further, but the benefits are lost if you have too many small files, each of which have to be included.

Advanced Error-Handling Techniques (try, throw, catch)

Calling functions and testing return values is acceptable in an application, but it isn't optimal. A better approach is to make function calls and use objects without continuously testing for results, and then include exception handling at the end of the script to catch whatever errors happen.

Beginning with JavaScript 1.5, the use of `try...catch...finally` was incorporated into the JavaScript language. The `try` statement delimits a block of code that's enclosed in the exception-handling mechanism. The `catch` statement is at the end of the block; it catches any exception and allows you to process the exception however you feel is appropriate.

The use of `finally` isn't required, but it is necessary if there's some operation that must be performed whether an exception occurs or not. It follows the `catch` statement, and, combined with the exception-handling mechanism, has the following format:

```
try {
...
}
catch (e) {
...
}
finally {
...
}
```

There are six error types implemented in JavaScript 1.5 engines:

EvalError
: Raised by eval when used incorrectly

RangeError
: Numeric value exceeds its range

ReferenceError
: Invalid reference is used

SyntaxError
: Used with invalid syntax

TypeError
: Raised when variable is not the type expected

URIError
: Raised when `encodeURI( )` or `decodeURI( )` are used incorrectly

Using `instanceOf` when catching the error lets you know if the error is one of these built-in types. In the following code, a `TypeError` is deliberately invoked, and then captured. The exception that's thrown has a message property that can be printed out to get information about the exception:

```
try {
  var somearray = null;
  alert(somearray[18]);
} catch (e) {
    if (e instanceof TypeError) {
       alert("Type error: " + e.message);
    }
}
```

You can also use multiple tests for the type of error, log the error, and even call a special exception handler—all within the catch block. If you have any functionality that needs to be processed regardless of success or failure, you can include this in the finally:

```
try {
  var somearray = null;
  alert(somearray[18]);
} catch (e) {
    if (e instanceof TypeError) {
       alert("Type error: " + e.message);
    }
}
finally {
    somearray = null;
}
```

This more sophisticated form of exception handling fits in with object construction because your object methods can throw exceptions using the associated throw statement, rather than having to fuss around with returning null or some other failed value. You can throw any number of exception types and then process them accordingly in the code that is working with the object.

In Example 11-7, the small object library and related example from Example 11-5 is modified so that it doesn't use the parseFloat function, which ensures that the opacity settings are treated as numbers before modifying the value. In addition, the two methods that set the opacity now test to see if the value is a number, and throw an exception if not. The calling function catches this exception and prints out the message.

Example 11-7. Testing opacity settings

```
<!DOCTYPE html PUBLIC "-//W3C//DTD XHTML 1.0 Transitional//EN"
"http://www.w3.org/TR/xhtml1/DTD/xhtml1-transitional.dtd">
<html>
<head>
<title>Exceptions</title>
<meta http-equiv="Content-Type" content="text/html; charset=utf-8" />

<script type="text/javascript">
//<![CDATA[

var div1;
```

Example 11-7. Testing opacity settings (continued)

```
function alphaOpacity(value) {
    if (typeof value == "number") {
        var opacity = value * 100;
        this.style.filter = "alpha(opacity:"+opacity+")";
    } else {
        throw "NotANumber";
    }
}

function cssOpacity(value) {
    if (typeof value == "number") {
        this.obj.style.opacity = value;
    } else {
        throw "NotANumber";
    }
}

function getOpacity() {
    if (this.obj.style.filter) {
        return this.obj.style.filter.alpha;
    } else {
        return this.obj.style.opacity;
    }
}function changeOpacity() {

    try {
        // div1
        var currentOpacity = div1.objGetOpacity();
        currentOpacity+=0.1;
        div1.objSetOpacity(currentOpacity);
    } catch (e) {
        alert(e);
    }
}

function DivObj(obj) {
    this.obj = obj;
    this.objGetOpacity = getOpacity;
    this.objSetOpacity = obj.style.filter ? alphaOpacity : cssOpacity ;
}

function setup() {
  div = document.getElementById("div1");
  div1 = new DivObj(div);

  // set initial opacity
  div1.objSetOpacity(0.0);

  // event handlers
  document.onclick=changeOpacity;
}
```

Example 11-7. Testing opacity settings (continued)

```
//]]>
</script>

</head>
<body onload="setup()">
<div id="div1">
<img src="fig01-1.jpg" />
</div>
</body>
</html>
```

The methods that set the opacity for the object don't normally return a value; doing so just for error handling is not the way to go. Instead, by throwing the exception, the calling program doesn't have to test the status of the method return, and the methods can trigger the error handling. Of course, without having any kind of exception handling, throwing the exception and not catching it triggers a JavaScript error. Even though that is appropriate, why have exception handling only to disregard its use?

As stated at the beginning of this section, exception handling in JS is relatively new. It's a product of the ongoing effort to improve the object-oriented qualities of a language that some people call chaotic and unruly. There's a move to put some controls on this wild child of the programming languages by issuing a new major revision of JavaScript: JavaScript 2.0. This effort is discussed in this last section.

What's New in JavaScript

Though the ECMA working group hasn't issued a new specification release, work on JavaScript continues. JavaScript 1.6 introduced new array methods such as `indexOf` and `lastIndexOf`, as well as iterators (methods to help one move through, or iterate through, a collection such as an array): `every`, `filter`, `forEach`, `map`, and `some`.

JavaScript 1.7, which is part of the Firefox 2.0 release, continues working with arrays, and includes additional iterators and generators for initializing them. It also expands scoping rules to include block-level scoping. Right now, there is function-level (local) and global scoping, and that's it.

At issue with these changes, though, is that they are browser-specific. At a minimum, they have no ECMA backing and again, push us off into a potential cross-browser dichotomy—just at a time when we're beginning to expect consistent behavior among the major browsers. Most of JavaScript 1.6 is covered by ECMA-262 revision 3, but there's no parallel ECMA specification for JavaScript 1.7.

More, there's no guarantee that Microsoft will concur with the steps that the Mozilla organization is taking with the language enhancements. However, unlike the issues with different interpretations of the DOM, which was the primary cause of cross-browser difficulties in past JS lives, we're now faced with a growing separation in the basic programming language itself.

I include a discussion of the future of JavaScript in this particular chapter because many of the proposed changes for JavaScript 2.0 (also known as ECMAScript Edition 4, or ECMA4) have to do with converting JavaScript to a true class-based language. This includes the ability to provide packaging and versioning, as well as true public and private keywords, and static typing through the use of const and final.

A second interest with JavaScript 2.0 is to improve its ability to communicate with other programming languages for multilanguage application development. This means types for object interfaces, as well as machine-level data types such as int.

The creator of the original JavaScript, Brendan Eich, formerly of Netscape and now a part of the Mozilla corporation, gave a presentation at XTech in May 2006 about JavaScript 2.0 and the future of the Web. The presentation is at *http://developer. mozilla.org/presentations/xtech2006/javascript/*. Unfortunately, there's no audio of the presentation, nor any document fleshing out the bullets. But going through the slides, you can draw several inferences about the whys and wherefores of this rather significant move in JavaScripting.

Change Just Enough

The original JavaScript 2.0 proposal was intimidating due to the extent the language would have to change. According to Scott McCoy's article on JS 2.0 (at *http://www. blisted.org/wiki/papers/opinions/JavaScript2.0*), we don't need to change the language much. McCoy provided a sound argument as to why classes aren't needed, and the current prototype-based system was very effective. What's needed instead is a better extension mechanism.

However, Eich's presentation lists some of the arguments for just minimal JavaScript changes and details why he feels these won't work in the long run. One of these reasons involves closures for data hiding, which I wrote about in an earlier chapter. As I noted then, closures can add to the memory burden, increasing it almost three times according to Eich.

Another argument for minimal changes to JavaScript is that we're finally at a point where browsers interoperate. Now is not the time to rock the boat. To this, Eich responds that browsers don't interoperate at the frontiers, which we must assume means at-the-edge cases (most likely Ajax-based). He also stresses that using namespaces for extensions requires cooperation. As for the current system of type checking, Eich argues that specific type checking is tedious, and frameworks must be shared and distributed.

Ultimately, Eich states that minimal changes don't scale.

Scaling and the Next 10 Years

There is a fork in the road for JavaScript usage. One path leads to the typical JS use we've seen for the last several years: form validation, setting and getting cookies, providing an interactive web page for the user, etc. We've added many more bells and whistles, but the underlying concept is that we're working with web pages.

Another path is one that sees the browser and the Internet as the new desktop of the future. Rather than view the document in which we work just as a web page, it's a whole new environment that requires a great deal more interactivity (storage, interfacing with a server, and so on) than we've had in the past.

When Eich talks about scaling, I'm assuming he means the latter and not the former. At Eich's roadmap weblog (*http://weblogs.mozillazine.org/roadmap/*), he begins to discuss some of the proposed changes, though most of the discussion is based on programming-language semantics, rather than what JS will look like for you and me in the end. In one comment, Eich talks about the scaling issue:

> There are at least 134 "Ajax" libraries, with line-counts in the 10KSLOC to 100KSLOC and beyond. These libraries are used by equally large apps. This *is* large scale programming—the horse is out of the barn.

We'll look at some of these libraries in the last two chapters, but the larger ones are focused on emulating desktop applications within browsers. Does the tail (in this case, Ajax and the desktop style of applications) then wag the dog (the entire community of web developers)? Eich seems confident that this is so, and believes Java-Script 2.0 will roll out in general-browser use by 2010.

When pondering the fact that Microsoft is just now coming out with IE 7, and it doesn't implement all of the DOM Level 2 functionality, which has been a released spec for years, I'm not so sanguine that we'll all be developing in JS 2.0 in four years. However, stranger things have been known to happen.

If you want a taste of the new JavaScript now, Adobe's ActionScript 3.0 (at *http://labs.adobe.com/technologies/actionscript3/*) is supposedly a close enough implementation of the changes that are to be incorporated into JavaScript 2.0. Brendan Eich, as convener of the ECMA TG1, which is working through the issues of ECMA4, has stated that he meets with the ActionScript folks monthly, sometimes weekly.

There's also work on a JS 2-to-JS translator that will allow you to write in JavaScript 2.0 and will then translate your writing to JavaScript 1.x syntax for use in current browsers. There's an online site that provides translation at *http://olav.dk/js2/*.

You can keep up with these and other changes in JavaScript at the *Learning JavaScript* web site (*http://learningjavascript.info*).

Questions

1. Let's say you want to create a new `Number` method, `triple`, which triples the current `Number` object's value. You also want this method available for all numbers. What are the steps you'd take?

2. How do you hide a data member with a new object? Why would you want to?

3. Create a function that wants a number argument and returns an error if the argument is the incorrect type. How would you implement this without having to use the return statement?

4. We've seen object detection used previously with events:

   ```
   var theEvent = nsEvent ? nsEvent : window.event;
   ```

   Why can't we use the same type of functionality when dealing with the `opacity` differences?

5. Create a custom object with three public methods—`changeState`, `getColor`, and `getState`—and two private data members, `background` and `state`. Set the data members to on for state, and set a color of `#fff` for background color. The `changeState` method will test to see if the state is on, and if it is, change it to `off`, and the color to `#000`. The `getColor` method returns the color, and the `getState` returns the state.

Answers are provided in the appendix.

CHAPTER 12

Building Dynamic Web Pages: Adding Style to Your Script

Back in 1996, I was invited to a confidential author introduction for a new technology that Microsoft planned to roll out within the year. I traveled up from Portland, Oregon to Microsoft's Seattle campus and joined with several other authors and editors from various book companies in a rather nice conference room (with a kicker buffet in the back).

One of the Microsoft managers appeared in front of a projected image of a web page, which wasn't anything to write home about. That is, until he clicked on a header in the page, and the material below the header was pushed down as a previously hidden paragraph. A small thing, and no big thing now, but back then, I was blown away.

This was my first introduction to the concept that became known as Dynamic HTML or DHTML. I eventually went on to write a book on DHTML, as well as several articles dealing with cross-browser DHTML. The key element to the concept was the introduction of a new W3C specification, Cascading Style Sheets, in addition to the concept of Document Object Model, though there was no universal model at the time.

It's through CSS that we can define the appearance of page elements without having to rely on external applications, plug-ins, or excessive use of images. It's also through CSS and stylesheets that we can separate the presentation of page elements from their organization.

However, it was through the DOM that we could access stylesheet properties from JavaScript, changing individual element properties even after the page had finished loading. Combined with CSS, it was a powerful means to make a web page far more interactive than it had been.

The only problem was that each company that then had a major browser—Netscape Navigator and Microsoft's Internet Explorer being the most popular—implemented a different DOM, and this made DHTML quite difficult. Although the Version 4 browsers were capable of some amazing effects, they came at a cost. The page had to include code to create the effect that would work in each browser and that would also work with older browsers that didn't have DHTML capability. Primarily due to this difficulty, DHTML languished without extensive use until the more modern browsers such as those that tested the examples in this book. Now, DHTML has awakened new interest, aided and abetted by the amazing popularity of Ajax (covered in Chapters 13 and 14).

> As mentioned in Chapter 11, I've had a set of cross-browser DHTML objects and animation objects built on them in one form or another since 1998. A modern variation can be downloaded, as well as several examples of their use, at my *Learning JavaScript* web site, *http:// learningjavascript.info*.

DHTML: JavaScript, CSS, and DOM

Cascading Style Sheets (CSS) had a rough start. The idea of putting the presentation of page elements into a separate specification was around before the beginnings of the Web, but was pushed aside by earliest browser developers. It wasn't until 1996—with the first release of CSS, followed by the first releases of the 4.x browsers—that CSS finally became a reality. None too soon, because web-page developers were getting quite frustrated with web-page limitations.

In those early days, most pages were laid out using HTML tables, which originally were not intended for page layout, but data organization. Problems associated with page layout included the entire page not displaying until all images were loaded, not to mention all of the cruft that was creeping into page development through the different browsers. If you worked with web pages then, you're familiar with font and, worse, blink.

CSS provided a clean alternative; with it, you could initialize and manipulate different categories of presentation properties. These include an element's background, font, colors, borders, and box size, margins, and padding, if applicable. These were a very nice addition to a web-application developer's toolbox, but there was something missing: the ability to position elements and control their layout, as well as their visibility and display. It wasn't until Netscape and Microsoft collaborated on an early release of positional CSS, called CSS-P, that these style properties were released. Eventually, they were rolled into a new release of CSS: CSS2.

> This chapter assumes you're familiar with CSS and how to add stylesheets to a web page. If you're unfamiliar with CSS, you may want to read a good tutorial or book on CSS first before reading the rest of this chapter. I recommend Eric A. Meyer's *Cascading Style Sheets: The Definitive Guide* (O'Reilly). There are also numerous tutorials online if you do a search on "CSS" and "tutorial." One popular site is W3 Schools at *http://www.w3schools.com/css/default.asp*.

The style Property

CSS style properties are typically retrieved and set via the style object. The concept of style as property originated with Microsoft, but was adopted by the W3C and included in the DOM Level 2 CSS module. Through the W3C DOM, any node has an associated style object as a property, which means any page element can have its style properties changed with JavaScript.

To change any style setting using JavaScript, you must first use one of the DOM-access methods outlined in Chapters 9 and 10 to get a handle on the individual element (or elements). To change the style attribute, use straight assignment:

```
element.style.color="#fff";
```

This works with any valid CSS2 attribute and on any valid XHTML object. Example 12-1 shows how to modify several CSS attributes, using our by now very familiar getElementById to access a DIV element, and the style object to set various CSS properties.

Example 12-1. Applying several style property changes to a DIV element

```
<!DOCTYPE html PUBLIC "-//W3C//DTD XHTML 1.0 Transitional//EN"
"http://www.w3.org/TR/xhtml1/DTD/xhtml1-transitional.dtd">
<html>
<head>
<title>Changing Styles</title>
<meta http-equiv="Content-Type" content="text/html; charset=utf-8" />
<script type="text/javascript">
//<![CDATA[

function changeElement() {
  var div = document.getElementById("div1");
  div.style.backgroundColor="#f00";
  div.style.width="500px";
  div.style.color="#fff";
  div.style.height="200px";
  div.style.paddingLeft="50px";
  div.style.paddingTop="50px";
  div.style.fontFamily="Verdana";
  div.style.borderColor="#000";
}

//]]>
</script>

</head>
<body onload="changeElement();">
<div id="div1">
This is a DIV element.
</div>
</body>
</html>
```

Notice in the example the naming convention used with the CSS properties? If the property has a hyphen, such as `border-color`, the hyphen is removed and the first letter of the second term is capitalized: `border-color` in CSS becomes `borderColor` in JavaScript. Other than that, the names of the CSS properties used in JavaScript are the same as the names of the properties in a stylesheet. Figure 12-1 demonstrates how the DIV element and its contents look after the style changes have been made.

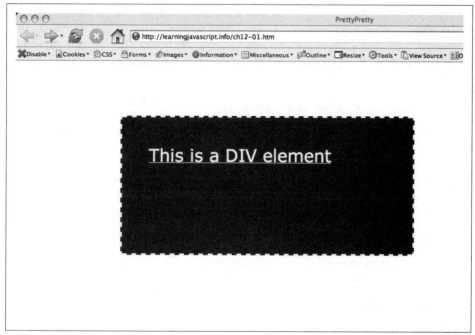

Figure 12-1. *Applying several style changes*

If modifying the `style` attribute is simple, reading it is less so. If the `style` property is not set through JavaScript or using the `style` attribute inline in the element, even if the value is set with a stylesheet, the property value will either be blank or undefined. This is important to remember because it will trip you up more than anything else when you're working with DHTML. The style settings used to render the object initially are internal to the browser and based on a combination of stylesheet settings, as well as element inheritance.

 To repeat: unless the `style` property is set via JavaScript or directly inline using the `style` attribute on the element, the value is blank or undefined when you access it via script, even if you set the value through a stylesheet.

To access the style, you need to use other properties, each specific to different types of browsers. Microsoft and Opera support a `currentStyle` property on the element, while Firefox, Mozilla, and Navigator support window.getComputedStyle. Unfortunately, these don't work consistently across browsers.

For the getComputedStyle method, you must pass in the CSS attribute using the same syntax you use when setting the style in the stylesheet. However, for the currentStyle method, you use the JavaScript notation. (It doesn't matter either way what you use with Safari, because it doesn't support any method.)

Example 12-2 demonstrates a variation of a function that gets the style settings for an object and a specific CSS property. It tests, first, whether window.getComputedStyle is supported, and if not, tests for getComputedStyle. If neither are supported, it just returns null. The style property is also accessed and printed out, both before and after it's set.

Example 12-2. Attempting to get CSS style information

```
<!DOCTYPE html PUBLIC "-//W3C//DTD XHTML 1.0 Transitional//EN" "http://www.w3.org/TR/
xhtml1/DTD/xhtml1-transitional.dtd">
<html>
<head>
<title>Shy Style</title>
<meta http-equiv="Content-Type" content="text/html; charset=utf-8" />
<style type="text/css">

#div1 { background-color: #ff0 }
</style>
<script type="text/javascript">
//<![CDATA[

document.onclick=changeElement;

function getStyle(obj,jsprop,cssprop) {
   if (obj.currentStyle) {
       return obj.currentStyle[jsprop];
   } else if (window.getComputedStyle) {
      return document.defaultView.getComputedStyle(obj,null).getPropertyValue(cssprop);
   } else {
     return null;
   }
}

function changeElement( ) {
    var obj = document.getElementById("div1");
    alert(obj.style.backgroundColor);
    alert(getStyle(obj,"backgroundColor","background-color"));
    obj.style.backgroundColor="#ff0000";
    alert(getStyle(obj,"backgroundColor","background-color"));
    alert(obj.style.backgroundColor);
}


//]]>
```

Example 12-2. Attempting to get CSS style information (continued)

```
</script>
</head>
<body>
<div id="div1">
<p>This is a DIV element</p>
</div>
</body>
</html>
```

Notice in the script that the syntax to get the computed value is document.defaultView.getComputedStyle rather than window.getComputedStyle. The reason is that document.defaultView returns the DOM AbstractView object, which is the base interface from which all views derive. This may be set to the window object, but there's no guarantee, and it could change from browser to browser, or version to version. As such, you'll want to use document.defaultView.getComputedStyle to get the style property.

Even when the style property is accessible, what exactly is returned also varies from browser to browser; for instance color, simple color. Opera returns the hexadecimal format for the color:

```
#ff0000
```

While Firefox returns the RGB setting:

```
RGB(255,0,0)
```

You then need to convert between the two formats if you want a consistent result.

Retrieving style settings from the page is fraught with interesting challenges. Perhaps more so than is fun, entertaining, or even useful. A good rule of thumb when working with DHTML is try to avoid retrieving information directly from the page style settings. Instead, whenever possible, use program variables to hold values and only use style to set attributes.

The CSS style properties tend to fall into families of like properties: fonts, borders, the container for elements, positioning, display, and so on. In the rest of the chapter, I'll cover several attributes, demonstrating how to work with each using JavaScript. Definitely take some time along the way to stop and improvise on all of the examples.

Getting style information through the document's stylesheet collection is not covered here. This is a newer collection and not part of the original BOM. Using this approach works around some of the compatibility and attribute-setting difficulties discussed in this chapter. To see an example and discussion on this approach, see "Modifying Styles" by Steven Champeon at *http://developer.apple.com/internet/webcontent/styles.html*.

Fonts and Text

One of the first presentation-specific HTML elements was font, and it's also one of the older HTML elements you still find, all too frequently, in web pages. It's not surprising that font and text properties were of such interest in building web pages. Few changes you can make to an element's style attributes can have such an effect as changing the text or font properties.

Notice I say text or font properties. The font has to do with the characters themselves: their family, size, type, and other elements of the characters' appearance. The text attributes, though, have more to do with decoration attached to the text and include text decoration, alignment, and so on.

Font Style Properties

There are several style attributes for fonts. Their CSS name and the associated Java-Script-accessible style attribute are given in the following list:

font-family
> Access it as fontFamily in JavaScript. This adjusts the font family (such as Serif, Arial, Verdana) for the font. When specifying a multiword font family, type the family name exactly; this includes spaces.

font-size
> Access it as fontSize in JavaScript. This sets the size of the font. You can use different units when setting the font size. If you use em or pt with the size (such as 12pt or 2.5em), the font is resized according to the web-page reader's personal settings. If you use px (pixel), the font is maintained at that size regardless of user settings. Specify some unit when setting font-size with JavaScript or use one of the predefined font sizes of xx-small, x-small, small, medium, large, x-large, and xx-large. You can also use relative sizing, smaller or larger, in addition to using a percentage based on the parent element.

font-size-adjust
> Access it as fontSizeAdjust. This is the ratio between the height of the letter x, and the height specified in font-size. This setting preserves this ratio, though it's rarely given.

font-stretch
> Access it as fontStretch. Expands or contracts the font. You can use one of the following: normal, wider, narrower, ultra-condensed, extra-condensed, condensed, semi-condensed, semi-expanded, expanded, ultra-expanded, or extra-expanded.

font-style
> Access it as fontStyle. You can use normal (default), italic, or oblique.

font-variant

> Access it as `fontVariant`. Use `small-caps` as a value if you want to use the small-cap variant of the font.

font-weight

> Access it as `fontWeight`. Set the font's weight (boldness). Use normal, `bold`, `bolder`, `lighter`, or a numeric of 100, 200, 300, 400, 500, 600, 700, 800, or 900.

As Example 12-1 demonstrated, changing the font of an element changes the font for all text contained within that element unless overridden by the style settings of a contained element—the cascade part of Cascading Style Sheets. This is inherent to the behavior of CSS; using JavaScript to change the font dynamically has no impact on this effect.

You can change many of the font attributes all at once using just font itself. In the following code:

```
div.style.font="italic small-caps 400 14px verdana";
```

The font attribute is used without any subproperty to set the style, variant, weight, size, and font-family. Many of the CSS properties have shortcut methods such as this. They're assigned in JavaScript just as they would be in CSS. In CSS, all the settings are to the right of the colon. In JS, everything that's to the right of the colon is included in the quotes on the right side of the assignment statement.

The Text Properties

For this chapter, I decided to group several attributes that affect the appearance of text, though unlike font, they're not part of the same family. The CSS text attributes I most often set are:

color

> Access it as `color`. Color for the text.

line-height

> Access it in JavaScript as `lineHeight`. The space from the top of one line to the bottom of another. Specify a value in a manner similar to specifying the font size, or use normal.

text-decoration

> Access it as `textDecoration`. Use none, underline, overline, or line-through. Please don't use `blink`.

text-indent

> Access it as `textIndent`. How much to indent the first line of text.

text-transform

> Access it as `textTransform`. Use none, capitalize (to capitalize every word), uppercase, or lowercase.

white-space

> Access it as whiteSpace. Use normal, pre, or nowrap.

direction

> Access it as direction. Use ltr (left to right) or rtl (right to left).

text-align

> Access it as textAlign. How the text contents are aligned. Use left, right, center, or justify.

word-spacing

> Access it as wordSpacing. Amount of spacing between words. Use normal, or specify a length.

What are typical uses for modifying font and/or text properties? You can expand a block of text to make it more legible, or highlight the data for some reason. In Example 12-3, clicking on one of two links will either make a text block very large, as well as justified, or will return it to what it was previously.

Example 12-3. Modifying a text block

```
<!DOCTYPE html PUBLIC "-//W3C//DTD XHTML 1.0 Transitional//EN"
"http://www.w3.org/TR/xhtml1/DTD/xhtml1-transitional.dtd">
<html>
<head>
<title>Read THIS</title>
<meta http-equiv="Content-Type" content="text/html; charset=utf-8" />
<script type="text/javascript">
//<![CDATA[

function makeMore( ) {
  var div = document.getElementById("div1");
  div.style.fontSize="larger";
  div.style.letterSpacing="10px";
  div.style.textAlign="justify";
  div.style.textTransform="uppercase";
  div.style.fontSize="xx-large";
  div.style.fontWeight="900";
  div.style.lineHeight="40px";
}

function makeLess( ) {
  var div = document.getElementById("div1");
  div.style.fontSize="smaller";
  div.style.letterSpacing="normal";
  div.style.textAlign="left";
  div.style.textTransform="none";
  div.style.fontSize="medium";
  div.style.fontWeight="normal";
  div.style.lineHeight="normal";
}
//]]>
</script>

</head>
```

Example 12-3. Modifying a text block (continued)

```
<body>
<p>
<a href="" onclick="makeMore( ); return false;">Make it more</a> <a href=""
onclick="makeLess( ); return false;">Make it less</a>
</p>
<div id="div1">
<p>
One of the first presentation-specific HTML elements was font, and it's also one of the
older HTML elements you still find, all too frequently, in web pages. It's not surprising
that font and text properties were of such interest in building web pages. Few changes you
can make to an element's style attributes can have such an effect as changing the text or
font properties. </p><p>Notice I say text or font properties. The font has to do with the
characters themselves: their family, size, type, and other elements of the characters'
appearance. The text attributes, though, have more to do with decoration attached to the
text and include text decoration, alignment, and so on.</p>
</div>
</body>
</html>
```

Chances are you wouldn't increase the text as large as this example, but it does show what kind of transformation you can create using JavaScript and CSS. Another typical use is to change the font color of a text field associated with a form element or block of text to show it doesn't apply; to literally "gray" out the font.

Position and Movement

Before CSS, if you wanted to control the layout of the page with any consistency, you had to use an HTML table. As for any form of animation, you either had to use something such as an animated GIF or a plug-in such as Flash.

Netscape and Microsoft together helped bring an end to all of this with the co-introduction of a specification called the CSS-P, or CSS Positioning. Consider the page as a graph, with both x- and y-coordinates. With CSS-P, you can set an element's position within this coordinate system. Add JavaScript, and you can move elements about the page.

The proposed CSS-P attributes were eventually incorporated into the CSS2 specification. The positioning properties in CSS2 include the following:

position

> The position property takes one of five values: relative, absolute, static, inherit, or fixed. static positioning is the default setting for most elements. This means they're part of the page flow, and other elements in the page impact the element's position, and it impacts all elements that follow. relative positioning is similar except that the element is offset from its normal position. A position set to absolute takes the element out of the page flow, allowing you to set its position absolutely in the page. This also allows you to layer elements, one on

top of another, just by positioning them in the same location. A `fixed` position is similar to absolute positioning, except the element is positioned relative to some viewport. For most DHTML efforts, you'll mainly use `absolute` or `relative` positioning.

top

In the web-page coordinate system, the value of x starts at the top and is zero. It increases as you travel down the container, whether that container is the page or another element. Setting an element's `top` property sets its position relative to the top of the container.

left

In the web-page coordinate system, the value of y starts at the left and is zero. It increases as you travel across the container to the right. Setting an element's `left` property sets its position relative to the `left` side of the container.

bottom

The `bottom` property has as its zero value the bottom of the page. Higher values move the element up the page.

right

The `right` property has as its zero value the right side of the page. Higher values move the element towards the left.

z-index

You may want to add the `z-index`. If you draw a line perpendicular to the page, this is the z-index. As mentioned earlier, with `absolute` positioning, elements can be layered on one another. Their position within the stack is controlled by one of two things: the first is its position in the page. Elements defined later in the web page are located higher in the stack; earlier elements, lower in the stack. This can be overridden using `z-index`. Both negative and positive integers can be used, with a value of 0 being the normal rendering layer (relative positioning), negative pushing an element lower than this, and `positive`, higher.

The `display` attribute also influences both positioning and layout, but it's covered later in the section "Display, Visibility, and Opacity." The attribute `float` is also involved in positioning, but it doesn't play well with DHTML so I won't cover it.

The `top`, `right`, `bottom`, and `left` properties, as well as `z-index`, work only if `position` is set to `absolute`. Elements can be set outside the page by setting any of the properties to a negative value. Elements can also be moved based on events, such as mouse clicks.

One DHTML effect is a *fly-in*, where elements seem to literally "fly in" from the sides of the document. This is a good approach for tutorials or other efforts in which you want to introduce one topic after another, based on a mouse click or keyboard entry from the web-page reader.

Example 12-4 demonstrates a fly-in with three elements coming from the top left. A timer is used to create the movement and reset each round until the x, the top value, is greater than a value (200 + a value × the number of the element, to create an overlap). The elements are hidden when they are originally positioned off the page, to the left and top, because setting elements beyond the page to the right or bottom results in a scrollbar being added to the page.

Example 12-4. Element positioning and movement with fly-ins

```
<!DOCTYPE html PUBLIC "-//W3C//DTD XHTML 1.0 Transitional//EN"
"http://www.w3.org/TR/xhtml1/DTD/xhtml1-transitional.dtd">
<html>
<head>
<title>Fly-Ins</title>
<meta http-equiv="Content-Type" content="text/html; charset=utf-8" />
<style type="text/css">

div { padding: 10px; }

#div1 { background-color: #00f;
        color: #fff;
        font-size: larger;
        position: absolute;
        width: 400px;
        height: 200px;
        left: -410px;
        top: -400px;
        }
#div2 { background-color: #ff0;
        color: #;
        font-size: larger;
        position: absolute;
        width: 400px;
        height: 200px;
        left: -410px;
        top: -400px;
        }
#div3 { background-color: #f00;
        color: #fff;
        font-size: larger;
        position: absolute;
        width: 400px;
        height: 200px;
        left: -410px;
        top: -400px;
        }
</style>
<script type="text/javascript">
//<![CDATA[

var element = ["div1","div2","div3"];
```

Example 12-4. Element positioning and movement with fly-ins (continued)

```
function next() {
    setTimeout("moveBlock()",1000);
}

var x = 0;
var y = 0;
var elem = 0;
function moveBlock() {
    x+=20;
    y+=20;
    var obj = document.getElementById(element[elem]);
    obj.style.top = x + "px";
    obj.style.left = y + "px";
    if (x < (100 + elem * 60)) {
        setTimeout("moveBlock()", 100);
    } else {
        elem++;
        x = 0; y = 0;
    }
}
//]]>
</script>

</head>
<body>
<p>
<a href="javascript:next();">Next slide</a>
</p>
<div id="div1">
Now is the time for all good wo-men to come to the aid of their country.
</div>
<div id="div2">
99 bottles of beer on the wall, 99 bottles of beer.<br />
Take one down, pass it around, 98 bottles of beer one...
</div>
<div id="div3">
web 2.0 WEB 2.0 WeB 2222....OOOO<br />
I'm so cool,
<h2>Learning JavaScript!</h2>
</div>
</body>
</html>
```

The text in the examples is a bit of nonsense, but with a little design polish and more appropriate writing, it's an effective presentation technique. Figure 12-2 shows a screen capture of the page, opened in Safari.

To make the page more accessible, the link can be changed to open up pages with the fly-in information. Alternatively, all three information blocks could be positioned in the page, and script used to hide them only if JavaScript is enabled.

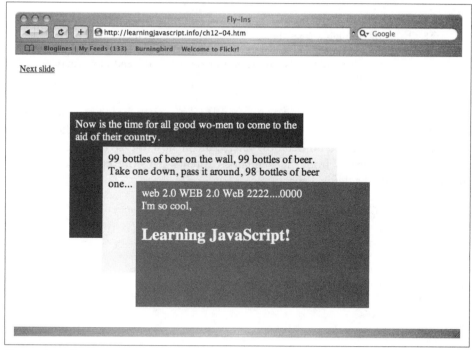

Figure 12-2. Fly-in page

Another common use of DHTML associated with movement has as much to do with tracking the movement of the web-page reader as it does elements in the page. The technique is called *drag and drop*, and it's discussed next.

Drag and Drop

One DHTML item that generated much interest when it was first introduced was drag and drop. Shopping-cart examples popped up all over, including a few variations of my own. I even created a drag-and-drop game.

Over time, though, we saw that much of the interest in drag and drop did not manifest itself in applications. I rarely see a drag-and-drop application in effect, and when I do see one, I tend to be irritated. Why? It's not always that easy to do drag and drop; especially if you're using a trackpad or a text-to-speech browser.

What reawakened the interest in drag and drop was Google Maps' use of the technique to allow you to move a map around within a constrained space. It was the first time I'd seen a really effective use of drag and drop. We'll take a look at Google Maps and its associated API in Chapter 13, but for now, let's look at implementing our own, very tiny emulation of drag-and-drop technology.

What makes the Google Maps approach really exciting is that as you scroll through a map, the application actually pulls up the next pieces from the server and integrates them into the page using a caching mechanism. With this, you seem to never reach the end of the map. It's really well done.

In Example 12-5, a DIV element is created, and a screenshot from the book is embedded within the element. In addition to drag and drop, it also uses the `overflow` attribute. You'll see more on overflow later, but for now the DIV element is set to hide or *clip* the overflow from the element's contents. This prevents any overlap of the image outside the defined space.

Example 12-5. The GoogleMap effect: drag and drop of object in a container

```
<!DOCTYPE html PUBLIC "-//W3C//DTD XHTML 1.0 Transitional//EN"
"http://www.w3.org/TR/xhtml1/DTD/xhtml1-transitional.dtd">
<html>
<head>
<title>GoogleMapEffect</title>
<meta http-equiv="Content-Type" content="text/html; charset=utf-8" />
<style type="text/css">
#div1 {
        overflow: hidden;
        position: absolute;
        top: 100px;
        left: 100px;
        border: 5px solid #000;
        width: 400px;
        height: 200px;
}
img {
        border: 1px solid #000;
    }
</style>

<script type="text/javascript">
//<![CDATA[

// global variables
var dragObject  = null;
var mouseOffset = null;

// capture mouse events
document.onmousemove = mouseMove;
document.onmouseup   = mouseUp;

// create a mouse point
function mousePoint(x,y) {
   this.x = x;
   this.y = y;
}
```

```
// find mouse position
function mousePosition(evnt){
  var x = parseInt(evnt.clientX);
  var y = parseInt(evnt.clientY);
  return new mousePoint(x,y);
}

// get element's offset position within page
function getMouseOffset(target, evnt){
   evnt = evnt || window.event;
   var mousePos  = mousePosition(evnt);

   var x = mousePos.x - target.offsetLeft;
   var y = mousePos.y - target.offsetTop;
   return new mousePoint(x,y);
}

// turn off dragging
function mouseUp(evnt){
   dragObject = null;
}

// capture mouse move, only if dragging
function mouseMove(evnt){
   if (!dragObject) return;
   evnt = evnt || window.event;
   var mousePos = mousePosition(evnt);

   // if draggable, set new absolute position
   if(dragObject){
      dragObject.style.position = 'absolute';

      dragObject.style.top    = mousePos.y - mouseOffset.y + "px";
      dragObject.style.left   = mousePos.x - mouseOffset.x + "px";
      return false;
   }
}

// make object draggable
function makeDraggable(item){
   if (item) {
      item = document.getElementById(item);
      item.onmousedown = function(evnt) {
                     dragObject  = this;
                     mouseOffset = getMouseOffset(this, evnt);
                     return false; };
   }
}

//]]>
</script>
</head>
```

Example 12-5. The GoogleMap effect: drag and drop of object in a container (continued)

```
<body onload="makeDraggable('img1');">
<div id="div1" >
<img id="img1" src="fig01-1.jpg" />
</div>
</body>
</html>
```

This is the most complex example we've had so far in the book, so let's take the Java-Script from the top:

- Two global objects are created: dragObject and mouseOffset. The former is the object being dragged; the latter is the object's *offset* value. The offset is the object's position relative to a container, in this instance, the page. We also capture the mousemove and mouseup events for the document and assign them to event handlers, mouseMove and mouseUp.

- The next is an object, mousePoint. This just wraps the two mouse coordinates: *x* and *y*. Creating an object makes it easier to pass around both values.

- The next function is mousePosition. This function accesses the target object's clientX and clientY values and returns a mousePoint object representing the object's *x* and *y* location relative to the client area of the window, excluding all the chrome. The parseInt function ensures the values are returned as numerics.

- Following is getMouseOffset, which takes as parameters an object target and an event. Once the event object has been normalized past the cross-browser differences, the mouse position of the event is set to the function just discussed, mousePoint. This is then modified against the object's offsetLeft and offsetTop properties. If we didn't do this bit of computation, the object would move with the mouse, but there would most likely be an odd jerking motion, and the object would seem to float above, below, or to the side of the mouse. Once normalized, it's used to create a normalized mousePoint, which is returned from the object.

- The next function is mouseUp, and all it does is turn off dragging by setting dragObject to null. Following is the mouseMove function, where most of the dragging computation occurs. In this function, if the dragging object isn't set, the function is exited. Otherwise, the normalized mouse position is found, the object is set to absolute positioning, and its left and top properties are set (after again being adjusted for offset).

- The last function is makeDraggable, which just makes the object passed to the function into a draggable one. This means adding a function for the object's mousedown event, which sets the drag object to the object, and gets the object's offset value.

Seems like a lot of code, but it's actually much simpler than it used to be with the older browsers because most modern browsers share the same properties when it comes to positioning. Rah for that, because drag and drop is hard enough without the extra challenge. Again, Google Maps adds an extra element of sophistication by using Ajax to continuously refresh the map, so you never run out. That's a little bit beyond this book, though. Consider it a future personal challenge.

Size and Clipping

An element's size is controlled through a set of six CSS attributes. The first two, width and height, are the most common and are used to set the absolute width and height of the element. The other four—min-height, min-width, max-height, max-width—are handy CSS attributes (particularly when working with images), but not commonly used in dynamic effects.

> Actually, an element's width and height are factors of several attributes, including the element's border, margin, padding, and content. All combined, these provide a CSS "box model" associated with block elements—elements that force a line break before and after. Read more on the box model at the W3C page, "Box model," at *http://www.w3.org/TR/REC-CSS2/box.htm*.

If the element's contents are too large for the element, the overflow is managed through the CSS overflow attribute, which can be set to visible (render all of the content and overflow the element boundaries); hidden (clip the content); scroll (clip the content, and scrollbars are provided); and auto (clip and provide scrollbars only if some of the content is hidden).

> Why even set the element's height? After all, if the height is not defined, and the overflow not set to clip, the element automatically resizes to fit the content.
>
> If you have content in two columns, laid out side by side, you might want to set the heights of the columns so that one isn't excessively longer than the other.

Overflow and Dynamic Content

When an element's contents are replaced dynamically, either through an Ajax call or some other event, the fit of the content within the element could change dramatically. One approach to ensure that the content is always accessible is to set the overflow to auto. If the content is too large, scrollbars are then provided. In Example 12-6, two blocks are given: one with a lot of text, one with little. The dimensions of both elements are set to safely hold their content when the page is loaded. However, there's a link that switches the content: small to large, large to small. In the CSS, the overflow for the second element is set to auto.

Example 12-6. Changing content and the impact of the overflow setting

```
<!DOCTYPE html PUBLIC "-//W3C//DTD XHTML 1.0 Transitional//EN"
"http://www.w3.org/TR/xhtml1/DTD/xhtml1-transitional.dtd">
<html>
<head>
<title>Overflow</title>
<meta http-equiv="Content-Type" content="text/html; charset=utf-8" />
<style type="text/css">
#div1 { width: 700px; height: 150px }
#div2 { width: 600px; height: 100px; overflow: auto }
</style>

<script type="text/javascript">
//<![CDATA[

function switchContent() {
    var div1 = document.getElementById("div1").innerHTML;
    var div2 = document.getElementById("div2").innerHTML;
    document.getElementById("div1").innerHTML = div2;
    document.getElementById("div2").innerHTML = div1;
}

//]]>
</script>

</head>
<body>
<p>
<a href="javascript:switchContent();">Switch</a>
</p>
<div id="div1">
<p>
One of the first presentation-specific HTML elements was font, and it's also one of the
older HTML elements you still find, all too frequently, in web pages. It's not surprising
that font and text properties were of such interest in building web pages. Few changes you
can make to an element's style attributes can have such an effect as changing the text or
font properties. </p>
<p>
Notice I say text or font properties. The font has to do with the characters themselves:
their family, size, type, and other elements of the characters' appearance. The text
attributes, though, have more to do with decoration attached to the text and include text
decoration, alignment, and so on.</p>
</div>
<div id="div2">
<p>Smaller item.</p>
</div>
</body>
</html>
```

When the content is switched, the first block contains little text and a large whitespace around it. The only way to alter this is to change the dimensions of the box. Unfortunately, in a real-world example, you may not be able to easily determine the appropriate fit for the new content.

The second box, though, suddenly has a scrollbar to the right, which allows you to scroll through the content. Rather than trying to resize the box by guesswork, setting the overflow to auto and triggering a scrollbar is a better approach. This way, the box is relatively stable in the page, other elements aren't continuously being pushed about, large blocks with whitespace don't result, and the content is still accessible.

Another approach to dealing with changing content is to resize the block using the read-only properties offsetWidth and offsetHeight to determine the actual size of the content. There is a cross-browser difference, though, when using these properties. Internet Explorer includes any border and padding in the block size, while Mozilla/Firefox provides just the size necessary for the content.

 You can also access the computed width and height of an element using the getStyle method defined earlier, using width and height instead of backgroundColor.

Though width and height control the size of the element, they don't always control what's visible of the element. That can also be controlled by the clipping rectangle associated with the element.

The Clipping Rectangle

According to the W3C, a clipping region:

> …defines what portion of an element's rendered content is visible. By default, the clipping region has the same size and shape as the element's box(es). However, the clipping region may be modified by the clip property. (From the W3C's "Visual Effects" at *http://www.w3.org/TR/REC-CSS2/visufx.html.*)

The CSS clip property specifies a shape and the dimensions of that shape. At this time, the only shape supported is a rectangle, designated with rect and defined by four dimensions: top, right, bottom, and left.

```
clip: rect(topval, rightval, bottomval, leftval);
```

The clipping region constrains how much of the actual element content is displayed. It also requires that the position attribute be set to absolute.

If an element is 200 pixels wide and 300 pixels long, a clipping region of rect(0px,200px,300px,0px) doesn't clip any of the block—depending, of course, on whether the element has a border or other setting that can alter the effective height and width. A clipping region of rect(10px,190px,290px,10px) clips 10 pixels off each side. Note that incrementing the value for the top and left sides, but decrementing the value for bottom and right, results in clipping.

From a DHTML perspective, clipping can be used to create any form of scrolling effect, whether paired with element movement or not. It can also create the new "accordion effect" that's become so popular (demonstrated in Chapter 14).

Example 12-7 demonstrates a simple use of clipping to create a drop-down animated item. Clicking on the header for the item either expands or collapses the item, depending on its current state. A timer is used to animate the effect; you can also set the full display or hide with each click, and skip the timer.

Example 12-7. Drop-down animation created using a timer and clipping

```
<!DOCTYPE html PUBLIC "-//W3C//DTD XHTML 1.0 Transitional//EN""http://www.w3.org/TR/
xhtml1/DTD/xhtml1-transitional.dtd">
<html>
<head>
<title>Simple Clip Scroll</title>
<meta http-equiv="Content-Type" content="text/html; charset=utf-8" />
<style type="text/css">

#data1     {
           position: absolute;
           top: 100px; left: 100px;
           padding: 0;
           width: 200px;
           height: 200px;
           background-color: #ff0;
           clip: rect(0px,200px,200px,0px);
           }

#data1 h3 {
           margin: 0; padding: 5px;
           font-size: smaller;
           background-color: #006;
           color: #fff;
           }

#contained {
           margin: 10px
           }

</style>

<script type="text/javascript">
//<![CDATA[

var bottom = 200;
var hidden = false;
var obj = null;
function clipItem( ) {
  obj = document.getElementById("data1");
  if (hidden) {
      showItem( );
  } else {
      hideItem( );
  }
}
```

Example 12-7. Drop-down animation created using a timer and clipping (continued)

```
function hideItem( ) {
   bottom-=20;
   var clip = "rect(0px,200px," + bottom + "px,0px)";
   obj.style.clip = clip;
   if (bottom == 20) {
      hidden=true;
   } else {
      setTimeout("hideItem( )",100);
   }
}

function showItem( ) {
   bottom+=20;
   var clip = "rect(0px,200px," + bottom + "px,0px)";
   obj.style.clip=clip;
   if (bottom == 200) {
      hidden=false;
   } else {
      setTimeout("showItem( )",100);
   }
}

//]]>
</script>
</head>
<body>
<div id="data1">
<h3 onclick="clipItem( );">Click to expand or collapse</h3>
<div id="contained">
This is the text contained within the div block.
</div>
</div>
</body>
</html>
```

Notice that rather than get the clipping value directly from the style property to test state, I use a global variable. You'll want to do this as much as possible with your animated DHTML effects; a variable get is cheaper than an object get, especially one that must work across browsers.

Display, Visibility, and Opacity

An interesting thing about web-page elements: they can be completely transparent and invisible, but still affect the layout of the page. The reason is that invisibility/transparency and display/lack of display are not the same thing in CSS.

An element can be hidden by setting visibility to hidden, or shown by setting visibility to visible. The property can also be set to inherit, and the element inherits its visible property setting from the containing element.

As demonstrated in Chapter 11, an element's opacity can also be altered until it is completely transparent, making it invisible. However, just as with the `visibility` property, the element still maintains its position within the page flow.

If an element's `display` property is set to `none`, it's also hidden; however, any effect the element has on the page layout is also removed. To make it visible, you have a couple of options. You can make it `visible` and have it act as a block-level element (line breaks before and after the element) by setting `display` to `block`. If you don't want block behavior, you can set `display` to `inline`, and it's displayed in-place and not as a block.

In addition, you can display the element using the default display characteristics of several HTML elements, which include `inline-block`, `table`, `table-cell`, `list-item`, `compact`, `run-in`, etc. It's a rather powerful attribute, and one worth playing around with until you're comfortable with its modifying results.

Right Tool for Right Effect

Given all these various ways to hide and display elements, which method should be used for what effect?

If you're absolutely positioning an element and then hiding and showing it based on an event such as a mouse click or form submission, use the `visibility` property. It's simple and easy to use, and an absolutely positioned element is removed from the page flow regardless. Use `visibility`, then, for just-in-time help.

If the content that's hidden should push down the page elements that follow when it's displayed, such as clicking a collapsed option list when filling out a form, then use `display`, switching between a display value of `none` and a display value of `block`. Use `display` to hide and show form fields to get user input.

If you're creating a fade effect or want to de-emphasize a page element, use the `opacity` property. You may eventually adjust it so that it's completely transparent, but usually only after an animated fade of whatever duration. Use `opacity` to empha-size and provide visual information. `opacity` can also be used to signal a transition, as demonstrated with the photo slideshow in Chapter 11.

 A note on using visual effects for information purposes: these effects should also include some textual element, so that people using non-visual browsers or ones with limited visual capability also receive the same level of notification. Never rely completely on a visual effect to provide feedback.

Time, then, for a little live action.

Just-in-Time Information

Some of the best sites I've visited provide some form of help any time information is requested from the web-page reader. Even if you're asking a person's name, you want to provide an explanation of the privacy controls in place and how that data is used.

You can provide a tooltip type of help by setting the `title` attribute of a link surrounding the field label, but this usually constrains how much information you can include. You can also pop up a dialog with information, and this is especially helpful if the information is long and detailed, with a description of options. But for those in-between cases where you have more than a little information, but less than a lot, it would be nice to include this information directly in the page.

For the most part, though, forms take up most of the space, and a lot of text can make the page seem cluttered. One approach then is to put the information in the page, but have it show up based on some event.

This is one of the more useful DHTML effects you can create, and also one of the easiest. Example 12-8 shows the page, including two form elements, each of which has a hidden help block. In the script, when the label for the element is clicked, if any item's help is already showing, the visible help is hidden and the new help block is shown.

Example 12-8. Using hidden help fields

```
<!DOCTYPE html PUBLIC "-//W3C//DTD XHTML 1.0 Transitional//EN"
"http://www.w3.org/TR/xhtml1/DTD/xhtml1-transitional.dtd">
<html>
<head>
<title>In-Place Help</title>
<meta http-equiv="Content-Type" content="text/html; charset=utf-8" />
<style type="text/css">

.help { position: absolute;
        left: 300px;
        top: 20px;
        visibility: hidden;
        width: 100px;
        padding: 10px;
        border: 1px solid #f00;
      }

form { margin: 20px; background-color: #DFE1CB;
        padding: 20px; width: 200px }
form a {color: #060; text-decoration: none }
form a:hover {cursor : help}
</style>

<script type="text/javascript">
//<![CDATA[

var item = null;
```

Example 12-8. Using hidden help fields (continued)

```
function showHelp(newItem) {
    if (item) {
        item.style.visibility='hidden';
    }
    item = document.getElementById(newItem);
    item.style.visibility='visible';
}

//]]>
</script>
</head>
<body>
<form>
<label><a href="javascript:showHelp('item1')" alt="get help">Item One</a></label>
<input type="text"><br /><br />
<label><a href="javascript:showHelp('item2')" alt="get help">Item Two</a></label>
<input type="text">
</form>
<div id="item1" class="help">
This is the help for the first item. It only shows when you click on the label for the
item.
</div>
<div id="item2" class="help">
This is the help for the second item. It only shows when you click on the label for the
item.
</div>
</body>
</html>
```

I also added a little CSS sugar to make the page taste better. The form is set with a color background, a help block is outlined in red, and when the mouse cursor is over the input label for each item, the cursor icon is set to the help icon. This typically looks like an arrow with a little question mark, or just the question mark itself. This is also a very inexpensive way to provide a hint to the web-page reader—as is the alt tag that says "get help." Figure 12-3 demonstrates this hidden help system.

Collapsing Forms

Having to split forms functionality across many pages is a pain, but a page with too many form elements displayed at once can be unreadable.

In addition, in-place editing of data has been growing in popularity; titles for data sections are activated for the person who owns the data, and clicking on these titles opens up a form or input fields in which that section of the data can be changed.

Both situations are rich with potential for using *collapsible forms*. These are forms or form sections that are hidden in the page; they display only when something is activated. And not just display: they push other data out of the way, occupying the same room the form would normally occupy if displayed.

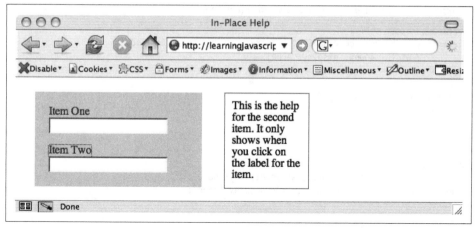

Figure 12-3. In-place help using the visibility property

Google, Flickr, and a host of companies use this type of collapsible content. Considering that it's also one of the easiest to make accessible, it's not surprising. If JavaScript is not enabled, the event handling associated with the titles that would normally display the content is not active, and the forms don't open. Menu items can be added to open a separate page for the form, or perhaps even displayed with the noscript tag.

The last example of this chapter, Example 12-9, demonstrates a collapsible form. In this case, it's a stacked set of form-element blocks. Clicking on the label for each either hides it if it's currently displayed, or shows it if not. For non-JavaScript-enabled browsers, the titles of both blocks are surrounded by hypertext links; clicking on the link, ostensibly, takes you to a separate static form. For pages with JavaScript, a return value of false as an onclick event for the links cancels its default behavior. You can actually see this when you disable JavaScript: clicking the link alters the page URL to reflect the URI fragment (*#name* or *#address*). However, when scripting is enabled, you won't see this, but you will see the form display.

Example 12-9. Implementing a collapsable form

```
<!DOCTYPE html PUBLIC "-//W3C//DTD XHTML 1.0 Transitional//EN"
"http://www.w3.org/TR/xhtml1/DTD/xhtml1-transitional.dtd">
<html>
<head>
<title>Collapsing Forms</title>
<meta http-equiv="Content-Type" content="text/html; charset=utf-8" />
<style type="text/css">

.label { background-color: #003; width: 400px; border-right: 1px solid #fff;
        padding: 10px; margin: 0 20px; color: #fff; text-align: center;
        border-bottom: 1px solid #fff;}
```

Example 12-9. Implementing a collapsable form (continued)

```
.label a { color: #fff }
.elements { background-color: #CCD9FF; margin: 0 20px; padding: 10px;
            width: 400px; display: none}
</style>

<script type="text/javascript">
//<![CDATA[

window.onload=setup;

function setup( ) {
    document.getElementById('one').style.display='none';
    document.getElementById('two').style.display='none';
}

function show(newItem) {
    var item = document.getElementById(newItem);
    if (item.style.display=='none') {
        item.style.display='block';
    } else {
        item.style.display='none';
    }
}

//]]>
</script>
</head>
<body>
<form action="GET">
<div class="label" onclick="show('one')">
<a href="#name" onclick="return false">Name</a>
</div>
<div class="elements" id="one">
<label>First Name:</label><br /><input type="text" name="firstname" /><br /><br />
<label>Last Name:</label><br /><input type="text" name="lastname" /><br /><br />
</div>
<div class="label" onclick="show('two')">
<a href="#address" onclick="return false">Address</a>
</div>
<div class="elements" id="two">
<label>Street Address:</label><br /><input type="text" name="street" /><br /><br />
<label>City:</label><br /><input type="text" name="city" /><br /><br />
<label>State:</label><br /><input type="text" name="state" /><br /><br />
</div>
</form>

<p>Other data or information.</p>
</body>
</html>
```

Again, this is the type of functionality you want to add to your web pages. It's simple, impressive-looking, and relatively easy to convert into non-JavaScript alternatives if scripting is turned off.

I've barely scratched the surface on what you can do with JavaScript and CSS. Hopefully, though, this provides you with a good starting point. Chapter 13 introduces you to the basics of Ajax; following, we'll look at combining Ajax and DHTML effects for powerful applications.

Questions

1. You access the text color of an element in JavaScript using `obj.style.color`, but no value is returned. You know it's been set in a stylesheet. Why is there no returned value, and how would you change the application to get a value?

2. Given text in a DIV block, how would you change it to display in a 14pt font, with a red color and a line height of 16pt?

3. If the above change didn't work, what could be causing the effect to fail?

4. What are two ways to cause a block to disappear?

5. If drag and drop isn't an effective shopping-cart technique, what DHTML effect would be handy for this type of service?

Answers are provided in the appendix.

CHAPTER 13
Moving Outside the Page with Ajax

Some consider it the next best Web; others consider it hype. Whatever the opinion, Ajax, or AJAX (Asynchronous JavaScript And XML), as some prefer, has led to a greater interest in JavaScript in general and dynamic JavaScript functionality specifically.

For all the shiny newness of the interest, none of the technologies associated with Ajax are new. It's dependent on JavaScript, which has been around since the mid-90s. It's also dependent on the Document Object Model; standard web technologies such as CSS, XHTML, and XML; and the XMLHttpRequest object, all of which were introduced years before the term Ajax was coined.

What is new is the fact that a concept was introduced for a type of development, coinciding with newer browsers, all of which enable the necessary functionality. In other words, the time was ready for the technology; all that was needed was someone to notice, package it, and promote its use. That someone was Jesse James Garrett in his publication, "Ajax: A New Approach to Web Applications" (at *http://www.adaptivepath.com/publications/essays/archives/000385.php*).

Where the Ajax examples in this chapter differ from examples in previous chapters is that Ajax does require a server component. Ruby is a popular choice of programming language for Ajax development, but any server-side language that can process the specialized Ajax requests will work. The examples in this chapter use PHP, primarily because of all the languages, it's most similar to JavaScript, as well as being one of the most common server-side scripting languages in use. In Chapter 14, we'll take a look at Ruby and Ajax libraries.

AJAX? Or Ajax? When Garrett introduced the concept, he used Ajax. If Ajax is an acronym, it should then be AJAX. Or perhaps, more accurately, AJaX. However, Garrett introduced the term as a nickname, not an acronym, and the acronym appeared later as people tried to figure out what led to the name.

There is no right or wrong choice—they're all just terms—and since the popular use is Ajax, I'll use this for the rest of the book. Besides, it's easier than having to hold down the Shift key every time I type the word.

Ajax: It's Not Only Code

Ajax provides a huge bang for the buck, especially when you really need the functionality. The first time your web-page form is validated in place, you'll see what I mean. When you can click on a button and collapse a huge form, clearing up the clutter on the page, you'll be convinced Ajax is the One True Way.

Well, yes and no. Ajax, like other JavaScript-enabled applications, has its pluses and minuses.

PermaWhat?

If you wanted to, you could create an entire web site in one page, using Ajax and other JavaScript-enabled and replace functionality based on your web-page reader's actions. However, the problem with this is that it becomes increasingly difficult to recreate a specific view of the content.

Ajax, like all DHTML functionality, does not create permanent page effects. They have to be recreated each time a page is loaded, or each time a person makes a sequence of movements. They may not be accessible via source or printable.

There will be no permalink to individual pieces, nor will your web-page readers have a history of their actions.

Most of all, when your web-page reader hits the Back key, rather than being taken in a reverse direction within the Ajax/DHTML display stack, chances are she will be taken completely out of the page.

There are entire frameworks that have taken on these issues, with solutions such as resolving an anchor-tag release into a sequence of Ajax calls and/or DHTML. However, for the most part, before you look into these, you should ask whether having this capability is essential to your work. Again, if Ajax and DHTML are complementary approaches available to help other more traditional work, then chances are you have what you need with existing technology; you won't have to add what could be large libraries. For instance, if Ajax and DHTML are used to dynamically validate a form as it's being completed, a bookmark to the form page should be sufficient.

One of the first and most common uses of JavaScript was to build menus. This is both sad and funny because one aspect of your site that should be completely accessible—no matter by whom or by what browser—is site navigation. JavaScript navigation breaks most accessibility tools.

One of the best pages on Ajax and accessibility is the WebAIM (Web Accessibility in Mind) page on the topic at *http://www.webaim.org/ techniques/ajax/*. In addition to covering the issues, it also links to other sites that provide additional information.

Security and Workarounds

One of the reasons Ajax achieved such quick popularity is because it is relatively safe to use—as safe as most web applications (and requiring many of the same safeguards). The reason for its safety is the JavaScript sandbox and how it impacts on `XMLHttpRequest`.

In the examples, the server page is on the same server and domain as the page that made the request to the server. If I tried to put that server on another domain, I'd get an error. Why? Because Ajax operates under the JavaScript same source/same domain rule: you can only invoke services on the same server (domain) as the web page.

Internet Explorer has a setting that allows requests to other domains, but other browsers don't. Firefox supports digitally signed script and cross-domain work, but again, other browsers do not. This means you'll have to either restrict page accesses to one specific domain or find a workaround.

One approach is to work through a proxy. If a proxy is installed on the web server, all calls to the service can be made through the proxy, and the proxy then distributes them accordingly.

Other web services, such as Google and Yahoo!, encode the web-service requests within the script tag rather than use the `XMLHttpRequest`. In addition, you can have your web server rewrite a web request and redirect the calls to a different location. This requires `mod_rewrite` with Apache and other services with other web servers, but most sites support this capability.

Ajax Best Practices

Aside from the usual practices outlined for DHTML and sanitizing data coming into the applications, there really is only one specific best practice for Ajax: use it when it makes sense.

I am really fond of Ajax because I think it's a great way to validate form input in-page, and it quickly populates lists and drop-downs. However, I don't use it for all of my applications; accessibility issues, lack of permalinks, and history are all good reasons why I don't. More than that, there are many other application components that are currently in use; they are stable, simple to implement, and should continue to be used.

For instance, I wouldn't recommend using Ajax to get a number of rows from a database and build a table of the values. Why? Because using the server application to generate a table of data (either by outputting the values or through a template system) is easier and faster; the page can, typically, be bookmarked; and the query can be stored in history and, possibly, in the bookmark.

Other than the whizbang factor, Ajax doesn't add much to this type of functionality. However, Ajax is terrific when it comes to validating a login or other form content because you don't lose what you've already typed in.

As for using Ajax to create applications to replace word editors, I already have a terrific editor: NeoOffice, the Mac frontend to OpenOffice. I don't need a browser-based alternative; the huge majority of people don't. However, when I use my online weblog-editing tool, I like some of the Ajax features; for example, I can pull up categories only when I click a toolbar, and thus select a category other than the default.

In other words, Ajax is a tool. It is not a mindset, philosophy, or badge of coolness. Definitely use it, but only when it makes sense. As *Star Trek's* Scotty would say, "How many times do I have to say it? Use the right tool for the job."

Beam me up, Scotty.

How Ajax Works

Ajax is not as complicated as it may seem at first. A request needs to be sent to the server, a service invoked, and data returned. However, instead of submitting a form and loading a new page with the response, Ajax handles all of this activity within the context of the same page.

A special object, either Microsoft's `ActiveXObject` or the more general `XMLHttpRequest`, manages the asynchronous communication between the server and the client. Asynchronous means that the request is sent, but the client doesn't have to stop, hold, and wait for the process to finish; there is no twirly icon to signal *working* while you twiddle your thumbs. Instead, the client provides a function to be called when the state of the request changes. In this function, this state is checked; then, based on its value, as well as the status of the request, the data returned from the service is processed and usually output to the page in some form.

To the web-page reader, all of this activity looks as if the processing is happening within the page, rather than through client/server interaction. The only indicator that server access is happening is if this information is specifically provided.

Now that we've had the 10,000-foot view, let's look first at an Ajax application, and then go through the individual pieces in the rest of the chapter.

 Ajax does require a server-side component. I'm using PHP for this book because PHP is probably one of the most common scripting languages used today. Also, in my opinion, of all the server-side scripting languages available—Perl, Python, Ruby, and PHP—I consider PHP to be the most JavaScript-like.

Hello Ajax World!

You can use Ajax to populate a drop-down box based on a selection in another box. It's an on-demand solution that limits how often a database is accessed. It's also a very simple Ajax effect to create.

Example 13-1 contains the web page, including the script used to make the Ajax server call. The page also contains a form with two select elements: one populated with two states, the other empty.

Example 13-1. First Ajax application

```
<!DOCTYPE html PUBLIC "-//W3C//DTD XHTML 1.0 Transitional//EN"
"http://www.w3.org/TR/xhtml1/DTD/xhtml1-transitional.dtd">
<html>
<head>
<title>Hello Ajax World</title>
<meta http-equiv="Content-Type" content="text/html; charset=utf-8" />

<style type="text/css">
div.elem { margin: 20px; }
</style>

<script type="text/javascript">
//<![CDATA[

var xmlhttp = false;
if (window.XMLHttpRequest) {
   xmlhttp = new XMLHttpRequest();
   xmlhttp.overrideMimeType('text/xml');
} else if (window.ActiveXObject) {
   xmlhttp = new ActiveXObject("Microsoft.XMLHTTP");
}

function populateList() {
   var state = document.forms[0].elements[0].value;
   var url = 'ajax.php?state=' + state;
   xmlhttp.open('GET', url, true);
   xmlhttp.onreadystatechange = getCities;
   xmlhttp.send(null);

}

function getCities() {
   if(xmlhttp.readyState == 4 && xmlhttp.status == 200) {
      document.getElementById('cities').innerHTML = "<select>" + xmlhttp.responseText +
"</select>";
   } else {
      document.getElementById('cities').innerHTML = 'Error: preSearch Failed!';
   }
}
//]]>
</script>

</head>
```

Example 13-1. First Ajax application (continued)

```
<body>

<h3>Select State:</h3>
<form action="ajax.php" method="get">
<div class="elem">
<select onchange="populateList()">
<option value="CA">California</option>
<option value="MO">Missouri</option>
<option value="WA">Washington</option>
<option value="ID">Idaho</option>
</select>
</div>
<h3>Cities:</h3>
<div class="elem" id="cities">
<select>
</select>
</div>
</form>

</body>
</html>
```

In the code, the second select is surrounded by a DIV identified by cities. When the results are returned, this element's innerHTML is replaced with the new contents: either a select with the options returned by the web service, or an error message. Figure 13-1 shows the page before the Ajax call.

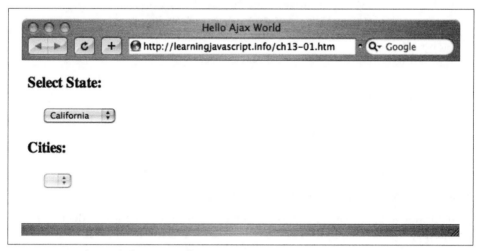

Figure 13-1. Web page before Ajax call

The server component of the application is listed in Example 13-2. Typically, this is a database request to look up cities, with more than two states listed. However, in the interest of keeping the example as self-contained as possible, the "cities" are created as a static string, based on the state selected.

Example 13-2. Server component of Ajax application in PHP

```php
<?php

//If no search string is passed, then we can't search
if(empty($_GET['state'])) {
    echo "No State Sent";
} else {
    //Remove whitespace from beginning & end of passed search.
    $search = trim($_GET['state']);
    switch($search) {
      case "MO" :
        $result = "<option value='St. Louis'>St. Louis</option>" .
                  "<option value='Kansas City'>Kansas City</option>";
        break;
      case "WA" :
        $result = "<option value='Seattle'>Seattle</option>" .
                  "<option value='Spokane'>Spokane</option>" .
                  "<option value='Olympia'>Olympia</option>";
        break;
      case "CA" :
        $result = "<option value='San Francisco'>San Francisco</option>" .
                  "<option value='Los Angeles'>Los Angeles</option>" .
                  "<option value='Web 2.0 City'>Web 2.0 City</option>" .
                  "<option value='barcamp'>BarCamp</option>";
        break;
      case "ID" :
        $result = "<option value='Boise'>Boise</option>";
        break;
      default :
        $result = "No Cities Found";
        break;
    }
    echo $result;
}
?>
```

Figure 13-2 shows the page after a state is selected.

In the next several sections, I'll go over each component of the page in detail, providing alternatives where appropriate.

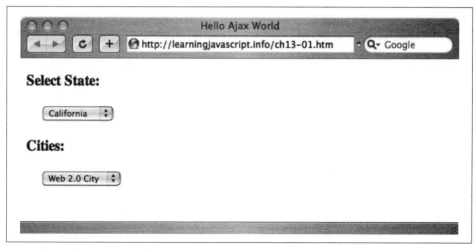

Figure 13-2. Web page after Ajax call

The Ajax Object: XMLHttpRequest and IE's ActiveX Objects

Microsoft was the first company to implement XMLHttpRequest as an ActiveX object. Mozilla followed with a direct implementation of XMLHttpRequest, and other companies have responded with their own browsers: Apple and Safari, Netscape and Navigator, and Opera. Though the constructor for the objects differs between the two formats, each shares the same functionality and methods. Once the initial object is created and assigned a variable, the one cross-browser issue is resolved. But taking care of this issue isn't as simple as it first looks.

Object, Object, Who Has the Object?

Example 13-1 demonstrates one way to create an XMLHttpRequest object: using a conditional statement and testing for its existence. If it doesn't exist, the object is created as an ActiveXObject; it passes in the progID (program ID) of the ActiveX object—in this case, Microsoft.XMLHTTP. However, a possible problem with this is that the object used in the ActiveXObject method call may differ from machine to machine. Among the various versions of the object could be MSXML2.XMLHttp, MSXML2.XMLHttp.3.0, MSXML2.XMLHttp.4.0, etc.

You can try to resolve every version of the XMLHttp object, but most Ajax libraries and applications focus on just two: the older Microsoft.XMLHttp, and the base version of the newer MSXML2.XMLHttp. In addition, since Microsoft throws errors if it attempts to create an ActiveX object that doesn't exist, developers use this to implement the correct version:

```
try
{
    http_request = new ActiveXObject("Msxml2.XMLHTTP");
}
catch (e)
{
    try
    {
        http_request = new ActiveXObject("Microsoft.XMLHTTP");
    }
    catch (e)
    {
        http_request = false;
    }
}
```

If the first object creation doesn't work, the next is tried.

The code is now more robust but a lot longer. It begs to be enclosed in a function, with the global value set to XMLHttpRequest or false to signal that it couldn't be created. In the end, our code is modified to include the following function:

```
function getXmlHttpRequest( ) {

    if (window.XMLHttpRequest) {
        xmlhttp = new XMLHttpRequest( );
        xmlhttp.overrideMimeType('text/xml');
    } else {
        try
        {
            xmlhttp = new ActiveXObject("Msxml2.XMLHTTP");
        }
        catch (e)
        {
            try
            {
                xmlhttp = new ActiveXObject("Microsoft.XMLHTTP");
            }
            catch (e)
            {
                xmlhttp = false;
            }
        }
    }
}
```

Of course, any cross-browser problems will soon be over because IE 7 supports XMLHttpRequest directly. In a few years, you can trim your code accordingly.

One other function call on the XMLHttpRequest object is to overrideMimeType. This is set to text/xml. Some browsers may require that the MIME type of the return be set to text/xml, and will fail if it isn't. You can either set the MIME type in the server application, or set the override value. Note that this is not a universally supported method.

Now that we have an XMLHttpRequest object, we'll cover the object in more detail next.

The XMLHttpRequest Methods

XMLHttpRequest is a rather simple object, with only a few methods and properties. However, it doesn't need to be complicated to provide a rather amazing amount of functionality.

Here are the methods, in the order most likely encountered in an application:

open
> The syntax for open is open(method,url[,async,username,password]). The open method opens a connection to a given URL, using a specified method (GET or POST). Optional parameters are async, which sets the requests to be asynchronous (true, and default), or synchronous (false); and a username and password if the server process requires these.

setRequestHeader
> The syntax for setRequestHeader is setRequestHeader(label,value). This method adds a label/value pair to the header in the request.

send
> The syntax for send is send(content). This is the heart and soul of XMLHttpRequest. This is where the request is sent with associated data.

getAllResponseHeaders
> The syntax for getAllResponseHeaders is getAllResponseHeaders(). Returns all HTTP response headers as a string. Among the information included is the Keep-Alive timeout value, content-type, information about the server, and the date.

getResponseHeader
> The syntax for getResponseHeader is getResponseHeader(label). Returns the specific HTTP response header.

abort
> The syntax for abort is abort( ). Aborts the current request.

Some of the mystique associated with XmlHttpRequest may be removed if you consider that the functionality used to process a form using a traditional form submission is the same technology used with Ajax and XMLHttpRequest, except that the page remains during and after the process.

In the example, the request is a GET, so the web-page URL has the associated parameters added as part of the URL. If the request had been a POST, the send method would be the following:

```
function populateList( ) {
    var state = document.forms[0].elements[0].value;
    var qry = "state=" + state;
    var url = 'ajax.php';
    xmlhttp.open('POST', url, true);
    xmlhttp.onreadystatechange = getCities;
    xmlhttp.setRequestHeader("Content-type", "application/x-www-form-urlencoded");
    xmlhttp.send(qry);
}
```

The content-type header is adjusted to urlencoded form, and a query is created and sent in the send operation. Other than these changes, the method is just the same as the Ajax call with GET.

 When do you use POST as opposed to GET? POST has cleaner URLs than GET, which doesn't matter as much with Ajax. POST also is more secure; GET can be called directly on the web service. POST is also typically used for posting data, as compared to GET, which is used for queries.

In addition to the six methods, there are also six properties associated with XMLHttpRequest, which are given in Table 13-1.

Table 13-1. XMLHttpRequest properties

Property	Purpose
Onreadystatechange	This property holds a handle to the function called when the ready state of the request changes.
readyState	Has one of five values: 0 for uninitialized request, 1 for an open request, 2 for a request that has been sent, 3 for when a response is being received, and 4 for when the response is finished loading. For the most part, we're interested in a readyState of 4.
responseText	Response as text.
responseXML	Response as XML, which can then be processed as valid XML.
status	Returns server status, such as 404, 500, and, hopefully, 200 for all is well.
statusText	Text associated with status.

Again, there isn't anything complicated or complex about Ajax. Probably the only area in which additional complexity enters the equation is how the data is returned. This is covered in the next section.

 If you try to run a Ajax application on your local system, you will most likely run into security restrictions. Browsers such as Firefox do not allow XMLHttpRequests on the local filesystem.

Working with XML—or Not

In Example 13-1, the response was returned as a text string, with contents formatted as HTML. When it was added to the page, the entire select element was replaced because Microsoft does not support innerHTML for select directly. A better approach would have been to take the response and generate options, which are then added to the page. However, returning the string as already formatted options isn't optimal for processing.

Rather than format the options, you can return a string with the options concatenated with commas in between, such as the following:

```
return "Seattle,Olympia";
```

However, this isn't very effective if the data is more complex. For instance, in our example, the value of the option item is different from the string that's printed out. When you start returning text more complex than simple strings, the response gets more complicated.

For more complicated data, or data that you don't want formatted as HTML, there are two other options: XML or JSON (JavaScript Object Notation). Let's look at each of these approaches in turn.

Yes to XML

One advantage to returning a response formatted as XML is that the data can be much more complex than simple strings, or preformatted in HTML. In addition, there are several DOM methods that can process the data. After all, a web page is typically valid X(HTML) (we hope), and these methods can work on web pages.

Of course, using XML adds its own burdens. For instance, it's important that the server-side application return the property MIME type of text/xml for the content, or it won't end up in the responseXML container. In addition, the XML has to be valid XML, which means it has a root element that contains all of the other data. Example 13-3 shows the server-side application, ajaxxml.php, after it's written to return XML. Note that there are two elements for each city: value and title. The value is what's included within the option, and the title is what's printed out to the page.

Example 13-3. PHP Ajax application now returning XML

```php
<?php

//If no search string is passed, then we can't search
if(empty($_GET['state'])) {
    echo "<city>No State Sent</city>";
} else {
    //Remove whitespace from beginning & end of passed search.
    $search = trim($_GET['state']);
    switch($search) {
      case "MO" :
        $result = "<city><value>stlou</value><title>St. Louis</title></city>" .
                  "<city><value>kc</value><title>Kansas City</title></city>";
        break;
      case "WA" :
        $result = "<city><value>seattle</value><title>Seattle</title></city>" .
                  "<city><value>spokane</value><title>Spokane</title></city>" .
                  "<city><value>olympia</value><title>Olympia</title></city>";
        break;
      case "CA" :
        $result = "<city><value>sanfran</value><title>San Francisco</title></city>" .
                  "<city><value>la</value><title>Los Angeles</title></city>" .
                  "<city><value>web2</value><title>Web 2.0 City</title></city>" .
                  "<city><value>barcamp></value><title>BarCamp</title></city>";
        break;
```

Example 13-3. PHP Ajax application now returning XML (continued)

```
      case "ID" :
         $result = "<city><value>boise</value><title>Boise</title></city>";
         break;
      default :
         $result = "<city><value></value><title>No Cities Found</title></city>";
         break;
      }
      $result ='<?xml version="1.0" encoding="UTF-8" ?>' .
               "<cities>" . $result . "</cities>";

   header("Content-Type: text/xml; charset=utf-8");

      echo $result;
}
?>
```

Once the server application is finished, the client-side application built into Java-Script must be changed. Example 13-4 shows the modified web page.

Example 13-4. Client application modified to work with an XML response

```
<!DOCTYPE html PUBLIC "-//W3C//DTD XHTML 1.0 Transitional//EN"
"http://www.w3.org/TR/xhtml1/DTD/xhtml1-transitional.dtd">
<html>
<head>
<title>Hello Ajax World, Too</title>
<meta http-equiv="Content-Type" content="text/html; charset=utf-8" />

<style type="text/css">
div.elem { margin: 20px; }
</style>

<script type="text/javascript">
//<![CDATA[

var xmlhttp = false;
if (window.XMLHttpRequest) {
   xmlhttp = new XMLHttpRequest();
   xmlhttp.overrideMimeType('text/xml');
} else if (window.ActiveXObject) {
   xmlhttp = new ActiveXObject("Microsoft.XMLHTTP");
}

function populateList() {
   var state = document.forms[0].elements[0].value;
   var url = 'ajaxxml.php?state=' + state;
   xmlhttp.open('GET', url, true);
   xmlhttp.onreadystatechange = getCities;
   xmlhttp.send(null);
}
function getCities() {
   if(xmlhttp.readyState == 4 && xmlhttp.status == 200) {
```

Example 13-4. Client application modified to work with an XML response (continued)

```
    try {
        var citynodes = xmlhttp.responseXML.getElementsByTagName('city');
        for (var i = 0; i < citynodes.length; i++) {
            var name = value = null;
            for (var j = 0; j < citynodes[i].childNodes.length; j++) {
                var elem = citynodes[i].childNodes[j].nodeName;
                var nodevalue = citynodes[i].childNodes[j].firstChild.nodeValue;
                if (elem == 'value') {
                    value = nodevalue;
                } else {
                    name = nodevalue;
                }
            }
            document.forms[0].elements[1].options[i] = new Option(name,value);
        }
    } catch (e) {
            alert(e.message);
    }
    } else {
        document.getElementById('cities').innerHTML = 'Error: No Cities';
    }
}
//]]>
</script>

</head>
<body>

<h3>Select State:</h3>
<form action="ajaxxml.php" method="get">
<div class="elem">
<select onchange="populateList( )">
<option value="CA">California</option>
<option value="MO">Missouri</option>
<option value="WA">Washington</option>
<option value="ID">Idaho</option>
</select>
</div>
<h3>Cities:</h3>
<div class="elem">
<select id="cities">
</select>
</div>
</form>
</body>
</html>
```

Let's walk through the code to process the return.

First, the DOM function getElementsByTagName is called on the XML returned through the request's responseXML property. This gives us a set of child nodes for each city in the XML. Each child node, in turn, has two of its own: one for value, and one for the title element.

Instead of assuming that the XML that's returned to the web page is positionally dependent (value is always first, then title), the application traverses the nodeList for childNodes and gets the nodeName for each. This is compared to value and if a match occurs, its nodeValue is assigned to value. If not, the nodeValue is assigned to title (though this value could be tested first to ensure it is title). Once the city childNodes are traversed, the value and title are used to create a new option, and the next city processed.

All of this code is enclosed in exception handling because the DOM functions throw errors that aren't processed as such by the browser. It's a good habit to get into when you work with Ajax.

With the approach just demonstrated, no matter how deep the XML nesting, this same process can be used to access the nodes. After a while, though, you can see that the code could become cumbersome and hard to read or modify. It is this issue that generated interest in a new format—JSON.

 If what you're after is an attribute and not a node, you can use the DOM getAttribute method to retrieve the value from the XML document. This is also part of the DOM Level 2 Core, as discussed in Chapter 10.

JavaScript Object Notation

As the web site that supports it claims, JSON, or JavaScript Object Notation, is "a lightweight data-interchange format." Rather than attempt to chain references as comma-delimited strings or have to deal with the complexity (and overhead) of XML, JSON provides a format that converts a server-side structure into a JavaScript object that can be used practically right out of the box.

JSON actually uses JavaScript syntax to define the objects. For an object, the syntax is curly braces surrounding members:

```
object{ } or object { string : value...}
```

For an array, it's elements and square brackets:

```
array[] or array[value,value,...,value]
```

The values specified follow the same rules for variables and associated values (strings or numbers) as defined for JavaScript in ECMA-262, Third Edition.

JSON, just as with the XML and HTML examples, can be manually encoded, because it is just another text string. However, there's growing support for JSON APIs in different programming languages used with web services, and most have encoders that encode or decode JSON transmitted data.

For our purposes, though, we'll manually create the data structure. Example 13-5 contains a new server application, ajaxjson.php, which now converts the data to JSON format. The structure used is an array of objects, each with a value and a title property.

Example 13-5. Working with simple JSON in PHP

```php
<?php

//If no search string is passed, then we can't search
if(empty($_GET['state'])) {
    echo "<city>No State Sent</city>";
} else {
    //Remove whitespace from beginning & end of passed search.
    $search = trim($_GET['state']);
    switch($search) {
      case "MO" :
        $result = "[ { 'value' : 'stlou', 'title' : 'St. Louis' }, " .
                  "{ 'value' : 'kc', 'title' :' Kansas City' } ]";
        break;
      case "WA" :
        $result = "[ { 'value' : 'seattle', 'title' : 'Seattle' }, " .
                  "  { 'value' : 'spokane', 'title' : 'Spokane' }, " .
                  "  { 'value' : 'olympia', 'title' : 'Olympia' } ]";
        break;
      case "CA" :
        $result = "[ { 'value' : 'sanfran', 'title' : 'San Francisco' }, " .
                  "  { 'value' : 'la',      'title' : 'Los Angeles'   }, " .
                  "  { 'value' : 'web2',    'title' : 'Web 2.0 City'  }, " .
                  "  { 'value' : 'barcamp', 'title' : 'BarCamp'       } ]";
        break;
      case "ID" :
        $result = "[ { 'value' : 'boise', 'title' : 'Boise' } ]";
        break;
      default :
        $result = "[ { 'value' : '', 'title' : 'No Cities Found' } ]";
        break;
    }

    echo $result;
}
?>
```

To use the data structure in the web page, access the JSON-formatted data from the
responseText property, and then pass it to the eval function to evaluate the structure
and assign it to a local program variable. Example 13-6 is our web page now adjusted
for a JSON data structure.

Example 13-6. Using JSON-structured data between server and client

```html
<!DOCTYPE html PUBLIC "-//W3C//DTD XHTML 1.0 Transitional//EN"
"http://www.w3.org/TR/xhtml1/DTD/xhtml1-transitional.dtd">
<html>
<head>
<title>Hello Ajax World, Too</title>
<meta http-equiv="Content-Type" content="text/html; charset=utf-8" />

<style type="text/css">
div.elem { margin: 20px; }
```

Example 13-6. Using JSON-structured data between server and client (continued)

```
</style>

<script type="text/javascript">
//<![CDATA[

var xmlhttp = false;
if (window.XMLHttpRequest) {
    xmlhttp = new XMLHttpRequest();
    xmlhttp.overrideMimeType('text/xml');
} else if (window.ActiveXObject) {
    xmlhttp = new ActiveXObject("Microsoft.XMLHTTP");
}

function populateList() {
    var state = document.forms[0].elements[0].value;
    var url = 'ajaxjson.php?state=' + state;
    xmlhttp.open('GET', url, true);
    xmlhttp.onreadystatechange = getCities;
    xmlhttp.send(null);
}
function getCities() {
    if(xmlhttp.readyState == 4 && xmlhttp.status == 200) {
        try {
            eval("var response = ("+xmlhttp.responseText+")");
            var sel = document.getElementById("cities");
            var name = value = null;
            for (var i = 0; i < response.length; i++) {
                name = response[i].title;
                value = response[i].value;
                document.forms[0].elements[1].options[i] = new Option(name,value);
            }
        } catch (e) {
            alert(e.message);
        }
    } else {
        document.getElementById('cities').innerHTML = 'Error: No Cities';
    }
}

//]]>
</script>

</head>
<body>

<h3>Select State:</h3>
<form action="ajaxjson.php" method="get">
<div class="elem">
<select onchange="populateList()">
<option value="CA">California</option>
<option value="MO">Missouri</option>
<option value="WA">Washington</option>
```

Example 13-6. Using JSON-structured data between server and client (continued)

```
<option value="ID">Idaho</option>
</select>
</div>
<h3>Cities:</h3>
<div class="elem">
<select id="cities">
</select>
</div>
</form>
</body>
</html>
```

As you can see, the JSON method is simpler than the XML method, though perhaps not as simple as the straight HTML approach. However, don't let that make your decision for you. You may have no choice in how the data is sent, and have to process the results regardless of the format. In addition, when dealing with increasingly complex objects, using XML with XSLT to transform the XML into viewable material can end up being less work in the end.

If you're working directly with a data structure, such as a relational database or Resource Description Framework (RDF), chances are you'll either be dealing with comma-delimited data or XML in the first case, or XML in the latter—and a specialized XML at that.

 One other thing to consider is using XML that uses namespaces. This can annotate an element name to prevent a conflict in vocabularies; use something like content:name. There is a DOM function called getElementsByTagNameNS that takes a namespace as one of the parameters, but not all browsers support this, including Internet Explorer.

The point is, and I hope it has been demonstrated in these examples, that Ajax is extremely easy and simple to use, and you have options with how your data is transmitted between the server application and the client page.

Now, time for a little fun: Google Maps.

Google Maps

One of the most famous Ajax/DHTML/JavaScript applications is Google Maps. It became even more popular when the company released an API that enabled people to quickly and easily add sophisticated mapping to their web pages. This one application, more so than probably any other, is what fires the imagination regarding Ajax and the ability to mix and mash technologies.

It's not unusual for people to record the longitude and latitude of a photograph's location into that photo (a process known as *geocoding*), which is then parsed out and passed to a Google Maps API call. A map is then created to show exactly where the photo was taken.

Geocachers, that group of passionate global positioning satellite (GPS) users, utilize Google Maps to mark *geocaches* (hidden objects of little or no value used as a way to mark the spot). Others use Google Maps to provide driving directions, to mark landmarks, or even play games. It's a rich and easy-to-use API.

To use Google Maps, you first need a free API key, which you can get at the Google Maps API web site (*http://www.google.com/apis/maps/*). This is used as part of the URL given in the src attribute of the script tag. For instance, the following shows how I use my key for *learningjavascript.info*:

```
<script src="http://maps.google.com/maps?file=api&amp;v=2&amp;
key=ABQIAAAAprpnCG3LM_SOd5dAqo4g7RThwcj_1x2ShM2_WlFws98yyiZZxRQyUhBJw9Ty1j6jpEUo_
v6PFZfJdQ"  type="text/javascript"></script>
```

That key has to match the *exact* domain *and* subdirectory location where you plan on putting your Google map pages. It's very picky.

There's an extensive set of examples and documentation at Google, and I won't take the time to cover what the company covers so well. When the key is generated, Google even gives you a small application you can use to start your development. That's what I'll use.

Google's small example just gives a map in a box, with no controls. I'll add on some functionality to create an application that puts markers on the page when the reader clicks the map, and displays an information window with the longitude and latitude. I'll also direct the map to the location of one of my favorite objects, the St. Louis Arch. It looks very impressive in the satellite view.

In Example 13-7, a new Google Maps object is created, passing in the DIV element in the page where the map will be located. Once created, two controls are added: one to zoom in or out in the map and one to switch between map, satellite, and hybrid views. Given the latitude and longitude, the map is then centered in St. Louis.

Once centered, an event listener is added for the click event on the map element. An anonymous function (all this should look familiar to you, because we've covered everything used so far) is attached to the event listener to test that the point where the click occurred already has a marker. If it does, it's removed. If not, one is placed, and an information window is opened above it, with the latitude and longitude of the point.

Example 13-7. Working with Google Maps

```
<!DOCTYPE html PUBLIC "-//W3C//DTD XHTML 1.0 Strict//EN"
  "http://www.w3.org/TR/xhtml1/DTD/xhtml1-strict.dtd">
<html xmlns="http://www.w3.org/1999/xhtml">
  <head>
    <meta http-equiv="content-type" content="text/html; charset=utf-8"/>
```

Example 13-7. Working with Google Maps (continued)

```
<title>Google Maps JavaScript API Example</title>
<script src="http://maps.google.com/maps?file=api&amp;v=2&amp;key=ABQIAAAAprpnCG3LM_
SOd5dAqo4g7RThwcj_1x2ShM2_WlFws98yyiZZxRQyUhBJw9Ty1j6jpEUo_v6PFZfJdQ"
    type="text/javascript"></script>
<script type="text/javascript">

//<![CDATA[

function load() {
  if (GBrowserIsCompatible()) {
    var map = new GMap2(document.getElementById("map"));
    map.addControl(new GSmallMapControl());
    map.addControl(new GMapTypeControl());
    map.setCenter(new GLatLng(38.624464, -90.18496), 15);

    GEvent.addListener(map, "click", function(marker, point) {
            if (marker) {
                    map.removeOverlay(marker);
            } else {
              marker = new GMarker(point);
              map.addOverlay(marker);
              marker.openInfoWindowHtml(point.lat() + " " + point.lng());
            }
            });
  }
}

//]]>
  </script>
</head>
<body onload="load()" onunload="GUnload()">
  <div id="map" style="width: 500px; height: 300px"></div>
</body>
</html>
```

Google Maps supports Ajax `XMLHttpRequests`, including the various formats discussed in this chapter.

Finally, Google Maps uses function closures. To prevent memory leaks, replace the body opening script tag with the following:

```
<body onunload="GUnload()">
```

This removes the circular references that can lead to leaks. Do take some time to enjoy Google Maps, and also make sure you click the satellite view with this example—the Arch is impressive.

Now that you're sold on web services, DHTML, and Ajax, we'll look in the final chapter at what others have been doing with JavaScript and how you can incorporate what they've created into your own applications.

Questions

1. Though it seems to defy the concept of Ajax, an XMLHttpRequest can be synchronous (wait for response). How would you open such a request?

2. Once a request receives a response, it needs to be processed. How do you attach a function to call when the service responds?

3. What are the two states for a successful, and completed, request?

4. What are the three data formats you can use with a response, and what are the advantages of each?

5. Modify the Google Maps application in Example 13-6 to include a custom icon stored in a file called *myicon.png*.

Answers are provided in the appendix.

CHAPTER 14

Good News: Juicy Libraries! Amazing Web Services! Fun APIs!

It's the lime effect.

Much of the new interest in JavaScript seems to run parallel with specific styles and page designs. Page elements have rounded corners; content is page-centered; and, for some reason, the color lime seems to predominate (followed by orange, yellow, and variations of sky or aqua blue). It's an oddly modern/retro feel.

Regardless of colors and corners, this new interest in JavaScript has generated a wealth of new scripting tools and toys—many of which are far more sophisticated than earlier efforts because the browsers themselves can support more sophisticated effects. And because the Web is an amazingly generous place, chances are if you need some functionality for your site, someone else has already created it or something similar, and put it on the Web for general use.

In this chapter, we'll look at several of these freely available libraries and frameworks. I'll explain how to access and install the library, as well as provide an overview and demonstration of some of the capabilities of the library or framework. Additionally, I'll cover the ramifications of using each library. As these become larger and more complex, there's an increasing likelihood of conflicts between your code, and even conflicts between using the library and using the built-in JavaScript objects and Document Object Model.

By the end of the chapter, you should have a good idea of what you can find on the Internet, when you should use a library, or when to just code the functionality yourself.

Before Jumping In, A Word of Caution

Many of the libraries covered in this chapter—many of the Ajax libraries, period—place some limitations on what you can and cannot do in JavaScript if you plan on incorporating them into your applications. It's important to be aware of how much of an impact they can have.

The Prototype library, the first we'll cover, is an excellent example of how much a library can affect even basic JavaScript development. At one time, it made a modification to the `Array` object, using that object's prototype property, that actually broke how associative arrays are manipulated when they are created using the `Array` object. Many Ajax developers believe that you should never create an associative array using the `Array` object, but instead should use the `Object` itself. Still, to break a built-in object such as this raised a hue and cry, and in the next version release of Prototype, this "enhancement" was removed.

However, Prototype still modifies basic JavaScript objects. After all, this is a feature of JS; expect that library developers will use it. This means you have to be aware of exactly what modifications have been made, and because many of the Ajax libraries have really poor documentation, discovering the gotchas could be a real challenge.

Another issue is event handling. Many of the libraries, such as Dojo, load functionality using the `window` load event. If you don't use DOM Level 2 event handling, you'll overwrite what Dojo creates and break the effects. When using an Ajax library, the best way to add a windows onload event handler is with code similar to the following:

```
// test for object model
if (window.addEventListener) {
    window.addEventListener("load",finish,false);
} else if (window.attachEvent) {
    window.attachEvent("onload", finish);
}
```

In general, when working with Ajax libraries, expect to use DOM Level 2 event handling for most or all of your own efforts.

Finally, there's a feeling among many of the Ajax developers that standards and accessibility are not big issues. More than one developer has disdained the need to provide effects that validate as XHTML, even XHTML transitional, which I used in the examples in this book. However, a page that doesn't validate as XHTML also won't be accessible, and there's no way I can condone disregarding the needs for accessibility just to add some pretties. There are always valid and accessible workarounds to any worthwhile effect—if you take the time to look for them, that is. In the Q & A sections at the end of the chapter, I cover one such, and once you accept that valid markup and accessible effects are achievable (and important), you'll find your own workarounds.

OK, enough of the caveats—on with the show.

Working with Prototype

No other library, toolset, or invention has led to the explosive growth of Ajax more than Prototype, the freely available Ajax/JavaScript library created by Sam Stephenson and available at *http://prototype.conio.net/*. It's become so popular, it's integrated as part of the Ruby on Rails (RoR) development environments. Several other libraries reviewed in this chapter and in previous chapters are based on Prototype.

What Prototype offers is a way to emulate a classlike behavior based on the JavaScript prototype; it provides a set of functions that hide much of the underlying JavaScript behavior. This is good because JS can be cumbersome when you're trying to access several elements in a page and have to get each one using something like getElementById. However, as has been noted frequently, Prototype also hides many of the underlying mechanisms, which can make reading any code that uses the library confusing—especially for newer JavaScript developers or those unfamiliar with Prototype. Luckily, this won't include you after the following brief peek.

Download, Install, Use

One aspect of Prototype I really appreciate is that it's one library, included in one JavaScript file, and easily integrated into a page. Just include a link to the downloaded Prototype library in your application:

```
<script type="text/javascript" src="prototype.js">
</script>
```

That's it (assuming you put the *prototype.js* file on your server). You're now ready to use Prototype functions in your own applications.

 The Ruby on Rails framework provides code support for Prototype, as well as Script.aculo.us. If you're a Ruby developer, find out how to include Prototype in your application at *http://api.rubyonrails.com/ classes/ActionView/Helpers/JavaScriptHelper.html*.

The Helper Functions and the JavaScript Extensions

Prototype is most known for its extensive set of utility or helper functions. I mentioned these in earlier chapters as being responsible for adding a series of cryptic operators into JavaScript, most starting with the dollar sign.

One of the more common functions is $( ), which can be used in place of document. getElementById, but with a kicker: if you specify a list of elements, it returns an array of elements:

```
var theDivs = $('div1','div2','div3');
```

The $F function returns whatever value there is for a specific form field, while the $H function converts an object into an enumerable Hash (one of Prototype's many new object types). In the following code, an object is converted to a Prototype Hash, and the values are then accessed and stored in a JavaScript array using one of the Hash functions, values:

```
var obj = {
                partA : one,
                partB : two,
                partC : three,
                };
var hshObj = $H(obj);
var arr = hshObj.values();
```

The $R function creates one of the new Prototype objects, ObjectRange. An
ObjectRange is a range of values, with given lower and upper boundaries that exclude
any specific values. The parameter objects are JavaScript Number objects, which themselves have been extended to include a new method, succ. This method, when called,
increments whatever primitive value the Number object wraps. ObjectRange inherits
behavior from the Prototype Enumerable objects that provide several enumeration
functions. These functions include each, find, findAll, entries; they convert the
object into an array, and so on. We'll look more closely at Prototype's enumeration
capabilities in a moment, but first, let's take these shortcut functions for a test drive.

In Example 14-1, two input fields accept numbers, which are then used to create an
ObjectRange. Once created, Prototype enumeration iterates through the collection of
values, creating a string. This string is then printed out using innerHTML to a DIV element, which is accessed by the generic $ function.

Example 14-1. Trying out the Prototype helper functions

```
<!DOCTYPE html PUBLIC "-//W3C//DTD XHTML 1.0 Transitional//EN"
"http://www.w3.org/TR/xhtml1/DTD/xhtml1-transitional.dtd">
<html>
<head>
<title>$</title>
<meta http-equiv="Content-Type" content="text/html; charset=utf-8" />
<script type="text/javascript" src="prototype.js">
</script>
<script type="text/javascript">
//<![CDATA[

function iterate() {
  var lower = new Number($F('input1'));
  var higher = new Number($F('input2'));

  var rng = $R(lower,higher,false);
  var div = $('div1');
  var strng = "";
  rng.each(function(value,index) {
            strng+=value + " ";
            });
  div.innerHTML = "<p>" + strng + "</p>";
}
//]]>
</script>

</head>
```

Example 14-1. Trying out the Prototype helper functions (continued)

```
<body>
<form id="form1">
lower: <input type="text" id="input1" /><br />
upper: <input type="text" id="input2" /><br />
<a href="javascript:iterate( )">Iterate</a>
</form>
<div id="div1">
</div>
</body>
</html>
```

Notice how the numbers accessed via the form are wrapped in a Number constructor? Without this, you'll receive an error about succ missing on the values. The reason you do so is because the values aren't returned from $F as Number objects, and it is the Number object that's extended with a succ method to aid in enumeration. You can also use parseInt or some other conversion function to ensure the values are the correct type when passed to the ObjectRange.

This example gave us a taste of some of the objects in Prototype. Let's look more closely at a few others.

Some Specialized Prototype Objects

Among some of the objects Prototype provides is a Class one-off object, which is used to manage the creation and initialization of the other objects. There's also an Element, which extends the functionality of DOM nodes; it basically merges many of the DHTML effects into method calls. The Form object extends the functionality of Form, providing methods such as getValue to get the value of a form field.

The Prototype Ajax object encapsulates much of the Ajax behavior demonstrated in the last chapter. To see how this object works, we'll replace the core JavaScript from examples in Chapter 13.

Example 14-2 is a recreation of Example 13-1, except this time we're using the Ajax object, as compared to doing the Ajax processing ourselves. Notice two things. First, we're using a lot less code. Second, we're providing an element that serves as a target for the Ajax results.

Example 14-2. Using Prototype Ajax object to make an Ajax request

```
<!DOCTYPE html PUBLIC "-//W3C//DTD XHTML 1.0 Transitional//EN"
"http://www.w3.org/TR/xhtml1/DTD/xhtml1-transitional.dtd">
<html>
<head>
<title>Hello Prototype Ajax World</title>
<meta http-equiv="Content-Type" content="text/html; charset=utf-8" />
<script type="text/javascript" src="prototype.js">
</script>
```

Example 14-2. Using Prototype Ajax object to make an Ajax request (continued)

```
<style type="text/css">
div.elem { margin: 20px; }
</style>

<script type="text/javascript">
//<![CDATA[

function populateList( ) {
   var url = 'ajaxprototype.php';
   var params = "state=" + escape($F('state'));
   var ajx = new Ajax.Updater('cities',url,{method: 'get', parameters: params, onFailure :
handleError});
}

function handleError(request,hdr) {
   alert(hdr);
}

//]]>
</script>

</head>
<body>

<h3>Select State:</h3>
<form action="ajax.php" method="get">
<div class="elem">
<select onchange="populateList( )" id="state">
<option value="CA">California</option>
<option value="MO">Missouri</option>
<option value="WA">Washington</option>
<option value="ID">Idaho</option>
</select>
</div>
<h3>Cities:</h3>
<div id="cities" class="elem">
<select>
</select>
</div>
</form>

</body>
</html>
```

Since we're specifying a target, and Prototype will insert the response in this object, I've also adjusted the PHP script to append the select element before and after the options list so that the whole object is replaced. In Chapter 13, we did this directly in the client JavaScript:

```
echo "<select>$result</select>";
```

I could have created an option in the Updater constructor, onSuccess, that passes in a function to be invoked on success, rather than sending it through a target. The function has one parameter, XMLHttpRequest, which I could have used to process the result exactly as processed in Chapter 13. In addition, how the data is inserted can be modified based on the insertion property. This represents an Insertion class object that determines how data is inserted: before, after, top, or bottom. There is also the Ajax.Request object, which gives even finer control in how the Ajax request/response is managed.

A Compliment and a Caveat

I've barely scratched the surface on what Prototype can do, but hopefully I've given you a taste, at least, of some of the functionality. There are many more objects, including objects that provide enumeration to many of our base objects. It is this fact that also forces me to issue a caveat when you're using Prototype or any of the libraries derived from Prototype (a few of which I'll be describing later in the chapter).

In Version 1.4 of Prototype, Stephenson made alterations to the Object.prototype that ended up breaking associative arrays. This was fixed in Version 1.5, but the Array object still breaks on associative arrays. According to an article at the web site *Ajaxian*, using the Array object conflicts with Prototype's array-management extensions. (See "Java-Script Associative Arrays Considered Harmful," at *http://ajaxian.com/archives/javascript-associative-arrays-considered-harmful*). The philosophy behind the decision to alter the Array prototype was that arrays should be numeric, and associative arrays should occur only directly through Object.

Regardless of whether you agree with this or not (and I'll go on record as saying I unequivocally do not agree with this), it's an important reminder that, because of the immensely flexible nature of JavaScript and the increasingly complex, functionally overriding nature of some of the JavaScript libraries, you may end up actually breaking any existing code just by importing another library. Definitely explore the use of such libraries, but always do so with caution.

 Like too many other Ajax libraries, Prototype is virtually free of any form of formal documentation. It's relatively easy to read, but this doesn't help when you're trying to get a quick overview of what it can and cannot do. Luckily, Sergio Pereira created a nice overview of the Prototype framework, in different languages, at *http://www.sergiopereira.com/articles/prototype.js.html*.

Script.aculo.us: More Than the Sum of Its Periods

The script.aculo.us library is one of several that's built on top of Prototype. It extends the available functionality and provides a higher level of interaction, as well as increasingly sophisticated effects.

You'll find documentation for script.aculo.us, which includes a usage page, at *http:// wiki.script.aculo.us/scriptaculous/show/Usage*. This covers where to get the library and how to install it. The library consists of multiple JavaScript files (*scriptaculous.js, builder.js, effects.js, dragdrop.js, slider.js,* and *control.js*), which need to be placed in your script directory, along with *prototype.js* and any other JavaScript file.

Usage

To use script.aculo.us, you'll need to link prototype as well as the new library:

```
<script type="text/javascript" src="prototype.js"></script>
<script type="text/javascript" src="scriptaculous.js"></script>
```

The *scriptaculous.js* file loads in all the other JS files. If you want only certain effects, though, you can specify this on the same line as the *scriptaculous.js* load, using the following syntax:

```
<script type="text/javascript" src="scriptaculous.js?load=effects,controls">
```

Once loaded, you can then use any of the libraries' specialized UI (user interface) effects.

> Script.aculo.us' libraries of effects, drag and drop, and auto-completion are integrated as a Ruby on Rails Ajax helper. This means you can automatically manage an effect using a tag such as the following:
>
> ```
> <%= text_field_with_auto_complete :contact, :name %>
> ```
>
> You don't have to be developing in Ruby on Rails to use script.aculo.us, but the documentation for doing so is sparse. Still, let's look at a couple of script.aculous.effects.

A Gander at Effects

One of the script.aculu.os libraries includes several visual effects: fades, clippings, and so on. These are extremely easy to use and quite fun to watch. In Example 14-3, I tried out several of the different effects, including ones to puff, squish, and pulsate a DIV element.

Example 14-3. Taking script.aculo.us visual effects for a run

```
<!DOCTYPE html PUBLIC "-//W3C//DTD XHTML 1.0 Transitional//EN"
"http://www.w3.org/TR/xhtml1/DTD/xhtml1-transitional.dtd">
<html>
<head>
<title>I want to have fun!</title>
<meta http-equiv="Content-Type" content="text/html; charset=utf-8" />
<script type="text/javascript" src="prototype.js"></script>
<script type="text/javascript" src="scriptaculous.js"></script>

<style type="text/css">
```

Example 14-3. Taking script.aculo.us visual effects for a run (continued)

```
div.elem { margin: 20px; padding: 10px;
           background-color: #C6B3FF;
           width: 400px; height: 200px;
         }

.elem a { text-decoration: none; font-size: larger; color: #6A38FF }
</style>

<script type="text/javascript">
//<![CDATA[

function pulsate() {
   new Effect.Pulsate($('theblock'));
}
function shake() {
   new Effect.Shake($('theblock'));
}

function slideup() {
   new Effect.SlideUp($('theblock'));
}

function slidedown() {
   new Effect.SlideDown($('theblock'));
}

function dropout() {
   new Effect.DropOut($('theblock'));
}

function appear() {
   new Effect.Appear($('theblock'));
}
function puff() {
   new Effect.Puff($('theblock'));
}
function squish() {
   new Effect.Squish($('theblock'));
}
function highlight() {
   new Effect.Highlight($('theblock'));
}
//]]>
</script>

</head>
<body>

<div id="theblock" class="elem">
<p>Testing the scriptaculous effects</p>
</div>
<div class="elem">
```

Example 14-3. Taking script.aculo.us visual effects for a run (continued)

```
<a href="javascript:pulsate( )">new Effect.Pulsate(obj)</a><br />
<a href="javascript:shake( )">new Effect.Shake(obj)</a><br />
<a href="javascript:slideup( )">new Effect.SlideUp(obj)</a><br />
<a href="javascript:slidedown( )">new Effect.SlideDown(obj)</a><br />
<a href="javascript:dropout( )">new Effect.DropOut(obj)</a><br />
<a href="javascript:appear( )">new Effect.Appear(obj)</a><br />
<a href="javascript:puff( )">new Effect.Puff(obj)</a><br />
<a href="javascript:squish( )">new Effect.Squish(obj)</a><br />
<a href="javascript:highlight( )">new Effect.Highlight(obj)</a>
</div>
</body>
</html>
```

Notice in the code that I pass the element in using the Prototype helper function, $.

The title of the example page says it all: I want to have fun. There's nothing wrong with making your web pages fun, but these effects go beyond just the coolness factor.

The Pulsate effect can be used to grab attention. Other means can still be used, such as an alert dialog when scripting is turned off. However, I find something like Pulsate preferable to using an alert to get attention.

The Shake effect can be used when a person enters a wrong value, and I've seen this used in login pages. If there's text that also provides feedback, the use of this effect is also accessible. The SlideDown and SlideUp provide the functionality demonstrated in Chapter 12 for creating an accordion effect. Again, if the layers are open when scripting is not supported, the page is accessible.

The Puff and Squish effects can show and hide a note to the web-page reader. I like this rather than using straight visibility because there's a warning that something is coming and something is going away, rather than just having them appear and disappear. One rule of DHTML is: don't disconcert your user too much.

The Appear function is a way to undo some of the other disappearing effects, and it also has a nice "here I come" feel to it. As for Highlight, this is the infamous blue-to-yellow fade that people are implementing in their applications to denote a successful form action. I'm still out on this one.

The point is how easy these effects were to use. Other script.aculo.us effects include the autocompletion, the sortables, and the slider. The library also implements drag and drop, though as discussed earlier in the book, use this effect sparingly.

Script.aculo.us isn't the only library built on top of Prototype. Another is Rico, discussed next.

 Take a look under the covers at how script.aculo.us creates its effects. This, combined with looking at Prototype's code, is a good demonstration of clever JavaScript object management.

Sabre's Rico

Rico is a rather interesting Ajax library. For one thing, unlike many other Ajax libraries, which are the inspiration of an individual or small group of individuals, Rico was created by a development team at Sabre Airline Solution. Developed by company personnel, it was released for general use via the Apache license.

Rico, like other libraries we'll examine, is dependent on Prototype. At the time this was written, Rico was at Version 1.1.2 and was dependent on Prototype 1.4.0. I tried the examples with the Prototype 1.5 release candidate.

After installing Prototype, access Rico from the library's web site at *http://openrico. org/rico/home.page*. Once downloaded, include both libraries in your page using the following in the head section of your document, before any JS that uses the libraries:

```
<script type="text/javascript"
    src="/pathto/prototype.js">
</script>
<script type="text/javascript"
    src="/pathto/rico.js">
</script>
```

What I especially like about Rico is the very easy-to-use cinematic effects. Among these are animators that position elements, fade colors, and especially, round corners, which I thought was rather unusual, but not surprising, with an Ajax library.

We'll take a couple of these effects out for a test drive, starting with that rounded-corner library.

Rounded Corners

The difficulty with the Rico library is that not all of the functionality provided is documented. However, the JavaScript library is simple to read (if you're familiar with Prototype), and the site provides a nicely organized set of demos.

The Rico rounded-corner effects are dependent on a one-off object, the `Rico.Corner.round`. You invoke it through the external interface object, `Rico.Effect.Round` class, passing in options to create the different effects:

```
new Rico.Effect.Round(tagname,classname,options);
```

It's interesting to look through the code for Rico (which is very readable). When the `Rico.Effect.Round` class is instantiated, the elements to modify are accessed using a function Rico adds to the document object:

```
document.getElementsByTagAndClassName = function...
```

The function takes a class and tag name and returns one or more nodes that match both constraints. Each element is then passed to the one-off object to actually create the effect.

Returning to the demonstration, Example 14-4 is a web page that rounds the corners of three DIV elements using the Rico API in combination with different options: ordinary rounding, rounding with border, and rounding only the bottom corners.

Example 14-4. Working with Rico's rounded-corner effects

```
<!DOCTYPE html PUBLIC "-//W3C//DTD XHTML 1.0 Transitional//EN"
"http://www.w3.org/TR/xhtml1/DTD/xhtml1-transitional.dtd">
<html>
<head>
<title>PrettyPretty</title>
<meta http-equiv="Content-Type" content="text/html; charset=utf-8" />
<style type="text/css">

.roundme { width:250px;background-color:#0f0;margin: 20px; }
.contents { padding: 10px }
</style>
<script type="text/javascript"
     src="prototype.js">
</script>
<script type="text/javascript"
     src="rico.js">
</script>
<script type="text/javascript">
//<![CDATA[

document.onclick=roundMe;

 rounded = false;
   function roundMe() {
      if ( !rounded ) {
         Rico.Corner.round($('div'));
         Rico.Corner.round($('div2'), {border: '#ff0000'});
         Rico.Corner.round($('div3'), {corners:"bottom"});
      }
      rounded = true;
   }

</script>
</head>
<body>
<div class="roundme" id="div" >
<div class="contents">
A div element with rounded corners.
</div>
</div>
<div id="div2" class="roundme">
<div class="contents">
Another div element with rounded corners.
</div>
</div>
<div class="roundme" id="div3">
<div class="contents">
```

Example 14-4. Working with Rico's rounded-corner effects (continued)

```
Another div
</div>
</div>
</body>
</html>
```

Clicking on the page calls the function that does the rounding. Figure 14-1 shows the page after the Rico effect has been applied.

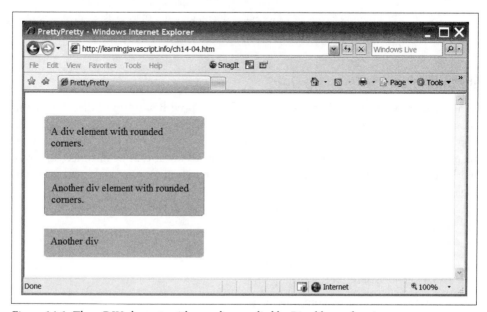

Figure 14-1. Three DIV elements with rounding applied by Rico library functions

The rounding effect can be applied as soon as a page loads. To make it less obvious, hide the elements until the page is finished loading, so that when they show, they show rounded.

Dojo

I hesitated about including Dojo. In some ways, it demonstrates how far you can take JavaScript away from the language, which makes it a good demonstration of the flexibility of the language. On the other hand, Dojo demonstrates how far you can take JavaScript away from the language, to the point where much of the simplicity of JavaScript is lost (not to mention some of the built-in DOM functionality).

Dojo really is a mastery of packaging and encapsulation. Much of the functionality has to do with keeping the amount of code loaded into a page to a minimum. Unfortunately, it also makes the code extremely difficult to read.

What sets Dojo apart is its focus on making desktop applications in the browser. It supports a Flash-based storage mechanism, including providing the Flash file used as a container. Two stellar demos of the library are Mail, a simple mail application, and Moxie, a web editor with persistent storage.

Another aspect of Dojo's library and framework that makes it stand out is its concept of widgets, which we'll get into later.

 The Dojo Toolkit web site is at *http://dojotoolkit.org/*. This includes the beginnings of a very nice set of documentation by Alex Russell, at *http://dojotoolkit.org/docs/*, and a manual at *http://manual.dojotoolkit.org/index.html*.

Installing and Setting Up Dojo

When you download and unzip Dojo, you'll end up with a group of directories and files. Just as with previous frameworks, you'll include *dojo.js* in your Dojo-enabled application, but you'll also need to load the secondary libraries based on your planned development activity. And there are a lot of libraries. For instance, if you're working with Dojo form widgets (a packaged functionality), you could end up needing to include the following script components:

```
dojo.require("dojo.widget.validate");
dojo.require("dojo.widget.ComboBox");
dojo.require("dojo.widget.Checkbox");
dojo.require("dojo.widget.Editor");
dojo.require("dojo.widget.DatePicker");
dojo.require("dojo.widget.Button");
```

Dojo then loads only those components you specify.

Like most of the newer libraries, Dojo has an Ajax component and drag-and-drop support, as well as an effects component, with slides, fades, and so on. In addition, it has three sets of widget libraries: ones for layout, form, and a general widget. It's actually the widget libraries that interested me most with Dojo.

Dojo Widgets

Dojo widgets are HTML elements bound to custom JavaScript objects. They're not unlike the added functionality associated with HTML elements in the BOM, except that widgets extend the base functionality. And they do so through attachment of a CSS class, which is a nicely different approach from the other libraries.

To demonstrate this capability, there's a rather nice fisheye component that magnifies content when your mouse is over the object. A demo of its use is included in the Dojo download, so I picked through the example to see what I could stea— …borrow.

Example 14-5 demonstrates how to use the fisheye widget. The key elements are the use of the class definitions for each DIV element that encloses the toolbar image, and the attribute for the image. Once the proper library is loaded, in this case, dojo. widget.FisheyeList, no other script needs to be used in the page. The reason is that the underlying code uses class definitions and attributes to decide what needs to be adjusted and when.

Example 14-5. Fisheye widget

```
<!DOCTYPE html PUBLIC "-//W3C//DTD XHTML 1.0 Transitional//EN"
"http://www.w3.org/TR/xhtml1/DTD/xhtml1-transitional.dtd">
<html>
<head>
<title>FishEye on Dotty</title>
<meta http-equiv="Content-Type" content="text/html; charset=utf-8" />

<style type="text/css">

.container { width: 800px;
             margin: 0px auto;
             border: 1px solid #00f;
           }

.content { padding: 30px }

.dojoHtmlFisheyeListBar {
        margin: 0 auto;
        text-align: center;
}

.outerbar {
        background-color: #CCD9FF;
        text-align: center;
        left: 0px;
        top: 0px;
        width: 100%;
}

</style>

<script type="text/javascript" src="dojo/dojo.js"></script>

<script type="text/javascript">
//<![CDATA[

        dojo.require("dojo.widget.FisheyeList");

//]]>
</script>
</head>
<body>
<div class="container">
<div class="outerbar">
<div class="dojo-FisheyeList"
```

Example 14-5. Fisheye widget (continued)

```
        dojo:itemWidth="60" dojo:itemHeight="60"
        dojo:itemMaxWidth="300" dojo:itemMaxHeight="300"
        dojo:orientation="horizontal"
        dojo:effectUnits="2"
        dojo:itemPadding="10"
        dojo:attachEdge="top"
        dojo:labelEdge="bottom"
        dojo:enableCrappySvgSupport="false"
>

        <div class="dojo-FisheyeListItem" onClick="load_app(1);"
                dojo:iconsrc="dotty.gif" caption="Dotty">
        </div>

        <div class="dojo-FisheyeListItem" onClick="load_app(2);"
                dojo:iconsrc="doomed.gif" caption="Doomed">
        </div>

        <div class="dojo-FisheyeListItem" onClick="load_app(3);"
                dojo:iconsrc="falling.gif" caption="I'm falling">
        </div>

        <div class="dojo-FisheyeListItem" onClick="load_app(4);"
                dojo:iconsrc="impatient.gif" caption="Impatient">
        </div>

        <div class="dojo-FisheyeListItem" onClick="load_app(5);"
                dojo:iconsrc="upright.gif" caption="Upright">
        </div>

        <div class="dojo-FisheyeListItem" onClick="load_app(6);"
                dojo:iconsrc="mad.gif" dojo:caption="Mad" >
        </div>
</div>
</div>
<div class="content">
<p><pre>
Forgive me, I'm no good at this. I can't write back. I never read your letter.

I can't say I got your note. I haven't had the strength to open the envelope.

The mail stacks up by the door. Your hand's illegible. Your postcards were

defaced. Wash your wet hair? Any document you meant to send has yet to

reach me. The untied parcel service never delivered. I regret to say I'm

unable to reply to your unexpressed desires. I didn't get the book you sent.

By the way, my computer was stolen. Now I'm unable to process words...

Excerpt from <em>All She Wrote</em> by Harryette Mullen
</pre></p>
```

Example 14-5. Fisheye widget (continued)

```
</div>
</div>
</body>
</html>
```

Figure 14-2 shows the page after the mouse is moved over the menu bar. The effect is very well done, providing just enough of the rollover feel of a fisheye toolbar magnifier. More importantly, if JavaScript is enabled, it's easy to include script to create the menu; if JavaScript's not enabled, it provides an alternative menu system in a NOSCRIPT tag.

Figure 14-2. Fisheye effect through Dojo Widget

You can also create your own widgets. One of the articles in the documentation section of the Dojo Toolkit provides detailed instructions on how to create your own widget (*http://dojotoolkit.org/docs/fast_widget_authoring.html*). Just like with Apple's Dashboard widgets, these JavaScript widgets are a package of XHTML page elements constrained by CSS and bound to JavaScript.

This is an idea well worth investigating further for your own libraries if you don't end up using Dojo.

 If there's one other major downside to Dojo aside from the difficulty in reading the script (outside of the use of compression), it's the fact that it doesn't load quickly. There is a noticeable lag in loading unless you strip the modules used down to the absolute minimum.

The Yahoo! UI

In Chapter 13, we had a chance to play with Google Maps' API, and in this chapter we'll give Yahoo! a chance to show its Ajaxy stuff.

The Yahoo! UI Library is a complete set of files that provides numerous functionality; some are basic DHTML effects, and others use Ajax to integrate with the Yahoo! search engine. To use the library, first download and unzip it from the Yahoo! UI site (*http://developer.yahoo.com/yui/*). This site also provides documentation, and there are numerous examples installed with the library.

Since there are well-documented examples and API calls included with the UI, I'm going to walk through one of existing examples rather than create any new ones. In this case, I'm going to take a closer look at the AutoComplete control being used with data accessed from Flickr, the photo-sharing service.

You can find examples of the AutoComplete control use in the examples/autocomplete subdirectory, and loading the *index.html* page allows you to pick whether you want to try out AutoComplete with JSON or with in-memory array, and so on. I clicked the "Query Flickr Web Services for XML" option.

Once the page opens, a logger console that can be collapsed is shown on the right side of the page, and a form field to enter Flickr tags is just below the application description. As you enter the tag information, the console provides information about the program's progress, and as you type, thumbnails of pictures that match tags with whatever letters you've typed are shown below the search field. All in all, a lot of activity is going on, and you can easily get lost playing with the AutoComplete control.

Looking under the covers (the bottom half of the example page shows the script) at the JavaScript, a data-source object needs to be created first. The Flickr XML example uses the Yahoo.widget.DS_XHR data control. This control processes XML Http requests (commonly referred to as REST requests). The URL for the request proxy and an optional object with configuration parameters are passed to the constructor:

```
oACDS = new YAHOO.widget.DS_XHR("./php/flickr_proxy.php",

    ["photo", "title", "id", "owner", "secret", "server"]);
```

Once the data source object is instantiated, several properties are set, including a parameter, responseType, maxCacheEntries, and the script query:

```
// Instantiate data source and define schema as an array:

//      ["ResultNodeName",

//      "QueryKeyAttributeOrNodeName",

//      "AdditionalParamAttributeOrNodeName1",
```

```
//      ...

//      "AdditionalParamAttributeOrNodeNameN"]

oACDS = new YAHOO.widget.DS_XHR("./php/flickr_proxy.php",

    ["photo", "title", "id", "owner", "secret", "server"]);

oACDS.scriptQueryParam = "tags";

oACDS.responseType = YAHOO.widget.DS_XHR.prototype.TYPE_XML;

oACDS.maxCacheEntries = 0;

oACDS.scriptQueryAppend = "method=flickr.photos.search";
```

I then took a peek at the proxy server application in PHP. It's a simple server application that uses the Flickr REST API to perform a query of photos based on whatever tag or set of tags is sent in the query. It then returns the results without any modification.

The AutoComplete widget is created next, and then several of its properties are set:

```
// Instantiate auto complete

oAutoComp = new YAHOO.widget.AutoComplete('flickrinput','flickrcontainer',
oACDS);

oAutoComp.autoHighlight = false;

oAutoComp.formatResult = function(oResultItem, sQuery) {

    // This was defined by the schema array of the data source

    var sTitle = oResultItem[0];

    var sId = oResultItem[1];

    var sOwner = oResultItem[2];

    var sSecret = oResultItem[3];

    var sServer = oResultItem[4];

    var sUrl = "http://static.flickr.com/" +

        sServer +

        "/" +

        sId +

        "_" +

        sSecret +
```

```
        "_s.jpg";

    var sMarkup = "<img src='" + sUrl + "' class='yui-ac-flickrImg'> " + sTitle;

    return (sMarkup);

};
```

The names of the form field and the container to hold the results are passed to the AutoComplete constructor along with the newly created data-source object. Next, a function to format the result assigns data fields to application variables, which are then used to build a return string suitable for embedding in the web page.

Behind the scenes, then, we can assume that traditional Ajax calls are being made between the Yahoo! UI library and the proxy PHP application hosted on my server, which then makes calls to the Flickr server. In addition, this same library most likely formats the XML that returns into a format suitable for easy access and display.

It's a lovely library, not only for the functionality provided but for the approach it demonstrates for working with external services. Since a direct Flickr API access violates the same-domain security rule, the server-side proxy application that manages the querying has no problem because there are no security restrictions on server applications accessing external web services. The UI then uses traditional JavaScript to communicate with this proxy.

In addition, the component-based nature of this library is one of the better I've seen, as well as being one of the best documented and demonstrated of the more advanced libraries. I give the Yahoo! UI a must-see rating for any new or experienced JavaScript developer.

MochiKit

As soon as you access the MochiKit web site, once you get past the ubiquitous lime color, you see the words proudly proclaimed across the top:

MochiKit makes JavaScript suck less

In my opinion, if JavaScript sucked that much, it wouldn't be used so extensively, and we wouldn't have the rich set of libraries and frameworks, of which I've only provided a sample in this chapter. However, be that as it may, MochiKit has a nicely organized web site that makes it very easy to find demos, documentation, and code. As with other libraries, MochiKit functionality is packaged into several different behavioral and UI components, including:

- `MochiKit.Async`: The Ajax component
- `MochiKit.Base`: Foundation for the MochiKit framework
- `MochiKit.DOM`: Wrapper around DOM functionality
- `MochiKit.DragAndDrop`: The ever-present drag and drop
- `MochiKit.Color`: CSS3 color abstraction
- `MochiKit.DateTime`: Date and time functionality
- `MochiKit.Format`: String formatting
- `MochiKit.Iter`: Adds iteration capability
- `MochiKit.Logging`: "We're all tired of alert( )"
- `MochiKit.LoggingPane`: Interactive logging pane
- `MochiKit.Signal`: Universal event handling
- `MochiKit.Style`: CSS API
- `MochiKit.Sortable`: Sortable effects
- `MochiKit.Visual`: The usual visual effects, such as rounding, visibility, and opacity

There are several interesting modules, all worth exploring. But the one that caught my eye was "We're all tired of alert( )".

I find that `alert` is handy to debug, but true, it isn't the most efficient. I decided to take a closer look at MochiKit logging.

Logging

As states in the MochiKit documentation, there is no print capability, which, in my opinion, developers have been dependent on for debugging. As such, the `alert` dialog is used for most debugging efforts.

MochiKit logging works with whatever console each browser supports. According to the documentation, it works with Opera 9, Safari, IE, and Firefox (if Firebug is installed). As an alternative, you can use the logging pane module. To do so, disable logging to the console and have the communications go to this pop-up window. I decided to try out the console option and also take Firebug for a test drive.

In Example 14-6, I have a copy of Example 13-3, which contains the Ajax example that processes XML. If any application is going to have something go wrong, it will probably occur in an Ajax request/response, when processing XML. When creating this small application, I had to use the alert function a lot, and it would be nice to use something else.

Firebug

What a great name for a Firefox debugging tool.

The Firebug add-on was created by Joe Hewitt and provides a line-by-line debugger, as well as a way to log messages from script. It also provides a JavaScript command-line tool and inspector to easily look at all page elements in context.

As you go over each element, the Inspector briefly highlights it directly in the page. However, it's the message console I found invaluable. When working with a script, I would keep Firebug open, and then have access to all error and information messages instantly, rather than wait for Firefox's very slow console to open. It's also a snap to keep it clean, but you have to shut it down when web browsing—there's an amazing number of bad JavaScript out there.

Firebug is a must-have tool for JavaScript developers. Download it at *https://addons. mozilla.org/firefox/1843/* and read more about it at *http://www.joehewitt.com/software/ firebug/*.

Figure 14-3 shows the application created by the Dojo fisheye effect, opened at the same time as the Firebug console, with inspection turned on.

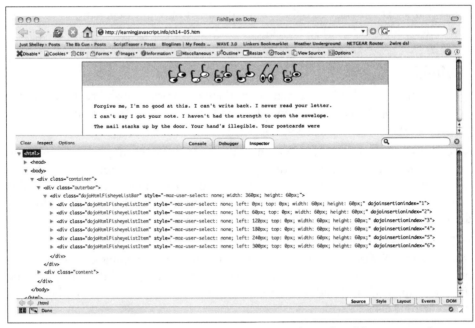

Figure 14-3. Dojo fisheye application opened at same time as the Firebug debugging console

Example 14-6. Ajax application with MochiKit debugging enabled

```
<!DOCTYPE html PUBLIC "-//W3C//DTD XHTML 1.0 Transitional//EN"
"http://www.w3.org/TR/xhtml1/DTD/xhtml1-transitional.dtd">
<html>
<head>
<title>Hello Ajax World, Too</title>
<meta http-equiv="Content-Type" content="text/html; charset=utf-8" />
<style type="text/css">
div.elem { margin: 20px; }
</style>

        <script type="text/javascript" src="mochikit/lib/MochiKit/MochiKit.js"></script>
        <script type="text/javascript" src="mochikit/lib/MochiKit/Logging.js"></script>

<script type="text/javascript">
//<![CDATA[

var xmlhttp = false;
if (window.XMLHttpRequest) {
   xmlhttp = new XMLHttpRequest();
   xmlhttp.overrideMimeType('text/xml');
} else if (window.ActiveXObject) {
   xmlhttp = new ActiveXObject("Microsoft.XMLHTTP");
}

function populateList() {
   var state = document.forms[0].elements[0].value;
log("INFO state is ",state);
   var url = 'ajaxxml.php?state=' + state;
log("INFO url is ",url);
   xmlhttp.open('GET', url, true);
   xmlhttp.onreadystatechange = getCities;
   xmlhttp.send(null);
}
function getCities() {
   if(xmlhttp.readyState == 4 && xmlhttp.status == 200) {
     log("INFO responseXML is ",xmlhttp.responseXML);
     var hdrs = xmlhttp.getAllResponseHeaders();
     log("INFO headers are ", hdrs);
     try {
        var citynodes = xmlhttp.responseXML.getElementsByTagName('city');
        for (var i = 0; i < citynodes.length; i++) {
           var name = value = null;
           for (var j = 0; j < citynodes[i].childNodes.length; j++) {
              var elem = citynodes[i].childNodes[j].nodeName;
              var nodevalue = citynodes[i].childNodes[j].firstChild.nodeValue;
              if (elem == 'value') {
                 value = nodevalue;
              } else {
                 name = nodevalue;
              }
           }
           document.forms[0].elements[1].options[i] = new Option(name,value);
        }
```

```
        } catch (e) {
            logDebug("DEBUG error message is", e.message);
        }
    } else {
        document.getElementById('cities').innerHTML = 'Error: No Cities';
    }
}

//]]>
</script>

</head>
<body>

<h3>Select State:</h3>
<form action="ajaxxml.php" method="get">
<div class="elem">
<select onchange="populateList( )">
<option value="CA">California</option>
<option value="MO">Missouri</option>
<option value="WA">Washington</option>
<option value="ID">Idaho</option>
</select>
</div>
<h3>Cities:</h3>
<div class="elem">
<select id="cities">
</select>
</div>
</form>

</body>
</html>
```

I've highlighted the lines of code where I've made changes based on adding in the logging functionality. What I find a relief with MochiKit is that, other than having to include the base functionality, most of the MochiKit modules are just that—modules that can be included only as needed.

Figure 14-4 shows the web-page application with Firebug opened, as well as Mochi-Kit's logging. As you can see, this is vastly superior to an alert dialog. And they're just in time to use for all of the JavaScript applications you've been itching to create.

Have fun.

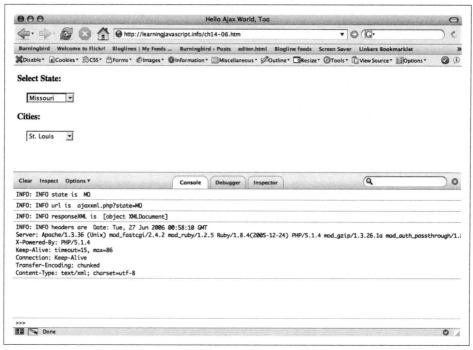

Figure 14-4. MochiKit logging in Firebug console

Questions

1. You're using a library such as Dojo in addition to your functionality. The Dojo effect, such as the fisheye toolbar, doesn't work. Where's the first place to look to see how there might be a conflict between your code and Dojo's?

2. In the Prototype library, what does the $( ) function do?

3. The fisheye application created using Dojo does not validate as XHTML. The custom attributes on the DIV elements are accountable for much of this. What is a workaround?

4. How does the Yahoo! UI Library work around the same-domain security policy but still allow access to web services at other domains?

5. So, does MochiKit make JavaScript "suck less"? Seriously, what's your view on the strengths and weaknesses of JavaScript now that you've read a book about it?

Answers are provided in the appendix.

Answers

Chapter 2

1. The following are valid:

   ```
   $someVariable
   _someVariable
   some_variable
   som&#232;variable
   ```

   The function variable uses a reserved JavaScript keyword, someVariable and 1Variable both start with invalid characters, and some*variable uses an invalid character, a JavaScript operator (*), as part of the variable name. All invalid names generate JavaScript errors.

2. The identifiers are converted as follows:

   The variable some-month becomes someMonth, using CamelCase notation.

   The function theMonth becomes getTheCurrentMonth, using relevant verbs and other distinguishing information.

   The const current-month becomes CURRENT-MONTH, using constant-width upper-case letters.

   The variable summer-month becomes summerMonths, maintaining consistency between the array of items and variable name.

   The MyLibrary-afunction function becomes mylibraryFunctionverbFunctionname.

3. Important point to remember: conjugation is the bane of coders. Use a backslash before the inner single quote so that it's interpreted literally, and not end-of-string:

   ```
   var someString = 'Who once said, "Only two things are infinite, the universe and
   human stupidity, and I\'m not sure about the former."';
   ```

4. The following code would work:

   ```
   var fltNumber = 432.54;
   var intNumber = parseInt(fltNumber);
   var octNumber = parseInt(intNumber,2);
   var hexNumber = parseInt(intNumber,16);
   ```

The function `parseInt` returns the decimal base integer of the floating-point number, which is 432. It can also take a second parameter, specifying base: 8 for octal and 16 for hexidecimal.

5. Ah, trick question here. Passing a variable that's not been declared to a function, user function, or JavaScript function results in a JavaScript error, so your function code will never need to test for this.

To test to see whether the value has been set, use a conditional statement:

```
function test(a) {
if (a) {
// some code
}
}
```

Chapter 3

1. The solution is:

```
var resultOfComp = (valA - valB) % 3 / 2 * (4 + valC) - 3;
```

2. The solution is:

```
switch(val) {
    case 'one','two' :
        result = 'OK';
        break;
    case 'three' :
        result = 'OK2';
        break;
    default :
        result = 'NONE';
}
```

3. The solution is:

```
if ((varOne == 33) && (varTwo <= 100) && (varThree > 0))...
```

4. and 5. In for loops, you don't have to start at 0 or 1, and you also don't have to increment the number. Here's how to count upward between 10 and 20:

```
for (var i = 11; i < 20; i++) {
   document.writeln(i + "<br />");
}
```

And here's how to reverse the count:

```
for (var i = 19; i > 10; i--) {
   document.writeln(i + "<br />");
}
```

Chapter 4

1. Use the `String.split` method, passing in a comma (,) as delimiter.

2. Word boundaries are particularly useful if you want a separate word, but being given a string that could match within another word:

```
var regexp = /\bfun\b/;
var str = "The fun of functions is that they are functional.";
var result = str.replace(regexp,"power");
```

3. There is no `Date` function that manipulates weeks, but we know that a week is 7 days at 24 hours a day, for a total of 168 hours. Use the `getHours` method to get the current date's hours, add this value, reset the hours, and then print out the date. Other approaches can also be used and are left for your own exploration:

```
var dtNow = new Date();
var hours = dtNow.getHours();
hours+=168;
dtNow.setHours(hours);
document.writeln(dtNow.toString());
```

4. `Math.floor` can be used to round the number down; `Math.ceil` can round the number up.

5. The answer is:

```
var str = "apple.orange-strawberry,lemon-.lime";
var regexp = /[\.|-]/g;
var result = str.replace(regexp,',');
var arrayValues = result.split(',');
for (var i = 0; i < arrayValues.length; i++) {
    document.writeln(arrayValues[i] + "<br />");
}
```

Chapter 5

1. Declarative functions are the traditional function forms, and should be used whenever possible because they're parsed just once (more efficient) and easy to spot in a page (readable). In addition, all browsers that support JavaScript support this type of function.

   Anonymous functions have no name, are assigned a variable or passed as a function parameter, and are parsed each time they're accessed. They're useful when some circumstance, such as user input, determines their behavior.

   Literal functions are useful for defining methods for objects, or to pass as a parameter. They're also useful in recursion, especially because if given a name, that name is available only internally in the code.

2. If an object, such as an array, is passed as a function parameter, modifications to the array in the function are reflected outside the function. A function can also return a value, and any modifications to global variables are also reflected outside the function scope.

3. Rather than define a parameter list, access the arguments array. With this, the number of arguments passed into the function can be easily altered:

```
function test( ) {
for (var i = 0; i < arguments.length; i++) {
    alert(arguments[i]);
}
}
test(1,2,3);

test(1,2,3,4);
```

4. The this property not only sets but accesses properties within a function.

5. An anonymous function suits these requirements:

```
function invokeFunction(dataObject,functionToCall) {

    functionToCall(dataObject);
}

var funcCall = new Function('x','alert(x)');

invokeFunction('hello', funcCall);
```

Chapter 6

1. The three approaches are inline, using syntax such as onload on the body element; using the traditional DOM Level 0 event capturing, such as window.onload; and using the newer DOM Level 2 events, such as addEventListener or attachEvent.

2. If using the DOM Level 0 event-handling system, you either access the event object on the window object or passed in as a function. For DOM Level 2, the event object is always passed into the function. From the event object, access the screenX or screenY properties.

3. The IE approach differs from that supported by most browsers, and as such, you have to support both it and the others. Test if the stopPropagation method is supported on the event object and if so, invoke it; otherwise, set the cancelBubble property to true.

4. The answer is:

```
if (window.addEventListener) {
        window.addEventListener("load",functionCall,false);
    } else if (window.attachEvent) {
        window.attachEvent("onload", functionCall);
    }
```

5. Though we haven't covered capturing keyboard events, typically you capture the keydown event and then access the Unicode key code from the which property on the event:

```
if (document.addEventListener) {
    document.addEventListener("keydown",getKey,true);
} else if (document.attachEvent) {
    document.attachEvent("onkeydown", getKey);
}

function getKey(evnt) {
    alert(evnt.which);
}
```

Chapter 7

1. If using the DOM Level 0 events, returning false from the event handler and the event-handler script cancels the submittal. If using DOM Level 2, set cancelBubble to true for IE, and call the preventDefault for other browsers, both based on the event object.

2. The blur event is triggered when the field loses focus. This is a good time to check the text field to make sure it has valid data.

3. The select options are stored in an array called Options. As such, you can add new options as you would add new array elements, making sure that the entry is a new Option object:

```
opts[opts.length] = new Option("Option Four", "Opt 4");
```

4. Here's one approach:

```
var rgEx = /^[A-Za-z\s]*$/g;
var OK = rgEx.exec(document.someForm.text1.value);
```

5. The code must first assign an event-handler function to each radio button's onclick event handler:

```
document.someForm.radiogroup[0].onclick=handleClick;
document.someForm.radiogroup[1].onclick=handleClick;
```

If there are several buttons, this can be managed in a for loop. In the handleClick function, test the check status, and disable the form element accordingly. For instance, to disable the submit button:

```
function handleClick( ) {
   if (document.someForm.radiogroup[1].checked) {
     document.someForm.submit.disabled=true;
   } else {
     document.someForm.submit.disabled=false;
   }
}
```

Chapter 8

1. There are actually several different ways to save material on a client machine:
   - Use cookies
   - Use a third-party plug-in such as Flash
   - Ask the user to right-click on an element and save it to his local directory
   - Attach a downloadable file to a link, where clicking on the link opens a dialog and tells the user to save the file
   - Create a browser extension, which is then downloaded and installed

2. A cookie name, a value, an expiration date for the cookie, and a path associated with the cookie.

3. Do not provide an expiration date.

4. Any data that can be invoked in the browser, or can be used to snoop around a client's cookies, or even run a server-side process. In particular, the phrase, javascript: or script tags should be scrubbed from input.

   However, this isn't as cleanly defined as you would think. For content-management tools, it may be feasible for a person to enter script into a specific posting or page. But in a multiuser environment, an individual could use script to find out information about the other users of the system.

   Look at any input field with suspicion and ask yourself, who can enter data through the field, and do I trust them 100 percent? Then scrub the data.

5. There is no right or wrong answer for this question. Here are some uses of cookies I've seen:
   - To maintain a person's username and URL and email for a comment system
   - To provide live feedback on data entries
   - To enable a spell checker
   - To store login information
   - To maintain a shopping cart

I've never run up against the 4 K cookie limit in any of these cases.

Chapter 9

1. The prompt dialogue.

2. Here's the timer:

```
setTimeout(callFunction,3000,paramA,paramB);
```

3. The location object can be used to change what's loaded in the browser. The individual items or the href property can be set to provide an entire URL.

4. The navigator object can be accessed to get information about the browser, whether cookies are enabled, and so on.

5. Here's the code for the window:

```
var newWindow = window.open("http://help.
htm","","width=400,height=400,toolbar=no,status=no");
```

Chapter 10

1. The attributes are: id, title, lang, dir, and className

2. Here's the element type:

```
var elems = document.getElementByName('elemName');
for (var i = 0; i < elems.length; i++) {
    alert(elems[i].tagName);
}
```

3. Here are the element types:

```
var children = nd.childNodes;
for (var i = 0; i < children.length; i++) {
    alert(children[i].nodeType);
}

divs = document.getElementsByTagName('div');
 for (var i = 0; i < divs.length; i++) {
    alert(divs[i].id);
}

var elem = document.getElementById("elem1");
var children = elem.childNodes;
var child = elem.getElementsByTagName('h1')[0];
var p = document.createElement("p");
var txt = document.createTextNode("hello");
p.appendChild(txt);

elem.replaceChild(p,child);
```

4. The solution is:

```
divs = document.getElementsByTagName('div');
 for (var i = 0; i < divs.length; i++) {
    alert(divs[i].id);
}
```

5. The solution is:

```
var elem = document.getElementById("elem1");
var children = elem.childNodes;
var child = elem.getElementsByTagName('h1')[0];
var p = document.createElement("p");
var txt = document.createTextNode("hello");
p.appendChild(txt);

elem.replaceChild(p,child);
```

Chapter 11

1. Use the Number's prototype property:

```
Number.prototype.triple = function () {
    var nm = this.valueOf() * 3;
    return nm;
}
var num = new Number(3.0);
alert(num.triple());
```

2. Declare the data member with var instead of this. The purpose behind data hiding is to control how the data is accessed or updated.

3. Use the throw statement to trigger an error. Then implement try . . . catch in the calling application:

```
if (typeof value != "number") {
    throw "NotANumber";
}
```

4. Unlike the event object, there are more than just model differences involved. Not only is the property different, but so is the value that's assigned to the property.

5. Here's one approach to creating the objects:

```
function Control() {
    var state = 'on';
    var background = '#fff';

    this.changeState = function() {
        if (state == 'on') {
            state = 'off';
            background = '#000';
        } else
            state = 'on';
            background = '#fff';
        };
    };

    this.getState = function() {
        return state;
    };

    this.getColor = function() {
        return background;
    };
}
```

Chapter 12

1. One approach is to set the style of the element inline using the style attribute. You can also use getComputedStyle or currentStyle, taking care to compensate for browser differences. A third approach is to store the current settings in a global variable and access it, rather than the actual setting.

2. You can set font size and line height at the same time:

```
obj.style.font="14pt/16pt";
obj.style.color="#f00";
```

3. If the text is in an element contained within the one whose style you've altered, and this inner element has a different style setting, it will override your setting.

4. One way is to resize it out of existence by setting either the `width` or `height` to zero. You can also clip the element to the top, bottom, left, or, right. You can also hide it by setting `visibility` to `hidden`, or turn off the display. Finally, you can make it move off the page, or move another element in front of it.

5. Try a mouse-click event handler attached to the image of an item, in combination with a "Buy me" hypertext link for keyboard events; this could move the item to a shopping cart using animation or instantaneously. This effect cuts the amount of coding, ensures the effect is accessible, and is still pretty cool.

Chapter 13

1. The third, and optional, parameter of `XMLHttpRequest.open` is a Boolean value. Setting this to true, the default, the request is asynchronous; setting it to `false` makes the request synchronous.

2. After getting a reference to the `XMLHttpRequest` object and opening it, assign the callback function through the `onReadyStateChange` property.

3. The `XMLHttpRequest` object's `readyState` property needs to have a value of 4 for completed; the request object's HTTP status property should be 200 for a successful service request.

4. Here are the three formats: HTML, which can be immediately added to the page without any formatting; XML, which can be formatted with XSLT; and JSON, which can be used in a `eval` function call to create a web structure ready for processing.

5. From the Google Maps documentation, create a new `GIcon` object and populate its properties. Then use the object when creating the new `GMarker` object:

```
var icon = new GIcon( );
icon.image = "http://labs.google.com/ridefinder/images/mm_20_red.png";
icon.shadow = "http://labs.google.com/ridefinder/images/mm_20_shadow.png";
icon.iconSize = new GSize(12, 20);
icon.shadowSize = new GSize(22, 20);
icon.iconAnchor = new GPoint(6, 20);
icon.infoWindowAnchor = new GPoint(5, 1);
...
marker = new Gmarker(point,icon);
```

Chapter 14

1. The first thing to check is to ensure you're using the DOM Level 2 event handling. If you use DOM Level 0, such as:

   ```
   window.onload=function;
   ```

   You'll overwrite the event handlers the Dojo library has assigned to this specific event.

2. The $( ) function returns whatever element has the identifier passed in as parameter to the function.

3. Dojo requires these element attributes, but they can be added using JavaScript before Dojo needs them (after the page loads). Create a function to add the attributes, and place a call to this function in the page body just after the toolbar is loaded. In the function, set the attributes using the DOM. Here's the code I've used for a web page:

   ```
   function setMenuProps( ) {
     var cont = document.getElementById("controller");
     cont.setAttribute("itemWidth","60");
     cont.setAttribute("itemHeight","100");
     cont.setAttribute("itemMaxWidth", "200");
     cont.setAttribute("itemMaxHeight", "300");
     cont.setAttribute("orientation","horizontal");
     cont.setAttribute("effectUnits","2");
     cont.setAttribute("itemPadding","10");
     cont.setAttribute("attachEdige","top");
     cont.setAttribute("labelEdge","bottom");
     cont.setAttribute("enableCrappySvgSupport","false");

     var menu1 = document.getElementById("menu1");
     menu1.setAttribute("onClick","load_page('http://scriptteaser.com/
   learningjavascript/')");
     menu1.setAttribute("iconsrc","/dotty/dotty.gif");
     menu1.setAttribute("caption","Learning JavaScript");

     var menu2 = document.getElementById("menu2");
     menu2.setAttribute("onClick","load_page('http://scriptteaser.com/threepsandr/
   ')");
     menu2.setAttribute("iconsrc","/dotty/doomed.gif");
     menu2.setAttribute("caption","Three Ps and your little R, too");

     var menu3 = document.getElementById("menu3");
     menu3.setAttribute("onClick","load_page('http://scriptteaser.com/webservices/
   ')");
     menu3.setAttribute("iconsrc","/dotty/falling.gif");
     menu3.setAttribute("caption","Web Services");
   ```

```
var menu4 = document.getElementById("menu4");
menu4.setAttribute("onClick","load_page('http://scriptteaser.com/misc/')");
menu4.setAttribute("iconsrc","/dotty/impatient.gif");
menu4.setAttribute("caption","Odds n Ends");

var menu5 = document.getElementById("menu5");
menu5.setAttribute("onClick","load_page('http://words.einsteinslock.com/')");
menu5.setAttribute("iconsrc","/dotty/mad.gif");
menu5.setAttribute("caption","Mad Tech Womon on the Loose");

var menu6 = document.getElementById("menu6");
menu6.setAttribute("onClick","load_page('http://scriptteaser.com/')");
menu6.setAttribute("iconsrc","/dotty/home.png");
menu6.setAttribute("caption","Home");
}
```
Now the custom attributes can be removed from the elements. Dojo is happy and XHTML validator is happy that they're gone.

4. Yahoo! UI creates server-side applications that provide the services for Java-Script in the pages and which make the web-service calls to the remote service. It's actually a good workaround, though performance should be monitored.

5. This is one I can't provide a answer for. I like JavaScript, and I hope that after reading this book, you do, too.

Index

Symbols

-- (decrement) operator, 48
- (negative) operator, 48
- (subtraction) operator, 47
< (less than) operator, 62
$( ) function, Prototype library, 293
$F function, Prototype library, 293
$H function, Prototype library, 293
$R function, Prototype library, 294
% (modulus) operator, 47
* (multiplication) operator, 47
+ (addition) operator, 47
++ (increment) operator, 48
/ (division) operator, 47
= (assignment) operator, 46
> (greater than) operator, 62

A

accessibility, 17
addEventListener, 126, 128
addition (+) operator, 47
AJAX, 270
Ajax
    best practices, 272
    Hello World, 273
    overview, 273
    permalink, 271
    security, 272
    XMLHttpRequest, 277
alert dialog, 165
all collection, document object, 188

alpha filter, 226
anchors, links and, 185
anonymous functions, 101
apply method, 231
arguments, functions, 99
arithmethic statements, 47
arithmetic operators, 47
arrays
    associative, 96
    constructing, 92
    queues, FIFO, 94
assignment statement, 46
assignment with operation, 50
associative arrays, 96

B

backslash in strings, 35
best practices, 17
binary operators, 48
bitwise operators, 50
BOM (Browser Object Model), 164
boolean data types, 33, 37
Boolean function, 38
Boolean object, 71
bottom property, 252
browser objects, 12
browsers
    DOM, 195–196
    supported, 3
built-in objects, 12

We'd like to hear your suggestions for improving our indexes. Send email to *index@oreilly.com*.

C

call method, 231
callback functions, 105–107
case-sensitivity, 26
catch statement, 235
CDATA section, 10
chaining constructors, 231–232
checkboxes
    introduction, 140
    JiT validation, 141
clipping region, 261
code
    examples, xiii
    location, 9
collapsible forms, 266
comments, 11
compatibility, 4
compression, 46
conditional operators, equality, 59
conditional statements
    if...else, 55
    program flow and, 53–59
confirm method, 166
const keyword, 42
constants, 42
constructors
    chaining, 231–232
    functions, 105
cookies, 149
    creating, 152
    Dojo and, 158
    erasing, 155
    escape function, 154
    LiveConnect and, 157
    path, 154
    reading, 152
    retrieving, 5
    setting, 5
    SO storage, 158
    storing, 152, 157
    XSS (cross-site scripting), 160–163
Core API, 195
cross-site scripting (XSS), 160–163
cross-window communication, 169
CSS (Cascading Style Sheets), 242, 243, 249
    bottom property, 252
    clipping and, 259–263
    color, 249
    direction, 250
    element size, 259–263
    fontFamily, 248
    fontSize, 248
    fontSizeAdjust, 248
    fontStretch, 248
    fontStyle, 248
    fontVariant, 249
    left property, 252
    lineHeight, 249
    position property, 251
    right property, 252
    text properties, 249–251
    textAlign, 250
    textDecoration, 249
    textIndent, 249
    textTransform, 249
    top property, 252
    whiteSpace, 250
    wordSpacing, 250
    z-index, 252
custom objects, 222
    functions and, 222
    private properties, 225
    public properties, 225
custom windows, 166

D

data types, 25
    boolean, 33, 37
    number, 38–42
    numeric, 33
    string, 33–37
Date object, 85–87
declarative functions, 105
declarative/static functions, 98
decrement (--) operator, 48
detecting objects, 226–228
DHTML (Dynamic HTML), 242–247
    drag and drop, 255
dialog windows, 165
display property, 264
division (/) operator, 47
do...while loop, 66
document object, 184
    all collection, 188
    DOM, 210–212
document.domain, 151

Dojo, 303
  cookies and, 158
  installation, 304
  setup, 304
  widgets, 304
DOM (Document Object Model), 193
  browsers, 195–196
  Core API, 202–210
  document object, 210–212
  DOM tree, 203
  Element object, 213–215
  event handler and, 116–133
  interfaces, 194
  methods, 204–208
  node properties, 204–208
  style property and, 244
  tree
    modifying, 215–218
    node and, 208–210
DOM HTML API, 194, 196
  browser differences, 200
  Element object, 197
  interfaces, 197
  Node object, 197
  objects, 197–200
    access, 200
DOM inspector, MouseOver, 183
drag and drop, 255

E

Element object, 213–215
encapsulation, 228–231
end-of-line terminator, 45
equality operator, 59
error handling, 235–238
escape function, cookies, 154
escape sequences, 34
event handlers, 13
  case, 117
  cross-browser, 128
  DOM and, 116–133
  this, 124
Event object, 119
  properties, 121, 130
events
  attaching to forms, 135
  bubbling, 122, 127
  generating, 132
  inline, 118

inline model, 117
introduction, 115
objects and, 115
exec method, RegExp object, 78
expressions
  function expressions, 105
  regular expressions, 78, 79

F

FIFO queues, arrays, 94
files, 11
  including, 11
finally statement, 235
Firefox
  DOM inspector, 22
  JavaScript console, 21
floating-point numbers, 38
fontFamily, 248
fonts, style properties, 248–249
fontSize, 248
fontSizeAdjust, 248
fontStretch, 248
fontStyle, 248, 249
fontVariant, 249
for loops, 67
form fields, validation, 5
forms
  accessing, 134
  checkboxes, 140
  collapsible, 266
  events, attaching, 135
  fields, 141
    hidden, 141
    JiT regular expressions, 145–147
    JiT validation, 143
    password, 141
    textarea, 141
  radio buttons, 140
frame object, 174
frames, 174
  iframes, remote scripting in, 177
function keyword, 98
Function object, 112–114
functions
  anonymous, 101
  arguments, 99
  Boolean, 38
  callback functions, 105–107
  closure, 109–112

functions (*continued*)
 constructors, 105
 custom objects and, 222
 declarative, 105
 declarative/static, 98
 function expressions, 105
 funtion expressions, 103
 introduction, 98
 literals, 103, 105
 naming conventions, 99
 nested, 109–112
 Number, 40
 parseFloat, 39
 parseInt, 39
 recursive, 108–109
 returns, 99
 user-defined, 13

G

generating events, 132
getElementById method, 210
getElementsByTagName method, 210
global variables, 29
Google Maps, 287–289
greater than (>) operator, 62

H

Hello World, 6
hidden field, 141
history object, 180

I

if...else statements, 55
iframes, remote scripting in, 177
images, 186
increment (++) operator, 48
inheritance, 231–232
inline events, 118
innerHTML property, 189
interfaces
 Core API, 195
 DOM, 194
 DOM HTML API, 194, 197

J

JavaScript
 compatibility, 4
 history of, 2

JiT validation
 checkboxes, 141
 list items, 138
 radio buttons, 141
 regular expressions, 145–147
 text fields, 143
JSON (JavaScript Object Notation), 284

K

keywords, 26
 const, 42
 function, 98
 var, 14
 variable identifiers, 26

L

left property, 252
less than (<) operator, 62
libraries
 including, 11
 Prototype, 292
 Rico, 301–303
 script.aculo.us, 297–300
 Yahoo! UI, 308–310
links, anchors and, 185
lists, selecting items, 136
 JiT validation, 138
 modifying selection, 138
literals, functions, 105
LiveConnect, cookies and, 157
local variables, 29
location object, 174, 175
logical operators, 64
loops
 do...while, 66
 for, 67
 while, 65

M

Math object, 87
 methods, 89–91
 properties, 88
memory leaks, 112
methods
 apply, 231
 call, 231
 confirm, 166
 DOM, 204–208

getElementById, 210
getElementsByTagName, 210
Math object, 89–91
resizeBy, 170
resizeTo, 170
setTimeout, 172
String object, 73
XMLHttpRequest, 279
MochiKit, 310–314
modulus (%) operator, 47
multiplication (*) operator, 47

N

naming conventions, functions, 99
navigator object, 181
negative (-) operator, 48
nested functions, 109–112
noscript, 18
number data type, 38–42
Number function, 40
Number object, 71
numbers, floating-point, 38
numeric data types, 33

O

Object constructor, 220
object detection, 8, 226–228
Object object, 70
objects
    Boolean, 71
    browser objects, 12
    built-in, 12
    custom, 222
        functions and, 222
        private properties, 225
    Date, 85–87
    document, 184
    DOM HTML API, 197–200
    encapsulation, 228–231
    Event, 119
    events and, 115
    frame, 174
    Function, 112–114
    history, 180
    introduction, 70
    libraries, 234
    location, 174, 175
    Math, 87
        methods, 89–91
        properties, 88
    navigator, 181

Number, 71
Object, 70
one-off, 233–234
Prototype library, 295
prototyping, 220
RegExp, 78
screen, 180
String, 73–77
window, 164
one-off objects, 233–234
opacity, 226, 264
operators
    = (assignment), 46
    arithmetic, 47
    assignment with operation, 50
    binary, 48
    bitwise, 50
    equality, 59
    logical, 64
    precedence, 49
    property, 14
    relational, 61
    ternary, 63
    unary, 48
overflow, 259

P

parseFloat function, 39
parseInt function, 39
password field, 141
permalink, Ajax, 271
position property, 251
precedence of operators, 49
private properties, custom objects, 225
program flow, conditional statements
            and, 53–59
properties
    bottom, 252
    Event object, 121
    event object, 130
    innerHTML, 189
    left, 252
    Math object, 88
    nodes, DOM, 204–208
    position, 251
    prototype, 220
    right, 252
    String object, 73
    style, 244
    top, 252
    visibility, 263

property operator, 14
Prototype library, 292
    $( ) function, 293
    $F function, 293
    $H function, 293
    $R function, 294
    helper functions, 293
    objects, 295
prototype property, 220
prototyping objects, 220
public properties, custom objects, 225

Q

queues, arrays, FIFO, 94

R

radio buttons
    introduction, 140
    JiT validation, 141
recursive functions, 108–109
RegExp object, 78
    exec method, 78
    text method, 78
regular expressions, 78, 79
    JiT validation, 145–147
relational operators, 61
removeEventListener, 128
reserved words, 26
resizeBy method, 170
resizeTo method, 170
returns, functions, 99
Rico library, 301–303
right property, 252

S

same origin security policy, 150
sandbox, 16
scope, 14
    variables, 29
screen object, 180
script tag, 7
    attributes, 9
script.aculo.us library, 297–300
security
    Ajax, 272
    same origin policy, 150
select element, 136, 138
setTimeout method, 172

SO (Shared Objects), cookies and, 158
statements, 15
    arithmetic, 47
    assignment, 46
    conditional
        program flow and, 53–59
    semicolons, 44
    switch, 56
string data types, 33–37
    backslash, 35
string literals, 34
String object, 73–77
style property, 244
styles, fonts, 248–249
subtraction (-) operator, 47
switch statement, 56

T

tags, script, 7
ternary operator, 63
test method, RegExp object, 78
text, 141
    properties, 249–251
text field, 141
textarea field, 141
this keyword, object properties and, 225
timers, 172
top property, 252
try statement, 235

U

unary operators, 48
user-defined functions, 13

V

validation, form fields, 5
var keyword, 14
variables, 25
    global, 29
    identifiers
        keywords, 26
        Unicode, 26
    local, 29
    naming guidelines, 27
        prototype effect, 28
    scope, 29
visibility property, 263

W

while loop, 65
whitespace, 45
window object, 164
    custom windows, 166
    dialog windows, 165
    open method, 166
    resizeBy method, 170
    resizeTo method, 170
windows
    cross-window communication, 169
    custom, 166
    dialog windows, 165
    modifying, 169

X

XML, 280–287
XMLHttpRequest, 277
    existence of, 277
    methods, 279
XSS (cross-site scripting), 160–163

Y

Yahoo! UI Library, 308–310

Z

z-index, 252

About the Author

Shelley Powers is a software developer/architect, photographer, and writer who has authored numerous computer books on web development and technologies, including the O'Reilly titles *Developing ASP Components*; *Unix Power Tools*, Third Edition; *Essential Blogging*; and *Practical RDF*. Through the years, Shelley has also contributed several articles on cross-browser development, standards, RDF, JavaScript, CSS, and XML for several publications, and has worked with some of the world's leading companies. Shelley's tech web site is *http://burningbird.net*.

Colophon

The animal on the cover of *Learning JavaScript* is a baby black, or hook-lipped, rhinoceros (*Diceros bicornis*). The black rhino is one of two African species of rhinos. Weighing up to one and a half tons, it is smaller than its counterpart—the white, or square-lipped, rhinoceros. Black rhinos live in savanna grasslands, open woodlands, and mountain forests in a few small areas of southwestern, south central, and eastern Africa. They prefer to live alone and will aggressively defend their territory.

With an upper lip that tapers to a hooklike point, the black rhino is perfectly suited to pluck leaves, twigs, and buds from trees and bushes. It is able to eat coarser vegetation than other herbivores.

Black rhinos are odd-toed ungulates, meaning they have three toes on each foot. They have thick, gray, hairless hides. Among the most distinctive of the rhino's features is its two horns, which are actually made of thickly matted hair rather than bone. The rhino uses its horns to defend itself against lions, tigers, and hyenas, or to claim a female mate. The courtship ritual is often violent, and the horns can inflict severe wounds.

After mating, the female and male rhinos have no further contact. The gestation period is 14 to 18 months, and the calves nurse for a year, though they are able to eat vegetation almost immediately after birth. The bond between a mother and her calf can last up to four years before the calf leaves its home.

In recent years, rhinos have been hunted to the point of near extinction. Scientists estimate that there may have been as many as a million black rhinos in Africa 100 years ago, a number that has dwindled to 2,400 today. All five remaining species, which include the Indian, Javan, and Sumatran rhinos, are now endangered. Humans are considered their biggest predators.

The cover image is from *Cassell's Natural History*. The cover font is Adobe ITC Garamond. The text font is Linotype Birka; the heading font is Adobe Myriad Condensed; and the code font is LucasFont's TheSans Mono Condensed.

Better than e-books

Buy *Learning JavaScript* and access the
digital edition FREE on Safari for 45 days.

Go to www.oreilly.com/go/safarienabled
and type in coupon code NQHY-XNGH-LD4W-DGHM-318F

Search
thousands of
top tech books

Download
whole chapters

Cut and Paste
code examples

Find
answers fast

Search Safari! The premier electronic reference
library for programmers and IT professionals.